D0463761

Intimately Betrayed

By
Roxanna P. Platt

Intermedia Publishing Group

Intimately Betrayed

Published by:
Intermedia Publishing Group, Inc.
P.O. Box 2825
Peoria, Arizona 85380
www.intermediapub.com

ISBN 978-0-9819682-4-7

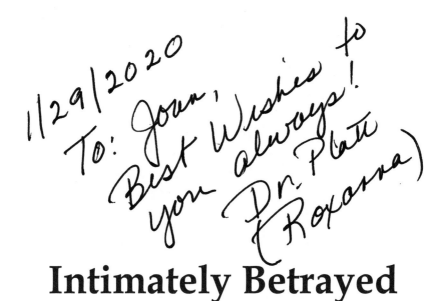

Intimately Betrayed

By

Roxanna P. Platt

Dedication

To my devoted mother, Justine Russell Platt, for giving me the gift of life, and for loving me unconditionally. It is she who taught me human stability, and instilled in me spiritual understanding, giving me the moral fiber that kept me from sinking during the most difficult and challenging times of my life.

To my father, Hamilton Carl Platt, Jr., who was an Air Force flyer, killed in action while fighting for a cause he believed in, the United States of America. I was two years old.

To my three beautiful, priceless children, Indira, Justin and Ariel, who completed my circle of love, and gifted me with much of the growth and strength to come this far.

To my beloved brother, Hamilton, who will always be my rock, and my sister, Cameron, thank you.

To my son-in-law, Charles, I love you for becoming one of us.

To my best friend, Carl, who has inspired and lifted me all my life to reach higher and higher and I'm still trying.

To all of the women in the world who have suffered misunderstanding or abuse. I pray that this story, woven with love and passion will be a small tool in helping guide you to safety.

Chapter One

𝓘t was four in the afternoon, and the air was still as Alyssa sat alone on the dock gently pushing the lounge swing back and forth with her feet. She clung to these few last moments, knowing that ultimately, she must let go. She gazed across the cove to the treetops on the other side. Their glistening leaves allowed the light to pass through them, sending a magical ray of diamonds dancing and sparkling across the water's calm surface. As if from its own magic, a dolphin appeared. He gracefully bowed his body again and again as he glided along the length of the sun's ray. Each time he came up to the air through the water's cool dimension, she could hear him breathe life's precious force. He swam and hunted and enjoyed while he lived those fleeting moments before her eyes.

It was almost as if he was leaving his message just for her. "I'm alive! See me, enjoy me, and love me. Know that this is beautiful, but when I leave, set me free to the ocean of mystery from where I came. Save my appearance as a message to your soul. We have met, we have bonded, and we have captured a perfect moment in time together, but now I must go."

With those few moments filling her senses, the dolphin was gone as quickly as he'd come, as Alex had come and gone from her life.

She quietly wept within her loneliness. "If we lived

within a perfect moment like a cove for dolphins, then how will I ever capture it again? I thought our love was forever."

She closed her eyes to shut out the blurring tears and stopped the swing from moving. How was it possible that not long ago they were together, each being total love for the other? They were best friends enraptured in a passion that was more than either one had ever known.

His voice still echoed in her memory. "Baby, you're so much deeper than anyone I've ever known. You are the love of my life."

She got up from the swing and turned her back to the water, passed by the swimming pool, and glanced under the dock bridge where they had made love time and time again under the stars. She entered the house and climbed the stairs to their bedroom. There she fell silently on the bed.

Curling into a fetal position and facing the window, she sobbed, "I need to be in your arms just one more time. There must be a way to get you back, Alex. I will get you back, because there is no way to live without you."

The afternoon passed and the evening came while she remained stunned on her bed, longing to fall asleep to join him. Only in sleep would the taste of his sweet lips, the smell of his skin, and the devotion in his beautiful eyes be hers once again. He was good and kind and gentle, which caused her to momentarily reflect upon the ladies at the shelter for battered women.

Even though love had been stolen from her, she knew only what good love was. She never had been abused mentally or physically. Her patients at the shelter suffered from lies and abuse from their boyfriends and spouses, and never knew the purity of grief after losing someone who was good. She mourned for them. Her agonized thoughts returned to her own sadness and love for her dead husband. Concern for anyone except herself faded, and she wanted to go where he was at any cost. Closing her eyes, she invited sleep as the empty pill bottle dropped from her hand onto the bed.

Chapter Two

*O*n the sixth anniversary of the day she awoke in the ICU, Dr. Alyssa Tennison-Kippler arrived at her Menlo medical clinic. She was thirty minutes late after hospital rounds and caring for an unexpected patient in the emergency room. The front of her lab coat had been splashed with betadine in the hospital, and its dried orange stains still reeked of pungent medicinal cleanser. She'd hoped for a more peaceful start that morning, but she was determined not to let its chaos interfere with her celebration of this second chance at life. Entering through the back door of the clinic, she smiled and added an extra bounce to her step.

After switching to a clean lab coat, she stood in front of the nursing station, mechanically twisting her long chestnut hair into a bun, momentarily reflecting on the clinic's earlier days.

Opening the clinic had been so exciting. She, with her toddler daughter in a playpen beside her, her mother, and Susanna—the clinic's nurse and Alyssa's best friend since childhood—had decorated the office with personal belongings from home. Four patients had come in the first day the office opened. Seemingly overnight, it became one of the biggest practices in the area.

Yet now, even in the exclusive beach village of Menlo, Florida, healthcare was trapped under the tragic change of times in medicine. The glitter of the new office opening had faded long ago, and reality had set in—medicine was no longer a profession of fulfillment. It had become a grueling and often not a rewarding chore.

Dionna, Alyssa's mother, entered the nurse's station, frowning as she faced her daughter and Susanna in private. "Honey, it's a lousy way to start the day, but the rudest patient just stormed out of the office because he couldn't be seen without an appointment. I told him you're overbooked, we'd try to fit him in, but it wasn't good enough. I thank my lucky stars that my little granddaughter will be with me tonight while you're gone, Alyssa. Her hugs and kisses will wash away today's depression."

Alyssa took in a slow, deep breath, understanding her mother's distress. Her child, Lisa, would be spending the evening with the most loving and devoted grandmother she could have. How lucky they all were to have each other. Alyssa vowed that Lisa would never suffer growing up. Her daddy had died when she was a newborn, she had never known him, but she had been given a great life so far, and everyone around her made sure of that.

Susanna rolled her eyes up in her head and leaned on the countertop, "Alyssa, I'm writing letters to him and the insurance company. We're dropping him as a patient. He's always nasty in the waiting room. He threw his five-dollar co-pay at your mom last week." Susanna glanced at Alyssa and continued in the same breath, "Your hair is a mess. Did you put your head in a wind machine? Maybe you should do a little better than a messy bun."

Alyssa chirped, "OK, Mother Sue, I'll put the bun a little to the left, OK?" She giggled, modeling her easy-care hairdo. "I like my hair. It's carefree like me."

But beneath the air of joy, Alyssa was fatigued after long

and late hours of work. She often wondered if there would ever again be a life even distantly related to the word *fun*. The patients had no idea that their meager co-pays and almost nonexistent insurance reimbursements weren't enough to keep the office open. Alyssa had to take out a loan against the practice to cover the last year's expenses, even before she could draw a salary. She had become more involved with charity work rather than profit. Dedicated to her medical commitment, she believed she owed her life to its cause.

Most frustrating was that while her quality of medical care was excellent, the reimbursement to the office was criminally low, and the patient's inflated premiums paid poorly with unfair medical coverage. The new system robbed the human purpose from medicine. Dr. Kippler was part of the major collection of doctors who longed for something to change.

Dionna shook her head in disgust of the office situation, and rushed back to the reception area to answer the phone.

Alyssa grimaced. "Sue, we can't take this much longer. How could an HMO refuse payment for a CAT scan of the brain ordered for a forty-year-old patient with a new onset of seizures? I had to send Gina to the ER two days after her episode in order to get her CT approved."

Susanna put her hand on Alyssa's back and lovingly patted it. "I don't know how much longer you'll continue to serve this dying art without slowly wilting away with it. "Anyway, enough philosophy. We're running forty minutes behind."

Alyssa reached for the next chart as Susanna whispered with a grin, "Better fix your messy bun, or maybe you should let it down. Don't you know who your first patient is today? Matthew Hunter, the boat designer, is right behind that wall. I almost fell over, he's so gorgeous. I can see why they make such a big deal over him."

With a playful giggle, Alyssa answered, "Shhh, he'll hear you. Is he really gorgeous? Maybe I should run home, fix my makeup, and get changed? Susanna, you're so silly, but you always make me laugh, and I love you so much."

Turning her back, she perused the chart.

Just then, Dionna called Alyssa back to the nursing station to take a phone call. An anxious voice spoke. "Alyssa, it's Denise from the Women's Hope for Harmony House. I know you're busy, but I just wanted to remind you that we have a meeting tonight. There are three ladies who need yearly exams, and remember I told you about the lady who came in last night who needs a rape exam. You're still able to make it?"

Alyssa replied with reassurance, "I'm coming. I've already filled a bag with office supplies and some sample birth control pills. I'll add the last sealed rape kit the office has left. See you tonight."

The human part of medicine was still the only worthwhile reason good doctors continued working. She had got involved with The Harmony House in order to give new beginnings to abused and battered women. She couldn't forget how lucky she personally was never to have known any kind of abuse from anyone. She was a strong and competent woman who had received many blessings in life, not to forget the loving family and friends who daily filled it. Lisa would grow up with those same stable blessings, and she would be groomed and protected from ever being mistreated. As a volunteer physician, Alyssa could help offer hope to those who were less fortunate, which gave her great pleasure.

Alyssa entered the Fish Room. She carried a green

chart labeled "Matthew James Hunter." Her patient was a handsome and distinguished man. Huge blue eyes dominated his face, and his gentle manner controlled the room. His quiet, confident presence left Alyssa feeling a little off balance.

"Good morning, Mr. Hunter. I'm Dr. Kippler. What brings you to our office today?"

"Well, ma'am, can you take this little spot off my eyelid." Pointing to a tiny skin tag on one of his upper eyelids, he continued, "I don't have a doctor here in Florida, because I've been travelin' a lot these last few years, and I'm never sick. But I'm about due for a good physical."

His adorable Southern drawl came straight from the romance of Rhett Butler and Scarlett O'Hara. He had the countenance of a senator in his gorgeous navy blue suit, yet the innocence of a boy. These qualities were so dramatic that she felt pleasantly dwarfed in his presence.

She glanced at his chart. "Mr. Hunter, we can take care of that little skin tag without a problem. However, I see that your blood pressure is a little high. Have you ever taken medication for that?"

She was careful not to alarm him, but his blood pressure was high enough to cause a stroke. Of note was that his father died from cardiac disease at the age of forty-six.

"Well, I have been told that it has been high in the past, but I never really took it seriously." He gave her a slow, easy grin. "My life has been really good to me, and I've always been healthy. I feel great. I never spent a day in a hospital and I reckon I never will."

She reached behind her head and tried to adjust her bun as Susanna had earlier suggested. Her heart leaped into his blue eyes, and at that moment, all she wanted was to be part of saving him in some way. He seemed untouched and lost, yet indefinable, with a presence that made her feel important. She snapped back to reality, and lifted her stethoscope to begin a brief exam of his heart and lungs through his opened shirt. She noticed a few silver hairs on his well-developed chest as she listened to the beating of his heart beneath the bell of her scope. She was separated from touching him with her hand by only a little round metal instrument, and felt privileged for that moment before moving the bell to his back and listening to the clear air passing through his lungs.

She continued to address his health. "I agree that you should have a good physical if you haven't had one within the last year. I'd like to order some routine blood work and start you on medication. Do you know if your cholesterol has ever been high?"

Mr. Hunter thought carefully. "It's never been really high, but I think it could be now. I've been doin' a lot a partyin' lately. My business kinda promotes that. I'm gettin' older and I need to start takin' better care of myself. Wait a minute. I'm not sick or somethin', am I? I feel fine. I just want this little guy taken off my eyelid."

"No. I think you're fine. I just want to bring your blood pressure down so you don't *get* sick. If you wouldn't mind, I'm going to ask my nurse to give you some medicine to bring it down before you leave today. You'll need to stay with us for a few minutes to let it work. I'll start you on a daily blood pressure medication today, and order fasting blood work for tomorrow to check your cholesterol and your sugar. I assume you've already eaten today?"

He looked at her with a restless uneasiness. "Yes. I'm goin' out of town for three weeks. Can we do all this when I get back? I'll have my blood pressure checked in South

Carolina next week."

"That's fine." She hid her disappointment. She was about to suggest he return in the morning for his physical and blood work. "Please also call me if you have any problems with the medication. Let's wait until your pressure comes down before we cause any further stress with a surgical procedure."

Matthew's eyes widened, "Surgical procedure? I thought you could just clip that baby off. It's no big thing, is it?"

"No, no. But any procedure, even putting in some numbing medicine and cutting off a little growth, is a big thing when it's yours, if you know what I mean," she smiled.

He smiled back, wrinkled his nose up, and nodded in agreement to show his satisfaction with her plan. She shook his warm and perfectly manicured hand. The heat from his eyes burning through the back of her dress felt good as she turned away and walked out of the room He had the power, that was for sure. What was it about this guy who made her feel so awkward that suddenly she just wanted him to disappear? Where was that self-assurance she'd had upon entering the exam room? Why was she not sure of her own medical skills in front of him? Was it just because his good looks overpowered her confident academics? Maybe he didn't trust her judgment. He was probably annoyed that she hadn't removed the skin tag. Her mind raced through several scenarios before she stopped herself.

"Anyway," she thought aloud as she readjusted her hair bun, "He's gone and I doubt he'll ever be back. Why should I be so concerned about what he thinks? I'm just oversensitive because I'm tired."

Alyssa returned to her office and placed his chart on the desk, and paused there for a minute looking out of the window, and watched Matthew Hunter's beautifully buffed, manly physique open the door to a white Mercedes convertible. His thick, brown curls with just a hint of silver gave him a distinguished, yet boyish look, rather irresistible. She remembered a few stories floating around town about him. Menlo was a small resort town. One of its drawbacks was the tremendous news chain that didn't distinguish between good and bad. Everyone knew everything about everyone else, even if it wasn't true. She thought about one article in the local *Post* that had called him "a most eligible bachelor, but an old-fashioned guy."

He started his engine and pulled out of the parking lot. She watched him drive away, and was glad he was gone, feeling restless when they'd met, and even more restless after it was over so quickly. She hoped he'd never be back.

She asked herself, again, "Who was that? Mr. Spicy Playboy in the flesh." Not the kind of guy any self-respecting woman would get involved with.

She returned to the hallway and reached for the next chart on the door.

She had begun to find some happiness after six long years of recovery from loss, and learned to drown pain, finding joy in moments at a time. Those moments had begun to expand to longer and longer periods of time. No, she didn't need someone like Matthew Hunter in her life. She had her practice, her friends and family, and her work with the Hope for Harmony House. She was grateful simply to be alive.

Chapter Three

*M*atthew left Dr. Kippler's office unaware that she was watching him walk to his car through her office window. At that moment he wasn't sure where he had been, but he knew where he wanted to be. Though half an hour from now he had a meeting scheduled with one of the most prominent figures in the cruise ship industry, he wanted to be right back in that exam room with her touching him again. This lady made him feel different about himself. Why had it taken so long to find a woman like her? She made him feel young and scared. She made him feel mature and brave and tall. He had never met a lady who was so strong, yet so soft and vulnerable beneath that starched white lab coat. She was beautiful and her body had to be incredible under all that material.

He got into his car, fastened his seat belt, turned the engine on, and he drove away from her. Arriving at the DeVinci Cruises Corporate Building, he took a deep breath, loosened his tie and removed it from his neck. Unbuttoning his top two shirt buttons, he looked in his rear view mirror and grinned at himself. But something was missing and he was lonely.

He stepped into the elevator and held the door for another gentleman. Pressing the button for the fourth floor, shivers went through his body as he relived her hands caressing his back while she listened to his lungs. "She knows what I need," he mused about the most beautiful woman he had ever met.

Antonio DeVinci sprang up from behind his huge

mahogany desk as Matthew entered the room, "Matthew, it is so good to see you again. Please, sit down. How has my good friend been?"

Matthew offered a firm handshake to his Italian acquaintance, a man whose partnership possibility would have been only a dream until now. "I couldn't be better. And how are you and your lovely family? Did your beautiful daughter, Antonia, get married yet?"

Antonio laughed. "We're all OK. My wife is my wife, and Antonia remains the most beautiful girl in Italy, still single."

Matthew had eyed Antonia, an Italian beauty of aristocracy, many times wishing he dared to move in on her space if only for a flicker. Just mentioning a beautiful woman brought back Alyssa in his mind. The shadows of his past would fade in her light, and maybe, finally, he could put to rest the part of him that couldn't forget the painful abuse of his childhood. His thought produced a broad grin.

"So, you're still not married? Such a handsome fellow can't stay out of the woman's web forever, you know," Antonio continued. "Matt, may I call you Matt?"

Matt nodded in approval. "My friends do."

Hardly pausing for Matt's response, Antonio said, "So, do you agree to design the prototype ship for the most incredible cruise line in the world?" DeVinci cocked his head in European style with a welcome signal for Matthew to be seated. It was also a signal to stop the small chat and talk business. DeVinci was a man of fewer words than actions.

Matthew sat, unbuttoned one sleeve of his well-pressed shirt, rolled it up his forearm, and cocked his head right back. "I'm ready, willin' and able. Let's get rollin' before I change my mind."

The mere fact that he had met Alyssa gave this meeting new meaning. He was prone to quick involvement and he had already decided that Alyssa would be his trophy in front of the world beside the new ship design. Her beauty, education, and charm would make him so proud, and their upcoming love would seal the image of stability he longed to know. No matter what Matthew James Hunter was up to, a woman's strength and love was always his greatest motivation for doing well.

The two men spread the charts and notes across DeVinci's desk. After a long and intense meeting of their minds, DeVinci seemed pleased. "Matt, let's have a drink and toast to our partnership. My father taught me that every important business decision should be sealed in friendship first."

Politely turning the drink down, Matthew responded, "Maybe another time. I'm drivin' to Charleston when I leave here. I don't want to drink and drive, I'll be tired." Though he used his trip as an excuse, Matthew had vowed to himself not to let alcohol screw up things this time.

It was still early in the day as Matthew took the elevator down to the lobby. He stood outside of the building before going to his car. Putting his hands on his hips, he took a deep breath, exhaled slowly, and exclaimed, "Yep, this is a very good day."

Chapter Four

*T*hat evening Alyssa left the office exhausted. She let her hair down to flow in the breeze and drove along the ocean in her convertible with the top down. The warmth of the fading tropical sun felt wonderful on her cheeks and the salt air smelled clean. The ocean view spread out before her like an infinite sea of crystal turquoise glass. Menlo had a monopoly on tropical beauty.

"Life is so lovely," she thought as she pulled the car in front of her beachfront home. Walking through the front door, she could hear her daughter's laughter ringing through the house. Lisa's grandmother was singing a song to her with childlike silliness, and it was obvious that the two of them were already full steam ahead with their fun night together. Coming home to a wonderful family was a great blessing of life, and Alyssa was grateful.

She immediately joined in the family fun, calling her little girl's name, "Lisa, Mama's home. Where is my kiddlepits?"

Lisa scrambled out from an unannounced corner and grabbed her mother's waist. "Kiddlepits is right here, Mommy."

They continued their playful interaction as Alyssa climbed the stairs to her bedroom with Lisa half pulling her down the steps. "Mommy, I'm ready for the big run with you and Uncle Marc. I just can't go yet, because my shoes won't run that fast. Take me to the store to buy some faster running shoes, please?"

"If you're ready, we can go right now before I get dressed to run. Want to go?" Alyssa loved the innocence of Lisa's belief that it was all in the shoes.

Lisa's bottom lip curled downward in a defeated pout. "No, Mommy. Tonight Grandmother and I are going to make pan cake in a can. What is that, Mommy? Grandmother said it's a surprise."

Alyssa wasn't sure. "I'm not sure. Maybe it means to make pancakes in a can?" She started to giggle and then it turned to laughter. How wonderfully ridiculous it all seemed.

Lisa, delighted by her mother's unusual silly giggling, interjected, "Mommy, I like it when you're silly. It's fun. I wish you could laugh all the time. Sometimes you're not very fun when you don't laugh."

Alyssa was stunned by her six-year-old daughter's observation. A simple remark by a child was like a picture telling a thousand words. It had never even crossed her mind that there wasn't enough laughter in their home. Lisa didn't think of her mother as happy. The hard work, love, beautiful home, kisses, and security lacked fun. Why hadn't that been obvious before now?

"Hey you, goochie-goo, I gotta go and run. You make that pancake in a can, and I'll plan on finding a store where they sell fast running shoes. I love you, pumpkin pie." Alyssa finished slipping on her other sock and slapping across her Velcro shoe tie. "Give Mommy a big kiss and a hug."

She kissed Lisa and ran out the back door to meet Jean-Marc Debussy for their evening run. This nightly event was the eagerly met, relaxing, and rejuvenating time spent with her childhood friend who lived next door. He was the man who had been there long before Alex or Lisa.

Evenings inspired family ties and memories of building blocks that had helped Alyssa create her beautiful palace on the ocean. There was so much in her home reflecting the years the Tennison family spent with the Debussys. Jean-Marc, her best friend, who had been part of her life in France since childhood, had earned his footprint in her sand. He was with her the day Lisa took her first step while he was helping place the palm trees and fragrant gardenia bushes along the back of the house. Jean-Marc actually sketched the curves of the mote-like swimming pool around the house, he poured the first gallon of chlorine into the pool, and he put the wooden gym set and swing together for Lisa in the backyard facing the ocean. He was the friend who had been there for Alyssa when she was drowning in quicksand after Alex died, because he loved her and he had become a dear friend to Alex. And Jean-Marc, her pal, had chased her around the French Riviera during their teen years, he had been there through thick and thin all of their lives, he loved her with all of his heart, and he promised her that it would always be that way, forever and ever. Nobody knew her so well as he did.

He fell into step beside her as she neared the water's edge, and they ran together on the beach, an exhilarating revival of life that lifted her up, already making her feel like a child born again.

As they ran along the shore, Alyssa puffed out a difficult question. "Jean-Marc, is it true that I never laugh?"

"What kind of question is that? Of course you laugh. Everyone laughs," he joked.

"No, really. Lisa said tonight that I'm not fun and I don't

laugh. Is it true that I'm not fun?" Alyssa was teary-eyed and stopped running not far from the back ocean access to her house. "It's so hard to be fun when all I do is work to survive. What is wrong with me?" Cupping her face with her hands, she began to cry.

Jean-Marc stopped short and pulled her toward him, cradling her in his arms. "Don't cry, you are lots of fun, a great survivor, and a very strong girl. We all love you. I bet you never see yourself as the beautiful sexual being that you are. Did you know that you're really sexy?"

Alyssa couldn't handle that from Jean-Marc, and she pulled away. "Now look who's silly. I'll see you later." She gathered her senses together, still breathing hard. "Thank you. I'm late to the Harmony House."

Running from Jean-Marc toward the beach entrance to her property, she felt her own sensuality. Momentarily, she flashed on how she had felt that morning when Matthew Hunter was with her. He made her feel sexy, and she liked it. He knew how to make her feel very alive. She wondered if she was emitting an energy during their run that encouraged Jean-Marc to tell her she was sexy. Her run on the beach that evening was better because she had met someone that morning who touched her spirit. She knew that her easy laughter that evening with Lisa was because she had met Matthew James Hunter that morning.

She took a quick shower and kissed Lisa. "Sweetheart, please mind Grandmother tonight and go to sleep at eight o'clock. I love you. As soon as I get home, I'll come into your room and kiss you while you're sleeping. If you want to, you can sleep in my bed tonight. I've got to go. I'm late."

Lisa reached for her mother's arms. "Hug me, Mommy. Help all those other sad mommies who got hurt, OK,

Mommy? Do they have little children, Mommy?"

Alyssa whispered, "Some of them do, sweetheart, and that's why Mommy needs to help them."

"I'm a little child. My daddy never hurt you." Lisa squeezed her mother's neck tightly.

"Your daddy never hurt anyone. Lots of daddies don't hurt anyone, and they love their families."

"Do you think we might have another daddy someday?" Lisa's lower lip quivered.

"I don't know, honey, but I promise that if Mommy ever found another daddy to be part of us, he would love us and be good. Now, tonight Mommy's helping people who aren't lucky like we are. I love you, honey, and I gotta go. You behave with those pancake cans tonight, OK?"

She kissed her little girl good-bye as she left her in her grandmother's arms.

Lisa had surprised her again, reaching another developmental plateau and getting brighter and more philosophical by the minute.

Alyssa walked up the short flight of steps, passed through a small courtyard bordered with tropical foliage, and entered the floral-sprayed patio that led to the front door of the Woman's Hope for Harmony House, a new shelter for battered and abused women.

As a family practice physician, she had become strength to a community of women and children who needed hope and guidance. The Hope for Harmony House was a place where abused people could find safety and support during a transition period between fear of domestic violence, and freedom.

Alyssa was met at the door by Denise Fortridge, a well-seasoned social worker, who had relocated from Harlem, New York, to spearhead the opening of the Harmony House program. Denise had been a victim of domestic violence, enduring beatings for almost ten years before ending up in an intensive care unit in critical condition. Since then, her focus had been on helping other women who might otherwise suffer the mental and physical pain from which she had escaped. Now she was married to a gentle and bright psychologist, Terrence Fortridge, who took great pride in his wife's fight against domestic violence.

Denise's eyes sparkled with enthusiasm. "Hi, Alyssa, we have a pretty good bunch here tonight, including four new ladies." Together they entered a small room decorated in rosy colors with a few cozy couches. Nine ladies, of various ages and ethnic backgrounds, filled the room. Some sat alone and withdrawn in quiet anticipation, and others talked with each other about their problems as they sipped coffee. Denise followed Alyssa into the room. Though the ladies who were there that night were lost women waiting to be found, their expressions brightened when they saw Dr. Kippler. Her heart ached for them, and she gladly would've given up all she had if that could prevent the circumstances that had brought them here. This was their evening of hope to gather the tools they needed to find their way out of their frightening death trap.

Alyssa placed a stack of reading materials on the coffee table in front of her and greeted the ladies, one by one, shaking their hands with warmth and reassurance. The ladies awaited their turns to greet her, most of them fidgeting with their purse straps or sitting very still with their hands clasped tightly in their laps.

One of the ladies was covered with facial bruises, which she had obviously tried to hide with heavy makeup. Alyssa noticed swelling around her eyes and paused to speak with her. She discreetly gestured toward her own eye. "Have you had that looked at?"

The lady blinked away tears. "It just happened a few hours ago. I came here first. I'll go to the emergency room after this meeting. I just wanted to come here first. I'm OK, honest."

Then she paused her rapid-fire excuses, falling silent for a moment. "Dr. Kippler, have you ever been abused?"

Alyssa knew most of the women would expect she'd suffered the way they had. "Not personally, but I connected with fighting domestic violence through Denise and Terrance when I referred one of my patients to them for counseling. At the time, I didn't know that my patient was a victim of domestic violence. She only opened up to me enough to confide that her marriage was in trouble and infidelity was an issue. After meeting with Terrance, she returned to me for antidepressants, which he had recommended as part of her treatment. Neither Terrance nor I ever saw her again. A few days later, after their last meeting, she was shot and killed by her husband. As a result of that tragedy, Denise, Terrance, and I teamed up. Maybe I should look at your bruises before the meeting." Alyssa was concerned because of the enormous swelling around her eyes. She called for an ice pack.

But the lady didn't want attention. She wanted to hear the meeting, and then go to the emergency room.

Denise called for everyone's attention, "Before we begin tonight, we must all promise each other that this is a secret club. Anything that goes on here is protected sharing. We have a lot of fears and concerns, and we might even be responsible for getting someone hurt if it becomes known that she was here talking. I want us all to sign our names on the enrollment sheet and please read the statement above before signing it."

Alyssa continued by passing out a copy of her poem for everyone to read. "Please read this poem very carefully. I think it's the story of why we're all here.

"Hey Baby, I Love You"

Hey baby, I love you.
I'll sing you a song,
And I'll dance you a dance.
I'll hold you all night,
For this is Romance."
Later that night he tried to hit me.
I don't understand. How could it be?
I don't understand. What did I do?
Why was I so black and blue?
The next morning he said,
"Hey baby, I love you."
We were in bed and things were OK.
"He loves me," I thought.
Then the pain went away.
"Hey baby, I love you.
I'll always love you.
If you'd be nice, we'd be fine.
I'd do anything to make you just mine.
Look into my eyes and get lost in just me.
I don't want to share you,
Why won't you see?
Your family and friends are just in the way.
They called you again and ruined my day.
Hey Baby, I love you." Again and again,

I wondered what love was, to have no friend?
We were moving away,
But he wouldn't say why.
I begged him to stay.
Then I began to cry.
"Why are we leaving?
My friends are all here."
"I hate them. They're bad."
He yelled in my ear.
"Hey baby, I love you,
We'll get a new life."
What was he talking about?
Was I truly his wife?
He ripped off my top because he was mad,
He said I should die because I was so bad.
I hated my life and I wished I could run.
Black and blue was my color,
What had I done? "Baby, I love you?"
This was no fun.
What was the matter with him or with me?
I had to get out and I had to get free.
I was calling a taxi and running away.
I'd rather be dead,
Than to live that way.
My body was shaking as I picked up the phone.
I had to be strong to go off alone.
But he heard my crying in painful despair,
And he killed me before my taxi got there.
If only I knew what he'd do to me,
It wouldn't take this for me to be free.

Silence and shock filled the faces of the room. Sadness and pain filled the air. Alyssa had never been abused; her experiences with battered women had prompted her to pen the poem as a way to reach out to them. She could only hope she'd captured even a small portion of what they were going through. Alyssa sat quietly for a minute and then began to speak softly.

"What is domestic violence? What is battering? What is wrongful behavior? These are questions that we will hopefully answer tonight. Denise is going to talk to you about some of these questions. I believe I am going to see about four or five ladies who need medical help. I know one of our ladies has a terribly swollen eye, and I want to take care of her first. Let's get started."

Three hours later, Alyssa gathered up her supplies and papers while talking with several of the ladies. She left that night with enthusiasm and hoped that the meeting might have made a difference in the fight against domestic violence. She flashed on Nicole Brown Simpson and Ronald Goldman, wondering if their deaths could in any way be atoned for. At least something could be done by committing to help other women so they might fight back and be heard, unlike Nicole, (who died with her innocent friend, Ron Goldman). Her pleas to the police for help were swept under the carpet until it was too late.

She stopped by the hospital on the way home to check in on a few patients. By the time she arrived home, Lisa was cuddled up in bed with a dozen dolls and stuffed animals around her. She looked like a little angel sleeping peacefully. Alyssa loved those tiny little blonde curls falling loosely over Lisa's delicate little face.

"Mother," Alyssa whispered, "Isn't she beautiful? She looks so much like Alex. She has that same adorable face he had."

"Yes, I see her father, but she has plenty of you in her,

too," Dionna responded.

Alyssa smiled. "Do you think so, Mama? I never see anyone but Alex in her face. I'm sorry I got home so late. I stopped by the hospital on my way home."

Her mother looked at her with loving, sad eyes. She hesitated and then spoke. "Honey, you need to go out and have some fun with friends. It's such a shame to stop living at your age. Alex would want you to move ahead with your life. You're not a machine who can just work and sleep and slave to keep enough money going to live and support the Harmony House. Nobody could be happy with that. Even Lisa would benefit if you had more of a social life. She'd become a little more independent, which she needs."

Alyssa rolled her eyes and exhaled heavily. "I really don't think there's anything wrong with the way I'm raising her. Please let's not talk about this here. She might wake up."

They quietly left the room and closed the door. Her mother's comments hit a nerve, especially after Lisa's observation earlier about Alyssa not being fun anymore. "She has lots of friends from school, and at least she knows I'm not out going to clubs and partying all night."

Dionna planted her hands on her hips. "You know that's not what I meant. You're not going to always be so young and beautiful. Life goes by so fast. I guess seeing that Matthew Hunter today just made me think a little. Sorry I spoke up."

Alyssa felt guilty for snapping. "I'm just not ready, Mother. Besides, you know how much money I need to help the shelter. Maybe if the office was pulling its financial weight, things would be different. I've thought a lot about it after talking with the accountant today. We need to let the practice go, and I need to go to work for someone else. A steady salary would help right now. I'm so tired. I think I'll go to bed and read a little."

Alyssa kissed her mother good night and gently squeezed her arm as she left the room for her quiet corner of the universe where she could close the world out for a little while. She lay in bed overlooking the eastern sky with its thousands of twinkling stars lighting up the water just enough to enhance the white froth of the surf splashing on the shore.

While she waited for sleep, she thought about the water and the moon and whether she was providing Lisa with a strong role model or just a harried, overworked mother who was barely around for her.

The phone startled her from her dreams, and she reached for it on the night table. "Hello?"

"Dr. Kippler," a voice rushed, "I'm sorry to bother you so late, but one of your patients, Matthew Hunter, is here with a gastrointestinal bleed. Dr. Smallwood is transfusing him two units now, but he wants to speak with you."

Alyssa got a quick update from the ER doctor. It was 2:00 a.m.

She arrived at the intensive care unit as Matthew was being transferred from the GI lab, where he had been scoped. He had an esophageal tear, esophageal varices, and severe gastritis. His condition, especially the bleeding tear, was presumed to be the effect of alcohol overuse. She had seen the devastating disease of alcoholism kill more than once, and prayed that Mr. Hunter wasn't another victim. The nurses were preparing to hang two more units of blood for transfusion.

"You're a lucky man, Mr. Hunter," she whispered. "You're doing well, and we'll take good care of you. You need to rest and let us do everything else."

A slight smile turned up his bottom lip. Alyssa sat with him briefly as he lay quietly next to the life support machines, sedated though he seemed to have understood her words enough to respond with that entrancing smile of his.

She held his hand for a few seconds before leaving the room, and his fingers tightened around her palm. His hand was big with long delicate fingers. She glanced down at his shiny fingernails, which enhanced her sense of being touched by a treasure. Without thinking, cupping his hand within both of hers, she felt as if she was his sweetheart, and when he got well she would be the one to take him home. The loving warmth and life in his soft palm consumed her. This man had touched her heart. Alyssa never thought of anyone as "just a patient," but Matthew was much more than just a patient. She was sure of that.

The concern was that he might begin bleeding again. His blood pressure was unstable, and it was being controlled with IV medication. If his pressure got too high, it could cause the tear to hemorrhage again which was easily fatal.

Alyssa sat at the nursing station after leaving Matthew's room, and she reflected about how it must be for him, the patient, lying on that bed. Six years ago she lay there as he was doing now, and she clearly remembered how safe she felt, but she could have died then as he might die now. It was all so surreal. She didn't know a lot about death and dying, but she did believe that she had lived because it wasn't her turn to die, and she prayed it wasn't his. She wrote some orders for the nurses, asked them to call her throughout the night for any problems, and returned home for a couple of hours to sleep before rising for morning rounds in the Intensive Care Unit.

Chapter Five

*T*he alarm's soothing sound of light jazz played at 6:30, and the golden-orange glow of morning opened the sky through her bedroom's large picture window, nudging her to awaken. Alyssa opened her sleepy eyes and gazed at the sunrise. Her mind quickly turned to the hospital and her patient in the ICU.

When she arrived, Matthew was awake, worn out, and disheveled after his all-night ordeal. But even with an NG tube in his nose, his body plugged into three IVs, with wires and medical instruments surrounding his bed, he looked good enough to photograph.

"Good morning, sunshine." She smiled at him, keeping her voice light and professional.

"Hey," he moaned. "I feel like I've been drug out and beat up, but I guess I should be thankful that you guys kept me alive. Believe me, I am."

He looked up at her standing beside the bed, and his instant grin and brightening eyes prepared her for his welcome speech. "Funny seein' you again so soon, Doctor. You sure are a pleasure for sore eyes." Matt looked away from her, pulled his sheet up over his chest and continued, a little self-consciously, "Thank you for bein' so sweet to me last night. I remember you came in and held my hand for a while. I didn't see you, I was so weak with my eyes closed, but I heard your voice and I smelled that great perfume you use."

Alyssa glanced at his chart, held it against her chest, and giggled. "Mr. Hunter, didn't you know that doctors aren't supposed to wear perfume? It could make some patients feel worse, you know."

He wasted no time. "Then it must be just you that smells so good."

She ignored his last remark, placed his chart on the corner of his bed, checked his vital signs, and listened to his heart and lungs. As she reached for his ankles to check for swelling, that same feeling she had in the office rushed through her body like a river. She examined his muscular, suntanned legs, his strong ankles, and his smooth manicured feet with her hands and it was if they belonged to her. Awkwardly, whatever she felt for him in the office was fourfold that morning. While she touched his legs, Matt's energy entered her as if he had been her lover forever.

"Good," she stated with a detached and clinical voice. "You don't have any swelling in your legs, and your pulses are great. You're still a little clammy, though."

"I wish you could stay here with me this mornin'," he mumbled. "I need you here to make me better. Dr. Kippler, am I gettin' crazy? This isn't just me, is it?"

"You're just very tired. You keep resting and you'll do fine." She knew he was feeling what she was, or she thought he was, but she quickly looked away from him in denial and grasped the chart from the bed. "What we need is to get you strong and help you change some of your lifestyle. That partying of yours needs a rest. You take it easy for a while, and we'll try to guide you to slow down so you can get better. I'll be back this evening after office hours. I'm a phone call away from the nurses." Alyssa backed out of the room with her arms still wrapped around his chart, as if for security.

She sat at the nurse's station to make a few more notes and noticed an attractive young lady walking toward Matthew's room. The curtain was drawn open and she could see the woman lean over to kiss him.

Alyssa was invaded by jealousy as she looked back at his chart and tried to concentrate on her notes. Suddenly her face flushed with embarrassment. She knew nothing about this man except the little information they had shared together and she didn't want there to be anything else. What was she doing? She had allowed a few exchanges with a stranger, a patient, to take her imagination out of her boundaries. Feeling ridiculous, confused, and inappropriate, she tried to rationalize her unfamiliar emotions. "That woman shouldn't be here," she told herself. "She's probably part of his party crowd that encourages his overindulgence. He needs my medical strength and guidance to get healthy. I need to let her know he needs rest and very little company right now."

Quickly getting up, leaving his chart on the desk, and returning to his room, she passed through the doorway and moved to Matt's bedside with the odd feeling that her presence was all that mattered to his well-being. His visitor stepped back in respect to allow room for the doctor to be in control.

Matthew offered introductions. "Dr. Kippler, this is my secretary, Margie. Margie, this is the wonderful doctor I told you about. I guess now you can see why I fell in love with her at first sight, right?"

Margie tittered at his forward comment. "Dr. Kippler, it's

great to meet you. Matt's been talking about you all day. You'll please forgive him for his poor judgment in conversation this morning." She laughed again. "It must be all that blood he lost. I just had a talk with him yesterday before he got ready to leave for Charleston about how he never takes care of himself. I hope you can do something to change his ways. I try, but he never listens to me."

Alyssa nodded, silencing any response. She had obviously jumped the gun as to the relationship between this woman and Mr. Flirtatious, who was lying in the bed innocently quiet, an effect that could never last with him.

Matthew crossed his hands on the pillow behind his head. "I think I'm in love. I admit it, because I am a new man with all that blood I got, by golly. Margie, stop tellin' her all that stuff about me. I know what I'm doin'. How am I goin' to win her over if you spoil it by makin' me look a fool?"

He chuckled a little and moved his hands to lay them across his chest, "I'm really tired. All this conversation is a lot for a poor bleedin' guy," he mumbled again without looking at either one of them. "Actually, I'm exhausted." Then he turned his gaze to Alyssa. "Do you believe people can fall in love at first sight, Dr. Kippler?"

Alyssa found her voice. "OK, you're having fun, Mr. Hunter. I'm happy to see you're strong enough to have humor after the last twelve hours. I came back in to let you know we'll be leaving that tube in your nose for a couple of days. You'll probably feel lousy without eating, but we need to be sure the bleeding is healing before we let you eat again. Some more tests have been ordered by the GI doctor." She carefully included his visitor in her eye contact. "We're not out of the woods yet, but we're getting there. Hopefully, we can transfer you to a regular room tomorrow."

She left the ICU feeling better. The lady visiting Mr. Hunter wasn't his girlfriend. That shouldn't matter to her, but it did. The ordeal left Alyssa numb. She felt as if a bolt of lightning had struck, and even though it wasn't possible, she was smitten with an almost total stranger.

The sun was high in the sky as she hurried to the parking lot. Her common routine was to do morning rounds early and return home to take Lisa to school. Dionna's living in the next house made it easy for her to arrive by seven o'clock to help her granddaughter get ready for school each morning before Alyssa returned. As she entered the kitchen, she apologized. "Mother, I am so late. I didn't finish morning rounds. I need to go back to the hospital before I go to the office." Even with that stressor, Alyssa was unusually lighthearted that morning as she helped Dionna prepare Lisa's lunch.

"Mommy, please don't forget to give me a piece of the pancake in a can for my lunch." Lisa pointed to the cake dish.

"Yes ma'am, and what was pancake in a can?" Alyssa lifted the cake cover and saw a regular cake.

"It was just a joke, Mommy, Grandmother made a joke."

Quickly wrapping a small piece of cake, Alyssa encouraged Lisa to take her last bite of cereal. "Come on, darling, we need to get you to school."

Dionna broke in, "Honey, I can take her to school this morning if it would help you get rounds done before office hours."

"No, Mama, it's really important to me to have at least those few minutes with Lisa every morning. I'd rather be a little late to the office than to miss kissing her and watching her jump out of the car each morning. It's a highlight for me."

It was true that Alyssa saw the world through rose-colored glasses. She had lost a great love to death and had seen unbelievable battlefields of life and death within her profession. But she had also seen unbelievable miracles of ongoing life leading to the beauty of human restoration, especially her own, and her daughter was a great part of that.

She still treasured the innocence within her, one that was as helpless as that of her new patient, Matthew Hunter.

It seemed that her future was an unwritten slate, and she had finally been forgiven for attempting suicide years before. A shudder always went through her as she recognized such behavior to be a terrible end to a temporary agony. Life was worth appreciating, even if it had to be without Alex. Such a little thing as taking Lisa to school every morning was bonding for her and her daughter, and Alyssa cherished that.

As Lisa opened the car door by the school playground, Alyssa reached over and kissed her. "I'll pick you up tonight and we'll have dinner at Sancho's Place."

Sancho's was a popular Mexican restaurant on the beach not far from their home. Alyssa and Lisa were particularly fond of the atmosphere and food there. Lisa's eyes always widened when the tortillas arrived at the table.

"Oh boy!" Lisa jumped out of the car and skipped away through the playground gate as Alyssa drove away toward the hospital.

Chapter Six

*M*r. Hunter recovered well, and his friend, Margie, remained by his side during his entire hospitalization. She seemed to be not only his secretary, but also his travel companion and very close confidant. Whether they had a romantic connection was hard to tell, but Alyssa suspected there was more to their relationship than business. She fought to pull her feelings back in continued embarrassment during the days that followed. Still, she was anxious to see him each morning, but when his condition stabilized, she avoided evening rounds. Instead, she hurried home early enough to spend just a little more precious time with Lisa.

Within a week, Matthew was released from the hospital. Alyssa wrote his morning progress note and signed the order to "discharge today" with pride and joy because her patient had recovered and was ready to go home.

He was beautifully shaven, wore his intoxicating Gucci parfum, and beamed with joy as he waved good-bye to the nurses. "I'll cater lunch for y'all tomorrow. Don't anyone a ya eat, ya hear me?" He looked up at Margie with that broad grin. "Send a great buffet to each shift, and add flowers, OK?" His joy at getting out of the prison hospital saturated the room around him. Alyssa lingered at the nurse's station writing notes on another patient when Matt's "pink lady" wheeled him by her.

Matthew stopped his wheelchair momentarily, and

addressed her in earnest, "Doctor, all kiddin' aside, I've never been more grateful to be alive. I feel like I owe you somethin' big. It's easy sometimes to forget what's really important in life, and this whole experience gave me a new chance to remember. I think it's changed me some. Thanks again, you're all great."

Alyssa smiled as any good doctor would do, encouraging him to leave in peace. She giggled and pointed her finger in his direction. "No more partyin', y'all hear me?"

She meant for her forced Southern accent to soften the rebuke, but his suddenly intimate gaze suggested she'd turned him on.

"I promise, Doctor." He laughed as he turned his excitement and fixed his attention on the glass exit doors.

She closed the chart she was holding, placed it in the orders rack, and left the building just behind Matthew. Passing his entourage of people helping load the flowers, presents, and personal belongings, she carefully studied Margie helping him into the car as if he were a fragile saint. She also noticed Matthew saw her and leaned toward the window as she passed. She hoped he wanted to say something, maybe to encourage whatever they had built so far, but to her consternation, he did nothing. She continued walking toward the doctors' parking lot, and with each step she felt more lonely and almost abandoned. He had planted the seed of her feelings for him, he had defied death, he had been a good and brave patient, and she felt as though she were falling in love with some kind of angel. Rest and change in lifestyle could make him better than ever, and Alyssa struggled with her emotions, wanting to be at his side throughout his recovery and beyond, yet knowing it was a ridiculous fantasy.

Three days after Matthew's discharge, Alyssa entered her office to find her waiting room filled with patients, their faces anxious. So many people with so many needs — and so many more she wouldn't be able to help because of the impending, smothering "universal healthcare," which was another fancy term for socialized medicine governing lives. More and more often, she wished it were possible to just move on to something new in life.

She greeted the staff while scanning the day's patient roster, and her eyes froze on Mr. Hunter's name. It was his hospital follow-up appointment that morning. Despite her previous pessimism, she quickened her steps, knowing the man would do his best to put a smile on her face. Alyssa entered the exam room where he sat comfortably and relaxed in a chair. His handsome face gazed up at her, and before she could close the door behind her, he was standing and broke into a warm smile, never missing a cue, as usual. "Hello, Doctor."

"Hi." She hugged his chart to her chest. Almost everything she knew about him was within those paper pages, now a small volume of medical information. "I'm glad to see you're looking so well after such a horrible ordeal. How do you feel?"

His lips widened with his trademark grin. "I feel better because I'm lookin' at you again. You saved me. I know I'm out of place, and you can kick me out of the office. I mean no disrespect, but you're all I think about night and day."

Alyssa flushed. "Mr. Hunter, I don't want to be disrespectful either. But you're my patient and I'm your doctor. Let's work on that relationship right now, OK?" She wondered how it could be so easy for him to always grin at everything. "Do you know how easily you laugh? That's a good thing."

Patting the exam table with her hand, she encouraged him, "Climb up here, and let's go over your progress." She opened his chart and scanned the discharge reports and lab values, his vital signs, and his weight. "Mr. Hunter, I think we need to go on a little health kick. How would you feel about trying to take off a little weight? It's not even that you look overweight, but it's the health issue I'm talking about." She had cooled off quite a bit since the hospital scenes and she was able to contain her professional demeanor on the outside quite easily until she started explaining that he didn't look fat. "It would be good to lose a few pounds because the extra weight is probably driving your blood pressure up. Now that you've had this type of bleeding, we need to be very careful that it never happens again." She smiled innocently to guard his ego.

"I'm an avid runner and swimmer, but I admit I've been partyin' heavily and entertainin' way too much. I know you probably think I'm an alcoholic or somethin', but I'm not. Doctor, I really wasn't drinkin' when that bleedin' started. I was gettin' ready to drive to Charleston to see my mama when for no reason I doubled over with belly pain. I guess that's when it happened. Now I need to go to South Carolina because my mama is pretty anxious to see me." He grinned that grin again, as he cocked his head and held one eye in a wink.

Alyssa looked him straight in the eyes and she didn't flinch. "I'm not assuming anything, but I'm not sure how seriously you've taken this. Alcohol is a deadly drug. When it causes your blood vessels to bleed, it's a wake-up call. You might have died."

As the appointment was coming to a close, Matthew seemed desperate to do something extra to stop her from going out the door of the exam room. She watched his eyes focus on her left hand and then glance back up at her face. "Excuse me, Dr. Kippler, but how is it that a lady like you isn't married? I'm sorry, that's none of my business."

He looked down as an ashamed little boy who had gone too far.

Reading through his attempt at innocence, she leaned forward and offered him her condolences. "It's OK, you can look back up. I'm a widow, and I live with my little six-year-old daughter who is the most important person in my life."

She realized he wasn't playacting as his voice cracked and his hands briefly covered his face. He was genuinely moved as his volume dropped and his voice softened. "Well, I'm very sorry about that. Your husband was one lucky man while he lived though, because he had you. Look, there I go again."

This time his bashful grin was familiar and she appreciated its honesty. She grinned back. "No harm done, Mr. Hunter. Thank you."

As they parted, she asked him to return in two weeks for another blood pressure check and repeat blood work. "I want to make sure your blood count stays up."

Matthew was apologetic as he stumbled for words. "I was hopin' you would clear me for a few weeks. I need to see my mother, then I need to go to Europe on business, and I want to see my children in England."

Alyssa agreed. "That's actually fine. So, your children live in England?"

She was surprised to get only a very brief nod in response. Returning to her train of thought with regard to his health, she repeated,

"I really think you're fine. Please try not to drink, and I'll see you when you return. We'll take that little tag off your eye when you get back, OK?"

"It's a deal." Matt nodded as he hopped down from the table. "That's all I ever originally wanted." He reached out for her hand and shook it with total doctor-patient respect. "Thank you, Doc, I can't thank you enough for everythin'."

This visit had gone well and Alyssa felt like she had taken professional control of the meeting much better than she had during the hospital visits. She felt professionally secure, and she didn't forget that he probably had a girlfriend. Her feelings toward him had, during the last couple of days, taken their appropriate place. When he left, she returned to her office once again to gaze out her window and watch him get into his Mercedes and drive away. This time she had a pleasant confidence that Matthew Hunter would be back.

Alyssa left the office with her mother for lunch.

They sat across from each other in a nearby quaint little restaurant and Dionna ordered a California chicken grilled salad, and Alyssa ordered a blackened chicken Caesar salad.

Dionna sighed. "What a busy morning, and boy, that Matthew Hunter is a good-looking guy. Honey, I think he has his eye on you."

"He does not." A wave of heat rose up Alyssa's neck. "Well, maybe. I'm not sure if he's interested in me or if his style is just to flirt with everyone. I don't want to read into it."

"I wouldn't be surprised if he calls you for something more than a health problem or an appointment."

Alyssa tried to read her mother's face. "Why, did he say something to you?"

Dionna shook her head. "He didn't need to. It's just obvious."

Alyssa's eyes lit up. "Mama, he had his secretary, Margie, with him the entire time he was in the hospital, and my guess is that she's his current toy. But he was so sweet and gentle with everyone. Who wouldn't fall for him a little just looking at those beautiful blue eyes?"

She playfully shrugged her shoulders. "Too bad he's taken."

Dionna nodded. "I'm glad you still have an eye for quality. And the way he looked at you in the office today, I doubt he's taken. There are still some great men out there, and one is waiting for you. You never know, maybe he's it. You might find out if you took just a little time away from your duties once in a while, and thought of yourself."

Alyssa's eyes welled up and she wiped them with her napkin. "Mother. We had this discussion the other night. You've got to notice that I don't feel beautiful, or even appealing. You notice everything else. I'm dead inside, except for the love I have for you and Lisa. I want to spend all my free time with you and Lisa. Besides, I do have Jean-Marc to keep me sparked up. He's the best man friend I could ask for, and I have dear Susanna for a girlfriend."

Dionna sighed and looked down, adjusting her own napkin on her lap. "Do you remember when we left Paris the day after your thirteenth birthday? You and Jean-Marc had a huge crush on each other that summer. I'll never forget how you stared out the plane window with tears running down your face. You both thought you were so in love. He still is, honey. It's not fair to him, and it's really quite sad. I hope for his sake, one of these days he meets a girl who loves him back the way he deserves. He'll never get over you unless that happens. When it does, you can't blame him for pulling away from you, because no woman would put up with a gorgeous friend like you as competition. It gets lonely later in life when you're alone. It's only natural that a mother would worry about her daughter the way I worry about you. All I can say is, if an older Matthew Hunter came my way, I'd go for it. Just think about it, honey, it can't hurt."

At the thought of her mother suggesting that she jump back in the dating game, a pain bubbled up in Alyssa's throat. She knew her mother was right, and this was the first time she admitted it to herself.

"Anyway, Mother, this is a silly conversation. I'm sure he won't ask me out, and if he did it would be wrong, because I'm his doctor, and besides, I'm not interested in a skirt-chasing international playboy." She wiped her mouth with her napkin and determinedly picked up her fork. "Now, how's your salad?"

As though her mother understood she'd pushed Alyssa a little too far, she gracefully allowed the conversation to stick to topics less controversial than her daughter's love life.

After lunch they walked back to the office. Dionna gave Alyssa an appraising look. "That new doctor next door, Dr. Garbo, surely does like covering our patients whenever possible."

"You mean he sure is eligible to buy the practice. I know he wants to buy our practice. Maybe he's better in business than I am, but the HMOs aren't going away."

"It's not that you're bad in business." Her mother clasped Alyssa's hand as they walked. "If anything, you care too much."

Alyssa's chest filled with warmth at her mother's

understanding. "You're right, you know. But I can't keep the finances up the way they are going, and . . . I'm tired."

"Admitting it is the first step," Dionna joked.

Alyssa laughed with her, and it felt good to be Mommy's little girl just then. It reminded her of childhood when it was so safe to share her worries with someone she trusted so completely.

"I'll talk to Dr. Garbo soon and see if we can work something out. Thanks for this lunch, Mama."

The next few weeks passed quickly. Alyssa continued to help at the Women's Hope for Harmony House. They were having difficulty raising money for the badly needed air conditioning repair. After exhausting other funding options, Alyssa ended up paying for it herself.

As she sat at her desk in her home office to write out the check, she listened to the eleven o'clock news. The sad state of affairs with the United States economy and world terror all made the general atmosphere a little gloomy. It had been eight years since the tragedy of 9/11, and so much had continued to change for the worse around the world. Iraq was in the news and Saddam Hussein's capture, trial and execution were in the past. Thousands of American soldiers continued dying in vain. Iraq never needed weapons of mass destruction, because with the help of international greed, Iraq and its tragic society had become a monster of mass destruction. The presidential elections had passed, and gender, race, experience, and hope had all been part of the competition.

The past was nothing like the present. Alyssa's mother sadly remarked how different things might have been if only her beloved husband had lived longer. She and her daughter understood the pain of losing a mate to an untimely death. Alyssa longed to be with her father, who unfortunately had died at fifty-six years old, after a long battle with leukemia. Dionna was forty-six, and Alyssa was a twenty-seven-year-old resident physician at the time. Her new husband was the surgeon who put in her father's port for his chemotherapy. Alyssa was always grateful that Alex was able to know her father, even if it was only during his illness. He was a loving and good father. She was proud to be his little girl. Everyone saw him as such an interesting man who was a brilliant correspondent respected by the best.

She believed he would be proud of her work against domestic violence, and contemplating the sale of her practice in Menlo, for that purpose was quite timely. Her teaching information at the Harmony House was taken from material she was compiling to write a book about the red flags of domestic abuse.

She didn't know what, but something needed to change in her life soon, and selling the practice would be a start toward moving into another direction professionally, and maybe her personal life was ready for a change, too. It was hard to believe that she and Lisa had already been without Alex for over six years. Losing him forever took just a split second. A careless and crazy decision of a teenage driver at an intersection snuffed out her husband's life, and all of Alyssa's dreams died with him.

But finally, she was experiencing new hope and she wanted to fulfill new dreams.

Chapter Seven

It had been a few weeks since Matthew left for England. Alyssa stopped at Barney's after dropping Lisa at school to meet Jean-Marc. They each ordered a large cappuccino and settled at their favorite table near the aromatic fresh coffees sold by the bag. "Alyssa," Jean-Marc said seriously, "Mother has asked me to come back to France because my father hasn't been all that well lately. They're both getting older now, and I need to spend time with them. I've decided to close my house up early this year."

The chatter of other customers faded into the background as the truth of her mother's warning sank in. "So soon? But—"

Jean-Marc reached for Alyssa's hands across the table, focusing his huge Kean painting eyes on hers. "You are doing really well and so is Lisa. I need to get serious about my life and go home to France for a while." He cleared his throat keeping his voice from cracking as he forced a painful smile.

Alyssa stretched her arms out across the table to reach him, her hands tightly grasping his, "Jean-Marc, you can't leave me right now. I'm getting ready to sell my practice so we can all have a better family life. I need your brains to help me negotiate. We'll do all sorts of things together because I'll finally have time and freedom. Life would be awful without you here to enjoy it with us."

"Alyssa, I wish I could believe that. Besides, it will take

some time to sell your practice, and I'm not leaving forever."
He laughed in that special awkward way she read through
so easily. "I'll always love you." He held her hands in his.
"But I need to get away from you in order to detach myself a
little. I need to meet other ladies, and as long as you're near
me, I have no desire for them. Your mother and I were talking
about that last night. I don't know what is wrong with me."
He laughed again and let go of her hands. "Last night while
you were at the Harmony House, Dionna, Lisa, and I made
dinner together. We ate outside by the pool, and I told them
that I'm leaving. Dionna wants to come with me to visit my
parents."

Alyssa's day was ruined with the news that brought back
that lonely void she felt when Jean-Marc wasn't nearby, and
they finished their drinks in stilted silence.

As she pulled up to her office a few minutes later, she
noticed Matthew Hunter's Mercedes parked in front.

"I guess Mr. Hunter is back from Europe," she said to
herself aloud.

After the discouragement of this morning's conversation
with Jean-Marc, the thought of seeing Matthew Hunter in her
exam room kindled an unexpected flicker of pleasure, which
she quickly snuffed out before it could turn into more.

She turned the key to the back door of her office and
entered privately as she so often chose to do. She buzzed the
front office and asked who her first patient was. It was Mr.
Hunter. Alyssa went straight to the mirror. She ran a brush
through her hair and adjusted her clothes.

"Oh, what am I doing? Who cares?" Again, she spoke
aloud to herself, which continued to be her incorrigible habit.
Looking in the mirror, she flipped her fabulous chestnut-

auburn hair, helping it fall over her shoulders.

With determined steps, she walked down the hallway to the room with Mr. Hunter's chart on the door. His presence was an intrusion into her most private world, which was supposed to be lonely and miserable right then. She tried to swallow away the big lump that was stuck in her throat left over from Jean-Marc's morning news.

Mr. Hunter's chart revealed that his blood pressure was perfect and he'd lost a little weight. Her attitude changed for the better. At least something was going right. She believed he was really trying to comply as a patient, and it was impressive. Cheerfully opening the door, she entered the room and shook his hand. "Mr. Hunter, it's nice to see you. Your blood pressure is great and you've lost six pounds. That's really good."

His expression brightened. "Every time I turned down a glass of champagne or wine, I thought of you. Every time I gave up a fresh-baked roll, I thought of you." He laughed easily and his humor was entertaining.

Alyssa chuckled. "I bet it's never boring to be in your company, is it?"

"I get bored sometimes, but then I never get away from myself," he answered. "Sometimes I could do with a change of scenery, ya know? Speakin' of scenery, you're quite a picture with your hair all long and loose like that. I like it."

Ignoring his comment, she listened to his heart and lungs and noted the little skin tag on his eyelid. "Are you still waiting for me to remove that little tag from your face?"

He answered lightly, "Yeah. It's about time we got to the real reason why I first came to see you. I think I've earned it."

"I think you have, too. You can just lie back, get comfortable and we'll be done in a jiffy."

While cleansing his lid and proceeding to prepare him for the tiny procedure, she continued, "How was your trip to England?"

She clipped off the skin tag.

He didn't flinch. "Did you already do it? I couldn't feel a thing."

"You weren't supposed to feel it. That's what numbing medicine is for."

"I'm flattered you remembered I went to England. It was OK, mostly business as usual. I was anxious to get back to the States. I have some important things cookin' here. But it was great to see my kids. I don't get as much time with them as I would like."

With Alyssa's encouragement, he sat back up and held the little gauze square over his eye as she directed him to do.

She kept the conversation going. "It must be hard to have your children living so far away. How many children do you have?"

Matthew beamed with fatherly pride. "I have three beautiful kids. Matthew Junior's twenty, Robert's seventeen, and my daughter, Dierdra, is fifteen."

"That's great." Alyssa turned away from Matthew as she disposed of the needles in the sharps container. "I would have liked more than one child. Unfortunately, I lost my husband shortly after my daughter was born."

"You're still young. You could fall in love again and have more children, ya know?" His voice had lost its humorous tone, and instead resonated with sincerity as she turned back to him.

He picked up a small paper bag he had tucked near his side while lying down. Opening it with one hand, he reached in and pulled out a delicate and beautifully sculptured figurine.

"This is a hand painted Juliet I picked up for you in London. Isn't she beautiful? Please don't think it's pushy of me for gettin' you somethin, I don't mean to be outta line. She just reminded me of you, so I bought her."

Alyssa was delighted that he'd remembered her while he was so far away. She held the little Juliet and smiled in appreciation for the gift.

He looked downward and spoke. "You know, Dr. Kippler, I want to thank you for the care you've given me. My blood pressure was really high. You never made me afraid even when I went into the hospital bleedin' to death. I just knew that you would fix everythin', and I would be fine as long as you were there for me. Thank you."

She felt her heart rush up through her chest and she was at a loss for words. She wanted to call him Matt or Matthew, or whatever his friends called him. For that second, she wanted to close the office doors and meet him during some beautiful frozen moment in time. It would be a moment when two people melt together and bond so deeply that they could command the universe as one. Unknowingly, he had awakened her sexuality again. Who knows what forces drive human desire. Last night she'd told her mother she wasn't ready for a social life, and right now she would give anything to just wrap her body around this person she hardly knew and be totally his.

She reeled under unfamiliar sensations. In the back of her mind, she knew a woman's sense of romance looks for sexuality in permanent bonding and security. It isn't usually about an orgasm, but rather, it's about many orgasms of love and nesting and holding and cuddling and being together forever. Yet this man she barely knew made passion and longing control her body.

Only human dignity and professional commitment held her intact. He leaned forward slightly as though sensing possible vulnerability, though he had no idea how vulnerable she was at that moment.

"Dr. Kippler, in a very respectful invitation, will you have dinner with me?" He melted into her with his eyes as he sped up his pace of speech. "Let's break the doctor-patient barrier. I'll find another doctor. You already saved me. I don't want to be your patient, I want to be your friend. I'm not lookin' for anythin' in particular. I want to know who you are as a person. I am very weak for gorgeous women, but you have all the ingredients. You have more than just your good looks. Frankly, I couldn't wait to get back here so I could ask you. I have nothin' to lose, 'cause if you turn me down nothin' will change, and if you say yes, I've won more than I could hope for. The most you can do is get rid of me as a patient, because I'm out of place. There now, I got it off my chest."

Alyssa was flustered. "Mr. Hunter, I'm truly flattered. But you know it would be inappropriate for me to date my patient. That's just something we never do. It's part of an understood code in medicine."

Matthew looked surprised that she'd turned his invitation down. She imagined his advances were rarely, if ever, rejected by a woman. He looked into her eyes again, quite bravely and without embarrassment. "Again, I said the wrong thing." He smiled.

But he hadn't said the wrong thing. Warmth and desire for him still suffused her body as she lingered near him. She wanted him as much as he wanted her.

"I'll see you here next month." Having set the boundary, she offered him a no-nonsense handshake.

Though Matthew's mother had imparted in him the importance of a Southern man's genteel treatment of women, the respectful handshake at his parting with Alyssa amazed him. He gave the Mercedes an extra shot of gas as he peeled out of the clinic's parking lot. "This lady isn't just some woman to take to dinner and then to bed. She needs to be earned," he thought, while concluding that he wanted her more than ever.

Matthew was always up for a challenge. The chase was usually the most fun part of any relationship and the chase was on. That old saying, "Expectation is greater than the realization," worked for him. He was easily bored with most women, but she was different and he was sure of that.

His appointment with Alyssa next month couldn't come soon enough for him. He contemplated calling her and insisting that she meet him after work. Maybe flowers? Realizing both ideas could be misconstrued as stalking her, he decided to be patient and wait.

Alyssa moved through the morning feeling much better than she had felt before seeing Matthew. That extra sparkle in her eyes was obvious as she placed the Juliet statue on the counter of the nurse's station.

Susanna couldn't hold back her intense curiosity as she ogled over the porcelain silhouette. "Alyssa, what happened with Matthew Hunter today? I bet he asked you out, didn't he?"

"Yes, but I turned him down." Alyssa's confidence was clearly too much for Susanna to bear.

"You did what? Are you crazy? Tell me you didn't, please." Susanna's scowl told it all. "All these years you haven't noticed anyone. This guy has had your head spinning since the first time he came into this office, and you turned him down."

"I think he'll ask me out again. If he doesn't, it wasn't worth it anyway. He'll be back next month." Alyssa sheepishly grinned. "I think he liked my hair down." She winked and wiggled her hips toward the next door with a chart hanging on it.

Susanna threw her hands into the air and shook her head. "I give up."

Dionna had just returned from her visit to France in mid-June and was back to work running the front office as she had for many years. She cheerfully looked up from her desk to greet the handsome man who was not so much a stranger to the office anymore. "Hello, Mr. Hunter, it's nice to see you," she bubbled. "We're running about thirty minutes behind. Do you mind waiting?"

"Not at all," he answered, "I'll just go get my newspaper. I left it in the car."

Her granddaughter's little voice suggested, "Oh, could you read to me instead?" Gazing up at him with sweet green eyes, she said, "I'm bored. I have a new book about Bambi that my mommy bought. Look Bambi pops out." Lisa held the open pages up toward Matthew, inviting him to share it with her.

Dionna quickly spoke up, "Lisa, why don't you come back here with Grandmother and I'll read to you?"

She looked at Matthew and apologized for Lisa's forward behavior. "She's the doctor's daughter, and lots of the patients play with her. Sometimes we need to slow her down. She thinks she owns this office and the patients."

Matthew looked delighted. "Oh, it's fine. I love children. Mine are older and I miss those ole times." He asked, "Are you Dr. Kippler's mother?"

"Yes I am." she smiled proudly. "And I've been her receptionist since she got out of medical school."

"I guess apples don't fall far from the trees. You're very pretty, if I may say so with respect. Ma'am, it's my pleasure to meet you. Your daughter is a wonderful doctor, and I'm sure you're very proud of her." Matthew returned the smile.

Dionna felt herself blushing. An adorable Southern gentleman stood in front of her. She thought, "Why can't my Alyssa take an interest in him?"

Matthew sat down with Lisa next to him. "Here, Lisa, let me read your book to you," he said. Bambi popped out of each page as the two new friends enjoyed the love story of the forest. They sat comfortably together musing over the pop-ups and had just come to the end of the story with a pop-up of Bambi and Faline, when the nurse called for him.

He looked down at Lisa, who was mesmerized by the pictures in her book. Her childlike innocence reminded him of times spent reading with his own children, when they seemed to delight in the pictures over and over again for the first time.

"I gotta go, honey," he said. "I hope I can read with you again sometime." She seemed to hardly notice his departure.

He got up and winked at Dionna, who was watching him leave the waiting room to once again see her daughter.

This visit was very short. Matthew's blood pressure was

120/78, and as Dr. Kippler read the numbers to him, her smile radiated soft warmth. Matthew felt his heart skip and he was sad that it didn't show up while she listened to him with her stethoscope. It would have given him an excuse to flirt with her. He just felt like all his charm had run out. There was only one thing he wanted to do, and that was to kiss his doctor. He almost took her face in his hands to do that, but he stopped himself from trying such a daring move.

He groped for conversation. "I met your mother and your beautiful little girl in the waitin' room."

"I hope she didn't pester you," Alyssa answered. "She thinks she owns our reception area. Most of the patients adore her, but once in a while she meets a sour person who would rather she go away."

"On the contrary, she's a little doll." Matthew again ran out of words.

All of that playboy style he'd worked so hard to cultivate just melted away, leaving him feeling as uncertain and awkward as an inexperienced teenager. "Dr. Kippler," he spoke very softly clearing his throat more than once as he fumbled to start his next sentence, "I sure would like to get to know you a little. We could just go for a walk on the beach or somethin." He cleared his voice once more and froze his gaze on hers. "I understand about socializin' with male patients bein' outta line. But we'll keep it a secret just between us that I've been your patient. I'll go to that doctor next door for my blood pressure." Breaking eye contact with her, he paused, and then caught her eyes in his one more time. "I'll beg you if I have to do it, by golly."

Chapter Eight

$\mathcal{M}$atthew arrived at the restaurant, pointed to his favorite table, and padded the host's palm. That evening he would meet Alyssa at the Bistro, a quaint little Italian restaurant on the water. Candlelit tables lined the cobblestone sidewalk outside and the smell of fresh-baked bread filled the air. The elegance of white linen tablecloths was mixed with the casual comfort of old wooden chairs and straw baskets filled with imported cheeses and fruit. Strolling Italian singers stopped here and there to quietly play a romantic song to would-be lovers in the night.

Moments later, Alyssa strolled into view. Her long auburn hair flowed loosely, framing her beautiful face and caressing her delicate shoulders. She had poured herself into a tiny, sensuous, black dress that clung to her hips and exposed just enough cleavage spilling forward to excite any man. He was stimulated to feel his best. His eyes undressed her and his mind followed her curves as she angled toward the table. He wanted her totally.

His back was to the water and its breathtaking view of Menlo's most beautiful yachts docked in rows one after the other. Directly behind him and staged perfectly was his world-class one-hundred-fifty-foot Sea Cliff. He stood as the waiter pulled out Alyssa's chair.

He was at ease with his perfect, romantic, and flirtatious Southern drawl rolling off of his tongue without missing a cue, "Dr. Kippler, you are beautiful."

"Please, it's time you call me Alyssa." Her nervous answer was an obvious attempt to avoid responding to the compliment.

The evening began with slight awkwardness, but after a glass of wine, the jitters decreased and more comfortable conversation ensued. Matthew was eager to tell her the things about himself that made him proud to be who he was.

He began, "You know, I started a boat company with a paper boat I built as a little boy. I glued papers together and created a fantasy about ownin' the biggest yachtin' firm in the world. That was back when Aristotle Onassis' yacht, Christina, was always in the news. I used to love hearin' about his adventures and all the famous people who got to be part of his shippin' empire. We always lived near water, and I used to gaze across the ocean thinkin' about how I was goin' to build the most wonderful ship in the world. I've done all right, but I've not built the best ship in the world."

He leaned over the table and changed his attention from yachts to her. His eyes met hers. "You know, what is it about you that makes me want to turn my guts inside out around you? I feel like I need to perform for you or somethin'. You're the kind of girl who just goes through life and probably doesn't even have a clue about how magical you are. I don't know. Maybe it's just me."

The moment of awkwardness that followed made him wish he hadn't said so much so fast. He wanted to take it back. He fumbled with the menu. "Have you eaten here before?"

Alyssa nodded with a smile that she had.

He continued, while hardly stopping to take a breath, trying to get away from the topic of his enchantment with her.

"I love the oysters here. My mother used to oyster hunt with us near the battery in Charleston when I was a kid. Mother loved to fish. We were very poor and fishin' and oyster huntin' were free. Besides, we lived right near the water. Seafood was everyone's main diet in Charleston. Isn't it weird how we're here now, and the past is just like tellin' a story?"

Just then the music in the restaurant heightened. A man sat down at their table and began to sing, "Amore, Amore." The violinists stood behind him playing beautifully and the discomfort of the moment melted away.

"This is the most romantic restaurant in Menlo," Alyssa sighed. "I love the beautiful boats in the background, the food is gourmet, and the whole atmosphere is just wonderful. You couldn't have made a better choice."

He grinned. "I hope you like the company best of all."

She lifted her wine glass. "Here's just one glass of wine, to best of all."

Their dinner went very well. His sense of excitement about her heightened as the evening progressed. Every new topic they each shared about themselves increased his awareness of common ground. Matthew easily impressed Alyssa with his diversity and in turn he was overwhelmed with her delightful and brilliant personality. With almost no effort, the stiff and formal lady became a natural, giggling girl. The evening passed too quickly. Everyone else had left the restaurant and the waiter politely awaited Matt's attention. Matt apologized for being last to leave and graciously paid the tab.

"Alyssa," he whispered, "let's go for a walk on the beach and get our feet wet."

The couple left the table arm in arm. They crossed the road where the restaurant opened directly to beach access, and Matt took off his shoes and helped Alyssa remove hers.

He hid them in a bush and said, "Now we can run along the shore like a couple of crazy kids splashin' in the surf. If your dress wasn't so pretty, I'd entice you to jump into the water with me and have a moonlight swim."

His suggestion, or maybe the warm summer night air, made Alyssa giggle. "OK, I'll race you to the water. The last one there is a rotten egg."

Off she darted toward the breaking tide with the moon right in front of her. He gave her a head start, passed her quickly, slid to a stop at the water's edge and waited for a second.

A wild impulse to jump in, pants and all, struck him. That's exactly what he did, and she followed him.

Both of them laughed as they splashed in the shallow surf. He swam out a few feet and she followed him again as if he were a magnet pulling her into his force field.

"This feels great. It's a perfect dessert after a perfect dinner," he sighed.

She swam next to him and floated on her back, looking up at the star-studded sky. "My dad used to bring me to the beach on nights like this. He spent hours teaching me the patterns of the constellations." She pointed to the North Star and followed the three-star pattern to the Dipper with her finger. "Do you ever look at the stars and believe you can be anything you want to be?" she breathed.

It was as though she could read his heart. "I have had such a great time with you tonight. Have you had fun?"

She glanced at him playfully, splashed water at him, and giggled again. "Yes I have."

They headed for the shore and both sat down on the sand with the water encircling their feet. She ran her fingers through her wet hair and turned her head toward him. He saw her as if he had just encountered an angel. He was mesmerized and couldn't speak. Without effort or resistance his arms enveloped her and he pulled her near him and lowered them both to lay their heads on the sand. He cradled her, allowing her arms and her breasts to melt into him, which completely broke the doctor-patient barrier. His firm body was aroused as he pressed himself against her. She gave a soft moan that sent a thrill through him. They caressed each other as the water's edge rolled up around her hair. Their lips began dancing together, tasting each other as if having found a fresh water stream after being thirsty for so long. Those few moments lingered all too briefly when the uninvited tide drove them back into a sitting position.

Once again he pressed his mouth to hers and tenderly kissed her. Pulling back so that their lips almost touched, he whispered, "I feel like we just shot that famous beach scene from that movie *On the Beach.*

She smiled. "I believe the movie was called *From Here to Eternity.*" He loved the way she never missed a cue. Usually, he spent an evening with a woman because it ended up in bed. Being with Alyssa was different from all that. She offered the excitement of brainpower, intellectual challenge, and sexuality. On other nights, if he wasn't after the tenderness of a warm body, he would choose one of his male friends for mental stimulation. Being with Alyssa was as satisfying as being with any man, yet she made him feel complete as a man.

He had to proceed with wisdom so he wouldn't lose her. With an instant flash of control, he changed the mood and pulled her to her feet. "C'mon. I want to show you where I live."

He was quick to pick up Alyssa's uneasiness. "No, no. I promise you that I have no ulterior motives. I just want you to know where to find me if ever you need me. You'll like my place. You were lookin' at it right behind me while we ate dinner tonight."

Her uneasiness turned to curiosity as she questioned, "You mean you live on a yacht?"

"Yeah," he answered. "You'll like it. C'mon, I'll show you."

With so much to share, where they each lived hadn't been mentioned during their dinner.

"How fun," she answered. "OK, I'd love to see your home. It looked more like a ship to me. I can't stay long, because I have rounds at the hospital early tomorrow morning. Don't forget, I'm a working girl."

He grinned, put his arm around her, and squeezed her shoulder. "Just relax," he said. "I have a plane to catch for Los Angeles at 9:15 tomorrow mornin'. We both need to call it an early night."

His next move would normally have been a perfect brunch served on his yacht, a small cruise out of the intra-coastal, a romantic swim, and who knew what else. He'd never been more disappointed to leave a town.

She hid her disappointment with, "Now I feel guilty for keeping you out so late. I had no idea you were leaving town tomorrow."

He reassured her, "I'll be back in three days. It's a business trip again, and I really wish I didn't have to go at all. I'd like to know we could have dinner again when I get back."

She didn't answer him. As they left the beach all sandy and dripping wet, he slipped his hand into hers. It was a perfect fit. Not a word was said between them as they walked along the short path leading to the display of yachts docked in perfect rows behind the Bistro.

"This is where I live when I'm in Menlo." He pointed to the unbelievably beautiful Sea Cliff yacht. It was definitely the one that had been docked directly in front of her while they dined.

He grinned in response to her mouth dropping, but said nothing.

Alyssa was caught off guard, "I gazed at that boat off and on during dinner, and wondered who owned it. It was you." She couldn't stop herself from imagining about the crazy parties he probably hosted there. She had just realized how he'd gained his playboy reputation. For a moment she felt threatened by her new emotions, but she caught herself realizing that a kiss was certainly not a commitment. There was no danger there.

He led her up the gangway to a glass door entrance with the large and perfectly polished letters, MJH, above it. To the right was another door leading to a small garden shower. Again, the perfect gentleman and host, his concern for her was sincere.

"Why don't you slip out of that wet dress. You can shower off here. Towels are over there on the shelf. I'll find you somethin' dry to wear home."

He left and she obediently removed her garments and showered away those moments on the beach. She reached for a large, soft, white bath towel with his gold insignia, MJH, on it. She wrapped it around her body and found a smaller towel to wrap around her hair.

Matt knocked on the door and handed her one of his T-shirts, humorously speaking from behind the door, "I'm sorry. I'm plumb outta lady clothes."

She wondered if he really had given away his last female garment to someone else before her.

She was envious of that lady. "But then," she told herself, "Why should I envy someone who was with him last? If it was a meaningful thing, it must be over now, or he's just a jerk and who would want that?"

She tried to stop herself from all the philosophy, but she hoped that there was nobody else in his life as she slipped into his T-shirt, fluffed her panties dry in a towel, and put them back on.

She opened the door to the inside cabin, which led directly to a massive bedroom. It had perfectly polished teakwood walls, plush carpets, a king-sized bed, and a large jet tub in the corner. Recessed lighting in the ceiling sent out a golden glow through the room. The color scheme of blue and gold in combination with the dark teakwood walls and matching furniture filled the room with the luxury of royalty. On one side was a desk displaying pictures of Matt's three children from early childhood to the present.

He entered the bedroom still sandy and wet. "I'm sorry. This is the only way in from the outside shower. If you'd like, you can come into the living room. I'll quickly clean off, and then I'll show you around."

He led her into the living room, again with dark teakwood walls and furniture, accentuated by recessed lighting of gold and blue tones. The overstuffed couches and chairs were white with accents of blue and gold on the many throw pillows. The carpets were white Berber. Alyssa was speechless.

"Please, make yourself comfortable," he encouraged. "There's anythin' you want to drink at the bar. I'll just be a moment." His response to her awe at his castle put her at ease.

Then he disappeared to the shower outside.

Moments later he reappeared, wearing shorts, a T-shirt, those beautiful big blue eyes, and the warm smile that came so easily to him. He gave her a grand tour of his pride and joy, which she imagined had been constructed for only his personal desires and fantasies. He explained that the interior detail and core rivaled those of other award-winning motor yachts from around the world. Matt had every reason to be proud of his masterpiece, and his pride showed in the gleam of confidence in his eyes and the rich authority in his voice.

They strolled along the deck and he pointed out details that separated his vessel from most other yachts. They stopped for a moment. Alyssa leaned on the rail and gently slid her hand back and forth across the perfectly polished wood. It was an excuse to take weight off of her slightly aching feet. He leaned on the rail next to her as he gazed into the distance. His expression softened, became introspective and his deep loneliness stood nakedly before her. It reminded her of that innocence she felt about him that first day in the office.

"I named her after my little girl, Dierdra," he sighed. "See, I'm like you. I love my children more than anythin' in the world. The difference is, I just got so strung out over my childhood dreams of makin' this company what it is, that I lost my kids durin' the process. I have one kid, Matt, Jr., whose havin' some problems right now. It hurts me to see his behavior because he's so bright and such a well-educated boy for his age. I know he's angry about a lot of things he saw that were wrong in his childhood. So much was my fault because I was abused as a kid by my father, and I never really could quite do the father thing just right." He stopped talking for a few seconds, and she silently urged him the courage to regroup his thoughts and continue sharing his emotions with her. "I have another kid, Robert, who's incredible. He's a genius in school. He's a soccer star, and he's headed for pre-med. And then I have little Dierdra. She's sixteen years old and she wants to live with Daddy. I'm up for it, but her mother isn't goin' to let go of her easily, not for one little minute. I understand, but I just want to be with one of my kids before they all grow up and it's over. I've missed so much. Grandchildren are great I'm sure, but I'm not sure I want to start real parentin' with my grandchildren."

He became quiet again. Then he turned his face to her and he cupped her chin gently in his hand. He once again melted into her with a perfect kiss. Their rhythm was in harmony as if they had created the art of a man and woman touching. Their lips parted as gently as they had touched.

He lingered near her with his mouth barely touching her ear. "I want you, Alyssa," he whispered. "I want you here tonight."

She could feel the invitation of his warm lips slowly brushing across her cheek, then down her neck and returning to her face until they fell onto her mouth again, this time with fervent passion. Their bodies turned toward one another and pressed together. Their human touch tortured desire. Innocence was disappearing quickly. Breathing a little harder, he repeated, "I want you here tonight." She momentarily reflected on that moment weeks ago in her office, when she wanted him totally for the first time. She basked in the luxury of actually experiencing a taste of it, teetering between desire and common sense.

He gently backed his body away from her and continued, "Tired little girl. I want you to be rested for your day tomorrow. I doubt you'd stay with me anyway, not yet. Alyssa, let's do this thing right or not at all. I tend to move in a little fast. It's my style to take what I want and when I want it. That's not always a good thing. Maybe we could make somethin' better than either of us has ever had before. Let's be careful with each other. Let's treasure whatever we have right now. Maybe this won't go any further than tonight. If it does, let's allow it grow to a crescendo. If I ever make love with you, I want it to be like the first and like the last woman I'll ever have. I want to bond so deeply that it controls us both."

Then he chuckled. "I'm very proud at this moment. I can be a romantic gentleman, and I just proved it."

"You sure did." She hadn't thought she could be so drawn to a man, and his gentlemanly patience for her sake only made the attraction stronger. Yet it was all happening so fast, and her work at Harmony House had shown her too many quick-involvement relationships that fell into disharmony or violence.

He hugged her. "It feels great."

She cautioned herself to take it one step at a time as he continued, "You know, I haven't been with a woman in six months? I just got some crazy notion that I don't want short affairs anymore. I'm tired of buildin' up the night for the big bedroom scene. Don't misunderstand me. I love sex. Sometimes, I just think I spent my youth as an oversexed fool. But what I really want is love. That's all anybody really wants, isn't it?"

Alyssa kept her dignity. "Matt, this is the first evening we've spent together. We have just met each other's representative tonight. We don't know each other at all. I have a philosophy about relationships. When two people meet, they show each other only their best sides. You know, the outer shells. I call that their personal representatives. As they spend more time together, the real person begins to come forward and the representative fades into the background. Only when that comfort zone is reached do people really begin to know each other. I think closeness begins there. The last man I was with was my husband, and the next man I want to be with, I will marry, if you know what I mean."

He grinned and shook his head. His masculine giggle washed over her, and a tremendous pressure valve was relieved. He continued to giggle. "What's wrong with us? We're livin' in the 2000s and we're action' like our grandparents used to act. Let's stop this before I get sick. Let me walk you to your car."

They walked to her car, again arm in arm, and again in silence. He helped her open the door and he brushed his lips across her cheek, "Good night, lovely Alyssa, thank you."

As she started her engine, she paused to watch him step back from the car. She was very turned on by his natural country boy demeanor. He truly was not phony, nor was he arrogant. His rural honesty and sweet demeanor mixed with his obvious cultured success created a very inviting package.

How wonderful she felt inside. Her whole body was alive and her feminine desire was willing to give, yet she was content. She smiled at him and he smiled back as she turned her wheels away from those perfect few hours. She couldn't help herself from watching him in her rearview mirror as he disappeared from view.

She wanted more, much more, than she had received from him that night.

Chapter Nine

*T*he next morning her mind combed through those few hours with Matt a thousand times. She relived each kiss and heard his voice in her head over and over again. As she lay in her luxurious bed, facing the sunrise with closed eyes, she realized the guilt she waited to feel wasn't there. Finally ready to take off her black veil, she believed that Alex was guiding her to do just that. Nobody could ever take Alex out of her heart, because he was her greatest love and the father of her child. Yet Alyssa was only thirty-four years old, with her whole life in front of her like Forest Gump's beautiful "box of chocolates," and she finally wanted the thrill of finding out what was inside the next piece.

The morning routine was particularly cheerful and everything fell into place. Jean-Marc, who had returned from France unexpectedly, surprised everyone for an early cup of coffee. Alyssa lifted the granola box. It was almost empty, but there was just exactly enough left to fill Lisa's bowl. The morning traffic moved smoothly, and every intersection greeted her with a green light.

As she dropped her little girl off at school, she kissed her good-bye and Lisa said, "Mommy, I like it when you smile. You're really the most fun mommy in the whole world, and I love you as big as the sky." Her little arms stretched out, grasping her mother's neck with a tight hug, and Alyssa was overwhelmed. Sharing her daughter's affection, she whispered, "Maybe this weekend we can go to Disney World like we've been planning."

Lisa performed her usual energetic leap from the car, "Yes, yes, yes! Mommy, will Uncle Marc still be here? He can go with us." Before Alyssa could answer, her happy child was skipping away from the car toward the playground.

Alyssa would rather not have been reminded that Jean-Marc's visit was for only two days. He'd told her that he had returned to check up on his three girls and make sure life was smooth in Menlo.

Her day was unusually light with an easy office patient load of twenty-two and nobody in the hospital. She left the office about 4:30 in the afternoon and stopped home to see her mother and Lisa before running on the beach. The three of them watched Rugrats together.

"What a cute show," Alyssa's mother said as the episode ended. She lifted her legs up and cradled them by wrapping her arms around her calves. Resting her chin on her knees, she continued, "So, I haven't talked to you since your dinner with Mr. Hunter. How did it go? Did you like him?"

Alyssa's voice bubbled over with bashful cheer. "Mother, he's great. It's almost too good to be true. We laughed and had so much fun. He's like the perfect man and he's so different from anyone I have ever met. He's almost more European than most Europeans with so much style and class. But with all of it, he's just a simple man. I've never met anyone like him."

"That's so good, honey," Alyssa's mother answered with a warm smile. "I'm sure you'll see him again soon."

Alyssa's giddiness continued, "He left for Los Angeles yesterday morning. He'll be back in a couple of days and he said he'd call me. I'm sure he will. You wouldn't believe his yacht. Mother, it's a ship. I've never seen anything like it. He's got it docked behind the Bistro, and he lives there when he's in town." She stopped short and dropped her mouth open for a second. "Wouldn't it be weird if he never called me again? Oh, that's ridiculous. Of course he will." Turning her attention to her work clothes she rushed toward the stairs, "I'd better change for my run with Jean-Marc. I can't wait to tell him all about everything. It's such a bummer that he's going back again so soon."

She began her run along the water alone, but seeing his figure running toward her, she slowed down and motioned for him to hurry and catch up. Shortly, he fell in beside her as he typically always had, and both of them automatically picked up speed together. They glided across the sand, caught in that runner's high that was heightened because they were together.

"Jean-Marc, I have so much to share with you. Did my mother tell you that I went out with Matthew Hunter last night?"

Jean-Marc sputtered out through his slight shortness of breath, "I heard."

"It's been five lonely years and thousands of my tears soaking the pillow at night. I've saved every fantasy in a secret corner of my heart that I closed off from myself since Alex died in my arms that awful, agonizing day. If I hadn't had you by my side during these years, I don't think I could ever have pulled through."

Alyssa made sure that Jean-Marc listened to her as they dropped their pace back to a slow jog. She knew he adored her and would support her in any way that she needed. But she had always denied that he could feel more for her than family ties.

He looked straight ahead as their feet slapped the wet sand. "Aren't you getting a little too excited, too fast?"

"What do you mean? I'm not that excited," she snapped back.

"I think you are. I just don't want you to get hurt." Jean-Marc picked up the pace a little. Alyssa continued talking about Matthew, while Jean-Marc brooded.

She realized that he was lost in his own thoughts, and she considered repeating the last two minutes of her monologue. "Jean-Marc, are you listening to me?"

"I'm listening to you. Maybe you're going a little too fast with your heart. Your heart is like a beautiful harp and your strings bring to life the finest music."

She noticed his French accent was getting stronger and his sentence structures were getting more awkward, sure signs that he was getting upset.

He groped the air as though searching for the right words. "You are a fine artist and you need your music to tune you. Oh, you know what I mean."

She understood his frustration.

"Please don't get broken again. You have been through a lot. I don't want to take a chance of ever losing you again like before."

"Let's change the subject. It's obviously a sore one, because you're forgetting your English. I'm sorry I brought it up."

Jean-Marc continued, "Do you remember when Alex and I lost all that money in Los Angeles?"

Alyssa couldn't have forgotten the business disaster that actually drove her to leave Alex for a time and return to Florida alone with their new baby. Soon after she met Alex, she introduced him to Jean-Marc, and the three of them became an instant trio. Alex often said he blamed himself for some of Alyssa's stressful lifestyle. The new changes in healthcare made it very difficult to survive financially in family practice, and unfortunately, his death had left behind very little monetary security for Lisa and her.

During their friendship, Jean-Marc joined Alex in a couple of business ventures, the last of which was a financial disaster. Together, they created a surgical adhesive paste to replace suture material. They patented the product, and instead of selling the idea, they decided to mass produce the paste in Thailand and import it back to the United States. Several hundred thousand dollars into the project, the overseas manufacturer closed its doors and the investment money disappeared. The financial loss had put a huge strain on Alyssa's and Alex's marriage. Jean-Marc had vehemently blamed himself for encouraging Alex to front half of the business with his own money. Alyssa tried to convince them to sell the idea instead of becoming distributors of the product, but they had visions of huge success with total control. They believed their product would revolutionize surgery. Instead, Alyssa and the baby left Los Angeles, the dream crashed, and Alex filed for California bankruptcy. Fortunately, he did have a fair life insurance policy, which Alyssa later used to build her home on the beach. Dionna gave Alyssa and Lisa the north side of her oceanfront property. Jean-Marc then bought the empty lot just north of it. He spent half his time in France and half his time in Menlo watching over Alyssa, Dionna, and Lisa. The three homes standing side by side facing the ocean created a small community with Alyssa's new home securely nestled between her mother and her best friend.

"Alyssa, when we lost all that money, Alex was really

ashamed. He made me promise to never let you down the way he believed he had. I have always tried to protect you from harm because I love you, and Alex would want me to encourage you to stop and take a deep breath before you get too excited about your dinner last night. Are you sure you should dive into this new relationship with such a famous playboy? It cannot be good."

Alyssa didn't answer him. She didn't want to put any dampers on the first romantic joy she had experienced in years. She clammed up because she wasn't going to let Jean-Marc's hang-ups poison their run. She decided to change the subject. "The sale of the practice looks very promising. Dr. Garbo is putting together his financials, and he'll give them to my lawyer next week."

"That's great."

As she slowed down to turn up the sand dune before her gate, she twisted toward him and pecked him on the cheek. "You know how much I appreciate you."

After he left Alyssa at her gate, Jean-Marc stopped running and walked back down to the water. He dropped down with a thud, sitting on the sand and digging his feet through it like a defeated boy, deeply in thought, pained and helpless.

"All these years, my darling Alyssa, you have been quite disconnected from reality. You are disconnected still, though today it was different. Why can't you choose me, Alyssa?" He dug his hands into the sand and filled them both, squeezing the moist granules through the webs of his fingers, as his fists tightened in painful anguish. He lowered his head to rest on solid ground and looking straight up to the sky, he groped for survival, "This is the kind of anguish that leaves a man feeling desperate because he can do nothing to change the truth. I am handsome and fun, and I am loving and kind to you. I am not so rich as he is, but you have never been after money. Why didn't you ever see me as your lover?" He was still as mesmerized by her sparkling energy as he had been as a boy. He had hoped during the last few years that he would someday be the man to fill that lonely void within her, but now he was convinced that it would never happen.

For Alyssa, there was no longer a void. Since meeting Matthew, wishing for a new world had dissipated and anticipation of her next meeting with him was all that mattered.

After their run, Alyssa darted upstairs to shower and get dressed for her lecture that night. She heard Jean-Marc downstairs, arriving through the back door a few minutes later. She quietly started down the stairs and paused while leaning on the wooden banister, where she could see into the great room. Her mother and Lisa were sitting on the couch and coloring on the coffee table. Alyssa could see her mother's puzzled face, but she could only see the back of Jean-Marc's head.

"Jean-Marc, you look like you've been hit by a ton of bricks."

"But of course." Jean-Marc was quick to answer, "You are the only one who knows how much I care for her. I want her happy. I just hope she won't go too fast. This guy is very smooth. She's been lonely and she likes him more than she admits. Maybe I am just jealous."

She wasn't surprised at their conversation, nor that they were hashing out her life. But the gist of their conversation annoyed her. It really was only her business whom she chose to love, and she wasn't going to let Jean-Marc or her mother interfere with her happiness. Instead of her usual cuddle with Lisa before she left for Harmony House, Alyssa bypassed the great room and closed the front door behind her.

Jean-Marc's vision blurred. "I think she just left. Dionna, I want to fight for her. But she doesn't love me. I must be crazy to have loved her for fourteen years, because she has given me no reason to believe she will ever love me back. She's going after this guy."

Dionna reassured him of her own loyalty by summoning him to sit beside her on the couch. As he sat, she put her arm around him and leaned close to him, "I've never understood why your relationship didn't change after Alex died. I'd love nothing better than to see you two together, and I've always been sure that sooner or later it would happen, but it didn't. Matthew's not a bad guy. He's very charming, and so far, he's being a total gentleman. I can't blame her for being interested."

"But why did you call me to tell me about her feelings for him if you don't believe we should be together?"

"Oh, Jean-Marc." Motherly concern creased her face. "I only wanted you to be happy for her."

"How can I be happy when Matthew Hunter is moving in for the kill?"

Jean-Marc couldn't let the gentleman phrase go. "A gentleman? A gentleman is nothing more than a clever man with patience." He smirked.

The sun was setting on the California coastline as Matthew arrived at the Beverly Hills Hotel. His excitement was transparent as he knocked on the garden hotel bungalow. Dierdra opened the door.

"Daddy!" She threw her arms around her father. "Mummy, Daddy's here." Her angelic-appearing mother, Carline, came out of the bedroom with a full smile across her face.

"Hello, Matt. I'm so glad this worked out that you were in Los Angeles while we're here." She reached out to offer a friendly handshake, and he returned the offer, and moved in for a peck on her cheek.

"Please, come in. We're just getting ready to go for dinner. You are joining us, are you not?"

"I'd like to, can Daddy come, Dierdra?" The famous Matthew Hunter grin melted the room.

Dierdra laughed and continued to cling to her father's arm. "You had better come with us. I've been waiting for you all day long, Daddy."

The formal ambience of the restaurant was toned down by the tropical display of foliage outside the window. As darkness overtook natural light, the outside garden came alive with torches and colored floodlights.

"Carline, let's toast to friendship. I am so happy to see you both tonight." He reached over and kissed Dierdra's head, then continued, "I have a huge deal goin' here tomorrow. I'm designin' a cruise ship for DeVinci. Wish me luck." Their glasses clicked, and the waiter lit the candle at their table.

Turning his attention again to his daughter, Matthew beamed with pride. "You're so beautiful. Are you sure I'm your daddy? You seem more grown-up than you were a few weeks ago. Tell me everythin' that's goin' on with you right now."

As Dierdra bubbled over with news from England, she included her brothers. "Matt and Robby wanted to come to see Auntie Amy with us, but they couldn't. Matt had to work and Robby has exams all week. None of us thought we'd get to see you or they probably would have come anyway. Oh, Daddy." She squeezed her father's hand and rubbed his forearm.

"If we could just talk your mother into lettin' you stay with me for the rest of the summer, it sure would be good. Maybe we can talk about it later tonight."

Carline glared into Matthew's eyes briefly and then broke contact. "Let's just enjoy a nice dinner together, OK? We're on our way to see Amy for one night, and then we're going to fly to Hawaii for a week. After that, Dierdra has lessons of her own to complete in England."

"One night? You've been here for three days and shoppin' on Rodeo Drive was more important than lettin' my sister spend a little time with her niece? Couldn't you a done a little better than one night?"

His territorial ex-wife's tightly closed lips illustrated the building tension and Matthew knew enough to back off. As the daughter of a British naval commander, she had a fiery power that had always attracted him to her, but it scared him a little, too.

Carline, Matt's first love, was a twenty-two-year-old English beauty when they met at a military party in London. She was petite and fiery and adorable with an English accent and lots of money. He was big, powerful, handsome, and the brand of America was written all over him as a naval officer stationed in Europe. He had joined the navy after graduating from the University of South Carolina, as a nautical engineer. There was no war, Vietnam was over, and there were no purple hearts or medals to earn. Instead, he served as part of an American-British team that spearheaded a new warship design, and Carline's father was his commander on the project. After serving four years for Uncle Sam, he was honorably discharged as an officer, with unchanged dreams in nautical design. Carline was a great encouragement for him, and used her father's political power to help Matthew forge ahead in business. Their relationship took off like a whirlwind, and within a year she was pregnant. He always swore he'd have married her anyway, because he loved her with all of his heart.

"Here we are, three beautiful children later—a divorce and almost twenty-three years have passed since we first met. Nothin' ever really changes, does it, Carline?" He raised his glass to Queen Carline, who sat across the table, as usual, protected by her royal country. A palpable chill was in the air, and he knew he had almost pushed her last button. "I'm sorry. Carlie, give me your hand as a sign of a truce. Let's do what you said, and have a nice dinner." Matthew reached across the table and took Carline's resistant hand in his. "I'm really sorry. That was cold."

After dinner, they all returned to the bungalow, and Carline offered Matt a glass of wine while Dierdra put on her bathing suit.

"I can't wait to go swimming. Mummy and I don't have this opportunity often in England."

Matt enthusiastically widened his eyes.

"I want to watch you swim, honey." He hoped his daughter would rescue him from Carline's company.

"I'll be right back, Daddy. Stay here with Mummy and convince her to let me visit with you this summer here in America."

The estranged lovers drank wine and laughed about old times. The tension that had started at dinner was held at bay until Carline's bitterness surfaced again. Matthew had noticed her face flush, though until now he thought it was from the wine. He prepared himself for her mental beating, and not too soon. She leaned forward and barked at him, "Here we are having a grand time, aren't we? No commitments, no responsibilities to each other, and we're able to enjoy each other without any reference to the past. Do you not find that a bit strange?"

Matthew shifted to one side and crossed his legs with increased uneasiness as she glared at him through squinted eyelids. "Why did you have to ruin our marriage? I had so many lonely years, and our children were raised without really knowing their father. Instead of having a normal family life, our world revolved around waiting for you to come home to England, something you rarely bothered to do."

Matthew passively allowed her feathers to fly until the "rarely bothered to do." Now he felt the heat rising in his own face. "And whose fault was that? You should have stood by your man, and come to America with me. I wasn't perfect, but you weren't so pure either. How do you think I felt when I came home unexpected and found you partyin' in my house with some strange guy?"

Carline's voice cracked before its volume heightened. "Oh, yes, Matt, it was always your house. It was never about us. You had affairs all over the world while I waited faithfully for you at home. But everything was always about you. Your house, your money, your children, your wife, your life, how many years did you think it would take before I would start looking for a life, too?" She was clearly shaken, and tears welled up in her eyes. Pointing her finger at him, she pursed her lips and continued her attack. "You never paid any dues. You'll never be close to our children, because you don't know how to be close to anyone. You're only here now because you have business in Los Angeles, coincidentally, while we're here, too. You couldn't even toast tonight without ending it with a mention of your new business venture. Sometimes I think I hate you." The anguish on her face turned to rage. She stood up, leaned toward him, and dumped her wine into his glass. "Here. You're the drunk. You need this more than I ever could."

As though moving of its own will, his hand raced forward and slapped her face. Protecting her cheek with her hand, she began to cry.

"Oh, Carline." Matt stood and grabbed her into his arms. "Oh, baby. I'm so sorry. I never shoulda done that. I'm not a violent man. I loved you more than anythin' in the world. I never wanted to hurt you. I didn't want to lose my family, but it just all went wrong with us. I'm so sorry. We gotta find a way to move on and forgive each other. It's the only way for our children's sake, Carline."

His own tears rolled down his cheeks and remorse was all encompassing. He knew she recognized his anguish. How could she not when she also had lived with this same pain for years?

Holding her tightly against him, he encouraged her to cry into his chest as if to wash the bad away. He ran his fingers through her hair and kissed the top of her sweet head. "I didn't mean it. I never wanted to hurt you. There's no excuse for what I did tonight. Did it really hurt, honey?"

"No," she whimpered. "It wasn't hard. I was just shocked. I probably asked for it."

Sliding her arms up around his neck, she raised her face toward his. Their lips met in a brief moment of lost love before Carline pulled away, hiding her face. "I need to wash and freshen up." She went into the bathroom while Matthew stood in the middle of the room, his hands in his pockets, a blank stare on his face, facing the closed bathroom door.

He felt like a hideous creature.

Dierdra came in rubbing her hair with her towel. "Where is Mummy?"

Matt pointed to the bathroom door, "She's in there. Honey, Daddy's gotta go. I have meetin's early in the mornin'. I'll call you tomorrow when you get to Napa. I love you. Come give me a hug."

He held his precious daughter with all the love in his heart, sheltering her in his arms for a prolonged moment before he left the bungalow.

Once again, alone and empty, he was compelled to go forward to repair his mistakes of the past. "How does anyone turn the past around when it's gone?" His remorse gnawed at him. "I need to keep goin', and look to the next thing I can do to make things better from here on. The past is over and I can't ever get it back, oh, how I wish I could."

Chapter Ten

$\mathcal{A}$lyssa entered the Harmony House with great news of her success in obtaining a business loan to fund the lease of the new medical clinic. A building less than a block from the Harmony House was vacant for lease. It was a perfect spot for the clinic and it even had a separate room in the front which could be used for a thrift shop. The proceeds from its sales would help support the needs of the clinic. She began emptying her personal clothes closets, shoes, jewelry, dishes, and anything else she could part with in order to donate them to the Harmony House Thrift Shop. Charity work was becoming more important than private practice, which had almost totally lost its human purpose for her. Her own financial obligations were quickly taking her into a deep hole, though she didn't consider that as she signed on the bottom lines for badly needed supplies and equipment.

She spent most of the evening giving well-woman exams to several patients and counseling on general women's issues and contraception. Denise held a small class on the red flags of domestic violence. The two girls worked smoothly together, each offering important aspects of women's health to ladies who needed special attention and appreciated it.

As she left the building on a spiritual high, she stopped to breath in the fresh air and communicate with the night. She raised her head toward the sky. "Oh, look at the stars!" On the way home, she passed the Bistro. On the other side of the street, the swooshing sounds of gentle waves breaking on the shore beckoned her to return. She turned the car around, parked on the beach side of the street, and walked to the edge of the sand. The warm water passing between her toes and encircling her ankles inspired her to ask herself out loud, "I wonder what he's doing tonight."

Matthew sat in a restaurant near the water in Los Angeles preparing to close the biggest shipping deal of his career. As he listened to the proposal being presented to him, he gazed into his Chardonnay. He circled the rim of his crystal glass with his index finger as if he were outlining the contours of Alyssa's lips with the moist wine. He tasted her kiss for a second as he lifted his finger and touched it to his tongue. Calculating the time differences, he decided to call her as soon as the meeting was over. It was six o'clock in the evening in Los Angeles. Menlo was three hours later. There was still time.

Alyssa got back in the car to sit quietly for a few minutes before starting the engine. Her cell phone rang and she answered, "Hello?"

A warm and heart throbbing Southern accent was on the other end of the line, "Alyssa, is this you? I've been wantin' to call you all night, but I've been caught up in a conference until just now. How are you doin'?"

She closed her eyes to avoid confronting her own nervousness and answered him quietly, "I'm doing very well. I'm glad you called."

"Alyssa, I sure wish you could be here with me tonight. Los Angeles is the kind of place where people shouldn't be alone. Hey. I'm leavin' tomorrow for San Francisco. I have a meetin' in the mornin', and then I'm leavin' to Napa Valley to see my sister. I was just thinkin', how 'bout I send a car around tomorrow, and you fly out here for a couple of days? No strings attached. My sister and her husband have a hot air balloon business, and I'll take you for a sunrise balloon ride over the vineyards. I mean, you said we should get to know each other better and this would be a great way to start."

Alyssa paused, her thoughts racing. She could leave the office a little early. Dr. Garbo could most likely cover her patients while she was gone, and of course, her mother would be happy to watch Lisa. Without further hesitation, she agreed.

"Great. I got you on a direct flight to San Francisco, leavin' Menlo at 4:50 tomorrow afternoon."

Alyssa turned the key to the ignition and started the engine. She shook her head and thought out loud almost babbling to herself, "What am I thinking?" Now that she had a chance to consider it, the whole thing felt a little weird. "I can't believe I said OK without thinking things out. After one date he can't call me out of the blue and expect me to package up my world and just go." She shook her head again. Actually he could, and he had.

Actually, she understood how his excitement to see her again led him to spontaneously seize the moment. That kind of spark, his ability to push buttons and make things happen quickly, was stimulating. Alyssa felt pampered as she drove home deciding which outfits to take, and making a call to Dr. Garbo, who agreed to cover her practice while she was gone.

That evening while she packed her suitcase, Lisa came into her bedroom. She stopped, staring at Alyssa's luggage. Lisa's own bags were conspicuously absent. The child was preparing to display a well-prepared temper tantrum with her famous bottom lip beginning to sag, "Mommy, we're going to Disney World this weekend. You promised."

Alyssa looked up in shock, reached out for Lisa and wrapped her arms around her. "Honey, I'm sorry, something has just come up. I'll be back in a couple of days. You know Mommy never goes anywhere without you, but this is very important to me. I'll try really hard to take us to Disney next week, OK?"

Lisa pulled away from her mother's arms, "Mommy, do you still love me?"

Stunned by such an unexpected question, Alyssa dropped the sweater she was holding onto the bed.

"Lisa, I love you more than anything in this world and nothing will ever change that, nothing."

Lisa's eyes searched her mother's face for an answer, "Then why are you leaving me to go visit that boat man you and Grandmother are always talking about? I hate him. I don't want you to go."

"Lisa." Alyssa again drew her daughter into her arms for a cuddle. "I am just going away for two days. He's my friend and I'm just going on a short trip to visit him. I'll be back before you know it. By the way, you don't hate anyone." She pretended to steal Lisa's nose, but the trick didn't bring the usual giggle.

Lisa had never had any man in her life except Jean-Marc. She was a little girl whose life was wrapped around her mother and her grandmother, and there was no such thing as sharing either one of them with anyone else. Daddy was a prince on a white horse that they told stories about, because she'd been an infant when he died. Now Lisa was six, and the introduction of a new man in their life was already proving to be problematic.

That night Alyssa, her mother, and Lisa went to dinner and then to the movies. Lisa still had a long face as Alyssa tucked her in bed hugging her stuffed animals. "Mommy," she asked, "Could I get a kitten?"

"I'll tell you what. You be good about Mommy going on this little trip, and don't be upset with me. When I get back, we'll go to the Preppy Kitty Shop in Coco Beach and buy a kitten, OK?"

Having won the tug-of-war, Lisa squealed with excitement and threw her arms around Alyssa's neck in an exuberant hug. "I'll be good, Mommy, I promise."

Alyssa's guilt swelled.

Chapter Eleven

*T*he next day Alyssa could hardly keep up with the clock, but everything fell into place. She was on her way home by 2:45 to meet the car that would whisk her off to the airport to embark on a huge adventure.

As she boarded American Airline flight 454 to San Francisco, she felt deserving of this treat. After all, hadn't she always been a perfect role model and sacrificial lamb, always giving? It was her turn to be a little crazy. She needed to be a little crazy right now. She was excited and wanted nothing to take this moment away from her.

The plane gained speed and momentum as it sped down the runway. It gracefully lifted off the ground and climbed into the sky heading westward. She gazed out the window in anticipation of the California sunset, which awaited her amazement as they would make their descent into San Francisco.

During the flight, she prepared for the next session at the Harmony House, and studied the various personality types that tended to be involved in domestic violence. The continuous thread that wove through all of her research was that domestic violence did have a pattern. This pattern was quite predictable, though one needed to be very well informed and analytical in order to predict the cycles of its occurrences. There seemed to be two very distinct prevailing characteristics, particularly among males. Many men who had tendencies toward domestic violence had characteristics of both manic behavior and alcohol abuse. Nothing was certainly clear-cut, but there was definitely a defining thread that ran through the behavior of violence. Alcohol was often used as an excuse for the dangerous physical aggression. It could be a contributor in the fact that alcohol was an inhibition reliever, it was a depressant, and it also could trigger chemical reactions in the brain that encouraged the negative behavior. Manic depression and alcoholism tended to run in families. Where mania was found, there was often alcoholism. She also noted that testosterone, the hormone of aggression and drive, was particularly high among many men with violent histories. With all this research pointing to heredity, addiction, and the effects of naturally occurring body chemistry, she could not accept the stereotype that violence in homes was just a by-product of evil people.

The plane was now on its last descent as the Bay Area's focus came closer to her. She put her notebook away and gazed out the window. The tiny moving dots on the ground began to take the shapes of moving boxes on lines, and the distant map of San Francisco coming closer began to look inhabited. The boxes became cars, the lines became roads, and before she knew it she felt the bump of the plane wheels touching down. The airline hostess welcomed the passengers to San Francisco and the plane rolled up to the terminal. Her stomach was queasy from nerves as she left the plane and walked toward the exit gate. She felt shy walking within the line of exiting passengers. As soon as he spotted her, his broad smile was easily picked out of the crowd. He was nervous, too.

"Hi," he said, "Did you have a nice trip?"

He put his arms around her and they exchanged a brief hug. He kissed her cheek and reached for her bag.

The hustle and bustle of the airport activity helped absorb some of their mutual anxiety. They walked briskly to the exit of the terminal, and a black stretch limousine was parked by the curb awaiting their arrival. The driver held the door open, and they slid onto the very comfortable velvet seats. Without delay, Matt reached for a chilled bottle of newly opened Crystal champagne. Obviously, it had just been popped open by the chauffeur. The car slowly pulled away from the curb and headed down the road toward the highway leading to Napa Valley.

Matt poured two perfect glasses, leaned over and gave her a tiny kiss, and whispered, "I'm so happy you came."

He handed her one glass and lifted the other to hers. "Here's to our health," he toasted.

She toasted with him to health, and then she commented, "How is your ulcer condition? I haven't stopped my concern . . ."

He stopped her, "I am gettin' scoped again next week. My appointment is set." He reached into his wallet and took out his appointment card to show her. "See? I'm really normal again. Besides, I've cut way back on the booze."

Alyssa relaxed back into her seat, feeling so much better now that the jitters of the trip were over. "I'm really proud of you, Matt."

The drive to Napa was a few scenic hours long. When they arrived in Calistoga, the sky had said good night to the day's brilliant orange setting sun, and was clear midnight blue and filled with stars. They pulled into a driveway lined with perfectly sculptured vines laden with deep purple grapes. As they drove along, the headlights lit up the vines and their succulent fruit was easy to see. A huge country home greeted them at the end of the drive. The limo pulled to a stop, and before Matt and Alyssa could get out of the car, Matt's sister appeared, clapping with excitement. "Matt, how wonderful to see you."

He quickly turned to Alyssa. "Amy, this is Alyssa. Alyssa, this is my sister, Amy."

Alyssa looked into Amy's eyes and sensed an air of discomfort.

"Hi, Alyssa." Amy smiled as she reached for her hand. "Matt has told me so much about you. I feel like I know you already."

Her southern accent was not so pronounced as Matt's. In fact, she barely had an accent at all.

Alyssa smiled in return, and shook Amy's hand. "Well, it's very nice to meet you."

Matt, with his head tilted, ran his gaze up to the house and back again. "Where is Peter?"

Amy fidgeted, and then turned to Alyssa. "Peter is my husband. Don't mind my brother, he always has issues." She grasped Alyssa by the arm and began strolling toward the house. "You know how brothers are. Anyway, Peter's just gone to the store. He should be back shortly. Come on inside and get comfortable."

The three of them entered the grand foyer.

Amy's eyes danced back and forth from Matt to Alyssa while she mused, "Now let's see. Where do you want to sleep?"

Matt answered, "We'd like separate rooms."

Amy turned one side of her mouth up and winked. "That's just fine. We have plenty of bedrooms here."

Alyssa assumed that Amy was accustomed to giving

Matt and his girl guests one bedroom to share. His sister led them both upstairs and down the hall to separate rooms next to each other.

Opening the first door, Amy pointed to the window. "Alyssa, I think you'll like this bedroom."

Alyssa entered the room and went straight to the open window. Taking a deep breath, she could feel the breeze and smell the clean air. "Amy, what a view of the vineyards. I can't believe how delicately the entire landscape is lit. The grapes look like purple jeweled clusters hanging from their vines, and the sky opens to reveal the brilliant stars. I thought Southern California was western heaven, but this beats all of it."

"I'm happy you like it. Mother stays in this room when she comes. It's her favorite spot in the house. Please get comfortable, and when you want to, we can all go downstairs and visit before dinner."

Alyssa was anxious to settle in, place a few things on hangers, and freshen up. She opened a door and oohed and aahed at the grandiose private bath equipped with a sunken Jacuzzi. She could hear Amy through the open door in the next room.

"She seems like a nice girl, Matt. It's not like you to invite someone across the country to meet your family during a business trip. This isn't serious, is it? You know Mama still hopes you and Carline will get back together someday. We had a great visit yesterday. You should be very proud of Dierdra."

"Yes, I'm very proud of how well Carline raised my daughter, Amy."

"I wish they could have stayed longer, but that would

have been awkward what with you two here today and all."

"Now, look. I didn't bring a guest to meet you for you to behave like this."

Alyssa could hear the annoyance in Matt's snapping intonation.

Amy interrupted him. "Mother and I thought we could invite Carline and all three children here for a visit soon, and maybe you would come at the same time. She's not dating anyone, you know."

His voice deepened and his volume increased, a little aggressive. Alyssa listened to an escalating sibling argument, which made her uncomfortable.

"You know Carline and I have no future together, and Mother needs to let go of the past. I've moved on and you guys need to move on, too. Look, I don't want to talk about Carline or anyone else this weekend. I had enough of Carline two days ago to last a long time. I've brought a very important lady to meet you, and as far as I'm concerned, you should be honored that I did. I really like this girl, and I want you to be nice to her. We came here to have a good time and if you're goin' to start with all this, we'll just leave. As soon as we got here, you were pretty obvious, and I'm sure Alyssa was uncomfortable."

An unfriendly vibe was brewing and penetrating the wall between Alyssa and the siblings.

"And I'm sick of putting up with your nasty temper. You might want to curb your appetite for it this weekend if you're worried about impressions. Mother and I always had trouble teaching you that family ties and responsibilities aren't just about you, but I'm not sure you'll ever quite get that."

"Let's not argue about this tonight. I don't want Alyssa

to hear any of this," he said in a soft voice. "Do you have any of Peter's special Vineyard Red?" Unable to let it go, he continued, "By the way, speakin' about family ties, marriage, and responsibility, where is Peter tonight really? Don't ever let me hear that he's messin' up again. He's not goin' to get away with it anymore. I swear I'll stop him if I have to do it with my own bare hands."

"I told you, he's at the store."

"Do you really think I buy that? You're talkin' to the seasoned pro, Amy. Our daddy taught me a whole lot."

A long silence was broken by the sound of the door closing.

Having heard this conversation through the walls, Alyssa was numb. She hoped this wasn't a Tennessee Williams type of family with a shutout valve to keep outsiders out. Obviously, Peter was shut out by Matt, who exerted significant control over his sister.

There was a soft knock on her door. Alyssa opened it, and Matt gave her a smile that subdued her newly formed apprehension. "Hey. Let's go downstairs and try Peter's great vintage Vineyard Red."

Matt, Alyssa, and Amy exchanged pleasantries together as they awaited Peter's arrival. Amy warmed up to Alyssa and Alyssa shed some of her discomfort. Peter finally arrived for a very brief appearance. It had taken him two hours to get back from the store, which apparently was five minutes away. Peter was stately, and quite an attractive man. Alyssa thought it was interesting that he was Australian. Both the brother and the sister of this Southern family had taken foreign spouses. Peter was very cordial, distant, shook Matt's hand, briefly addressed Alyssa, and excused himself, explaining that he felt sick. It was obvious that he had little interest in entertaining people that evening and it was also obvious that he wasn't sick, not physically anyway. Nobody in the room could miss the huge chill between Peter and Matt.

Amy made sure that before Peter departed he committed to taking Matt and Alyssa up in one of the balloons early in the morning. There was also tension between Amy and Peter, and it was more than just a little spat. Matt leaned forward, placing his elbows on the table and holding his crossed fisted hands in front of his mouth. His staring at the table in front of him was an obvious display of his discontentment with the situation.

Everyone agreed to get to bed early, and awaken before dawn in order to heat up the balloon, and lift off at sunrise. Matt and Alyssa parted with ease.

"I'm right next door if you need anythin'. You just knock and I'll be right there."

He reached toward her and kissed her forehead. "Good night." Then he turned toward his own room.

The moment of discomfort earlier had nothing to do with her and Matthew, and Alyssa rushed to call her mother and Lisa from her cell phone to wish them good night and let them know she was safe and having a great time. After taking a quick shower and slipping into her short silk nightgown, she lay alone in bed thinking about her new acquaintances. It was odd that Peter was so antisocial with his wife's brother. Maybe Matt was in Napa for more than a fun weekend . . . Voices from down the hallway interrupted her thoughts. The altercation between Amy and Peter was only briefly audible. Alyssa thought she heard a thud against the wall and then whimpering sounds, but she wasn't sure. She couldn't decipher any of their conversation and was grateful for that. There was something weird going on, and her association with the Hope for Harmony House always put her on guard.

Unable to sleep, she turned her pillow toward the wall that separated her from Matt. She imagined his lying in a bed near the other side, longing for her. Her heart pleaded for him to leave his room and come to hers. She closed her eyes and imagined her door opening, Matt quietly entering her room and standing at the foot of her bed. She'd pretend to be sleeping, and he'd kiss the tips of her toes with soft, gentle lips. She'd slowly make him aware that she was arousing, and her arms would reach down to him, her fingers barely touching the hair on top of his head, coaxing him to move from her toes to her lips. Alyssa's fantasy stopped abruptly, and she got out of bed and went to the closed window to open it again, just enough to let northern California's cool night air into the room. As she gazed out the window at the cloudy western sky, a slight crisp breeze kissed her cheek. She wondered what the eastern sky looked like right then through her bedroom window in Menlo. The California vineyard certainly had a different atmosphere from Florida's star-studded, tropical ocean breeze. She liked California.

Four thirty a.m. came early, but Alyssa, looking forward to the balloon ride with great anticipation, jumped out of bed, washed her face, brushed her teeth, combed her hair, and put on a pair of jeans and a sweater. She tied a windbreaker around her waist, put on her tennis shoes, and went downstairs to meet the others.

Matt, Amy, and Peter were solemnly sipping coffee and waiting to pour her a cup before leaving for the park where the balloons were ready to be fired. Matt was speaking very softly yet appeared angry.

Alyssa did catch him saying, "Peter, I came here to see the books. It's enough that you bought two new balloons without my permission."

Their conversation was hushed as Alyssa entered the room. She first greeted Peter. "I hope you feel better this morning."

Peter smiled, and then looked at his coffee cup and took a sip.

It was still dark when they got in the van and pulled out of the driveway. Alyssa sat close to Matt as his arm automatically wrapped around her.

"Baby, did you get a good sleep?"

"Yes, I did, thank you. How about you?"

"I did OK," he whispered. "But I had a hard time knowin' you were just on the other side of the wall. I wanted to hold you all night. It would have kept me warm."

He chuckled, and she knew what he meant.

"Alyssa, I'm really startin' to care about you. I know it's fast, but I can't help it. It'd feel so natural to be with you all night."

She invited him to turn her face toward him and gently plant a soft, brief kiss on her lips, and then her cheek. His warm hand gently rubbing her shoulder felt so good.

Amy turned around from the front seat. "Alyssa, have you ever been up in a balloon?"

"No I haven't, but I've always wondered what it would be like."

"These balloons hold up to six people each," Amy explained. "It's really great. The only part I never have enjoyed is touching down. You just won't believe how hard it can be on your joints. You're fixing to have a real surprise."

The park was about a fifteen-minute ride from the house. Eight balloons were spread out around a huge field, and tremendous torch fires filled them with gas as they slowly, one by one, lifted into the air. They were gorgeous with brilliant colors and each with its own design. Each balloon was attached to a huge basket that was tied and weighted to the ground.

Alyssa could feel the adrenaline rush through her. "They're beautiful. I can't believe we're actually going up in one."

Matt took her hand in his and led her to the balloon that would carry them far above the vineyards to offer a spectacular, one-of-a-kind view of Napa Valley. They stepped up into the basket and Peter took a photo of them as they slowly lifted off the ground.

Matt grinned and squealed like a young boy, "Up, up, and away. We're off. Remember when we were kids, that movie came out with those guys in a balloon goin' around the world in eighty days? Well that's us."

Alyssa playfully batted his shoulder. "Is there any movie you liked that you don't later pretend you're part of?"

He laughed. "Yeah, Old Yeller." I loved that dog, but I don't want to be Old Yeller, and I wouldn't want to be the boy who lost his dog, either."

They enjoyed a glorious two-hour glide through the sky, looking down at the spectacular vineyards thriving for miles all around them. The view was first almost surreal with the Napa Valley mist covering everything below. As the sun rose, the mist cleared, and the healthy vegetation came alive in multiple colors and shades of green as if it were all a breathtaking painting. Miles of vineyards continued to surround them as they floated over the countryside with the wind carrying them all the way.

Suddenly one of the other balloons behind them displayed a banner that read, "Will you marry me?" The pilot, a very friendly and humorous man, got on the communication system and contacted the balloon with the banner.

"What's going on over there? You know, Bob, I'm already married."

Everybody in the basket laughed.

"You're kidding. A guy in your balloon is actually proposing to someone? They're in the blue balloon next to us? Well, what's she got to say? She said she'll marry him? All right."

Everyone in all the balloons cheered and clapped. In the excitement of the moment, Matt swept Alyssa in his arms and tenderly pressed his lips on hers.

He whispered, "Isn't love a beautiful thing? I think I'm fixin' to fall in love with you, Alyssa." He pulled her into his open jacket and tightly closed his arms around her. "I'd want to write it across the whole sky."

She leaned into his chest and gently relaxed her head on him, marveling at the wonderful feeling of union between new lovers that she could feel was beginning to grow.

The ride was filled with comedy, fun, and jokes from the pilot. He was very curious to know something about all of his passengers.

He noted that Matt and Alyssa looked like newlyweds. "You two have a little magic of your own cooking," he remarked.

Matt laughed without any embarrassment, "We're gettin' real serious real fast."

"All right," the pilot exclaimed. Then he manually pumped the extra energy into the balloon and it climbed to seven hundred feet. They continued across the sky until they reached a road where they could land safely.

Like a magician, the pilot brought the basket down. "I warned everyone to bend their knees upon landing in order to save their joints, so don't forget. Also hold the side of the basket for support. Even the softest landing has a tremendous jolt," he continued. "These baskets don't have very good shocks. You really have to have a strong back and strong joints to fly these babies often. Brace yourselves on the basket with your hands before we land and bend your knees."

It hit the ground with a thud, and there was no mercy for weak joints. Everyone climbed gingerly out of the basket and got into a van that carried them back to the field. When they arrived, Peter was absent, but Amy was waiting for them. She enthusiastically greeted them. "How was your ride?"

Alyssa praised the trip as she squeezed Matt's hand. He pulled his arm up around her neck and kissed the top of her head, which sent that thrill through her chest that happens only with falling in love.

Matt took in Peter's absence and the guilty expression on his sister's face. "Amy, it was really great. I wish you could have come with us," he said. "Doesn't Peter help put the balloons away?"

Amy reassured him that Peter had been plenty busy and was home helping get breakfast ready. He and Lena, their partner, were preparing the food out on the veranda.

As they drove down the road they passed rolling

vineyards, and many wineries came into view as they wound around bends canopied with lush trees. The sunlight shone through the leaves and glistened like gold. This beautiful scenery continued for miles and followed the picturesque road to Amy and Peter's home in Calistoga. Every inch of the way, Matthew found Alyssa's glowing face far more attractive than the view outside. He held her close to him during the drive, and as he sensed her mutual yearning, he guessed she must have tossed a bit last night, too, though only he had admitted it.

The veranda was beautifully set up with fruits, pastries, and covered dishes filled with eggs, sausages, bacon, grits, biscuits, and gravy. The morning air was crisp yet comfortable. Alyssa looked cool and fresh, obviously enjoying this contrast to Florida where the heat and humidity forced tiny beads of sweat to form on most people's cheeks by this time of the morning.

Amy wasted no time in introducing her best friend, Lena, to Alyssa, and then disappeared back into the house.

They exchanged greetings and Lena politely welcomed Alyssa, adding, "I hope you enjoy your stay with us. Napa is really a great place."

"Lena, you made everything so beautiful for us this morning," Matt exclaimed.

"Oh Matt, gracias." Lena blushed. She glanced at Matt with her flashing eyes and then she turned away from him and addressed Alyssa. "Is this your first visit to Napa?"

Matt picked up that something was troubling her, and she was trying very hard to hide whatever it was. He knew her well; they shared deep secrets together, especially family ones. At this moment, she was transparent to him as she flashed what Matt devoured as still the prettiest, sexiest brown eyes he had ever seen. He couldn't help remembering those passionate nights in the vineyards with the most beautiful Latina in California, but Lena was not the woman he was dreaming of now. Alyssa was the only woman for him.

Matt left that moment of thought about Lena as quickly as it came and he turned to his new love. "How's everythin'? Isn't this the greatest place in the world?"

Alyssa whispered back in awe, "Lena's really beautiful. I don't think I've ever seen eyes quite like hers."

"Nobody would argue there. Isn't she unbelievable? She's a perfect-lookin' woman."

"Has she been with Amy and Peter long?"

Matt tried to cool down his fervor. "About twenty years ago, she came from a little Mexican fishin' town called Guaymas. Her father brought his family across the border as migrant workers, and it was his inspiration and hard work that built the political stability of the Mexicans in California. Lena is the daughter of Emilio de la Cruz."

Alyssa visibly perked up. "You mean the migrant labor leader?"

Matt chuckled, anxious to share some of Lena's background. "Yeah. Can you believe that? It's a long story how she joined our family, but she's the only sister Amy's ever known. She's the backbone in their balloon business and she's earned every right to be the equal partner she is. Anyway, Lena wrote a book about the Mexican migration ordeal, and her father's political power will probably insure its publication. She has a bunch of statistics about the Latin population takin' over the country or somethin' like that."

Questions flickered in Alyssa's eyes. And for you, is she

like a sister, too? But Lena had never been like a sister to him, and answering that question would lead to others, ones he didn't want to discuss with her.

Just then Peter and Amy entered the veranda and sat at the table. "I'm sorry I've not been a very good host. I have a lot going on running the business and all."

Peter was a nervous liar, and Matt was onto him.

The brunch was delicious, Peter displayed his best side with good conversation, a couple of good jokes, and generous laughter, but Matt became more serious than usual, grinning only rarely as they sat around the table. Lena floated around everyone, the perfect hostess, allowing Amy to relax.

Amy lovingly reached for Lena's arm. "Please sit down with us."

Lena declined. "I'm fine, don't worry. I've already eaten. I'll go get more champagne from the kitchen."

Matt excused himself for a moment and followed Lena like a bee to honey while sensing Alyssa's keen awareness of him. He knew she didn't miss the charisma between Lena and him. Seeing her behavior during times like this was also part of his getting to know her better. He loved confidence in a woman. Insecurity and jealousy annoyed him. He liked it that she was self-assured enough to ignore them, and continue conversing with Peter and Amy about the balloons.

Matt entered the kitchen. "Lena, what's goin' on? This place isn't its usual happy hideaway. Somethin's creepy."

Lena broke into soft tears, and Matt wrapped his arms around her. "Oh, my little chica, que es la problema?"

She kept her voice low and spoke Spanish as he held her. "Matt, Peter isn't right. He's drinking too much, and who knows what else he's doing. He stays out late and half the time he doesn't even come home. Amy thinks he has another woman. The business is going really poorly. He doesn't even take care of the balloons anymore."

She touched the palms of her hands on Matt's chest, unconsciously causing him to quiver. "Our books are so bad, money disappears, and I can't figure them out anymore. You know Amy. She wouldn't tell you, but we get up at four in the morning to get the balloons ready to fire up. This week alone we lost three flights because he didn't put them in the schedule book. You know how bad it is for business in this small town when your company leaves vacationers hanging over and over again?"

Matt grabbed onto her hands. "Why wasn't I told about any of this?"

Lena slipped her hands away from his. "Amy is too scared to tell you that the bank is ready to foreclose on the balloons."

"Foreclose?"

"Yes. We still owe over three hundred thousand dollars on the loan. I bet we've lost fifty thousand during the past six months, and soon we're going to lose the whole business. I could go to Father, but his temper is as bad as yours. Besides, I would be afraid of what could happen to Amy if I left her alone with that animal. I don't know what we should do. You are Amy's brother, you financed this venture, and we're all going to see the investments fall away for no good reason."

Matt felt the boiling begin inside.

"There's more," she continued. "Peter comes home drunk, and goes after Amy for no reason. He has left her black and blue several times. I wanted to call you, but Matt, I know you too well. You would break his neck with your own temper.

I was afraid to call you, but now it has gone way too far. Amy doesn't want Mother to know and that's why she hides it. What's wrong with her that she puts up with abuse from him?"

Matthew's anger released.

He saw red with memories of childhood terror and he vowed under his breath, "I'll kill him if this is all true."

Lena's face turned chalky white.

Matt wildly flashed his eyes at her. "Lena, has he ever touched you? Tell me he never put his filthy hands on you or Annie."

"Oh, don't start with that kind of stuff." Lena shuddered and pulled away. "He wouldn't dare touch me. He's overly protective of Annie, and never even reprimands her over anything. He leaves all the parenting to Amy and me."

"Don't worry, Lena. I won't mess up here. This just has to stop. That cockroach was never good enough for my sister. I never should have gone along with this whole balloon thing. Don't worry. I'll do the right thing."

He knew she didn't buy his reassurance, because she knew him too well. Matthew always took charge when his territory was threatened, and this was his territory. For sure he would need a plan . . . For sure it wouldn't be a simple say-you're-sorry type of plan.

Matt grabbed a fresh bottle of champagne and returned to the veranda. Peter was already gone. Amy and Alyssa were sampling cheese and fruit.

As Matt came up to the table, Amy said, "When are you taking Alyssa to meet Mama?"

Matt enjoyed the enthusiasm in Alyssa's face, "I think

Mother will really like her, don't you?"

Amy smiled and nodded her head. She got up to help Lena clean the kitchen.

Alyssa reached for some dishes, "Please, let me help."

"Absolutely not. Matt, why don't you take Alyssa on a tour of the property? Lena and I are going into town for a few hours. You two could just relax and get rested up for tonight."

Matt liked the idea. He playfully asked, "Whatcha got cookin' for tonight, Sis?"

Amy grinned, her single dimple very apparent. "Dinner and a hayride under the stars."

Alyssa clapped her hands in approval. Matt still felt a tightness in his chest over his conversation with Lena.

He gazed at Amy, calling attention to the one dimple on her left cheek, "That little dimple will never have a partner, will it?"

Amy laughed and disappeared back into the kitchen.

Matt showed Alyssa the vineyards and they sampled grapes together off the vines. He taught her about the cabernets, the merlots and the zinfandels on their way to a small wooded area where there was a tire swing hanging from a branch near a pond. They sat down and Matt practiced skipping pebbles over the water. He was making very poor conversation and knew Alyssa read his body language shutting her out, which forced her to retreat.

She sprang to her feet, brushed off her bottom with her hands, and moved toward the swing. The moment was awkward, and Matt knew he had created a bump in the road.

"Who does that swing belong to?"

"Maybe it wasn't such a good idea bringin' you here so early on." Matt felt his own pressured speech. "We have some family issues to clear up right now, and I don't like anyone seein' us while we're problem solvin', that's all."

Alyssa reassured him, "All families have lots of problems. Mine does. It's just life."

Matt hadn't planned to expose his family's flaws to her so soon, but he needed her to understand a few things from the start.

"Amy hasn't had an easy life. We had a real mean father, and he tore into her childhood. I'm surprised she's as good as she is today. A lot a women wouldn'ta survived. Then her first little baby died at three months old, ya know, crib death. Her second child has Down syndrome. They keep her in a special school three days a week. They went into town just now to pick her up. She comes home Saturday and goes back Wednesday every week. Lena and Amy hover over her like mother hens together. She's a great kid. Those children sure do know a lot about love. They may be missin' some things, but not how to show love. Her favorite thing is a hayride. She gets to sit up with the driver. I think Amy has hayrides just for Annie. That's her name, Annie. That's Annie's tire swing."

"How old is Annie?"

Matt thought for a minute, "Well, Amy was somewhere in her early forties when she had Annie. Amy's fifty-four, and I guess Annie must be about twelve now."

As he described his niece, Alyssa's eyes welled up.

He playfully reached for her. "Come on. Let's be happy. It's not right bein' here on the edge of the pond talkin' about ugly things. People need to come here to get close to one another. Give Daddy a little sugar."

He brushed his lips over her cheek then lay back on the grass. "Lie down here beside me, Lys. I want to call you Lys. Is that OK?"

Stretching her back and turning onto her stomach, facing him, Alyssa felt weird realizing that his family really did have issues uncommon to most others. She never had a brother to protect her and care for her as Amy had. Lisa never had a real uncle to love her as Matt obviously cherished his niece. Alyssa saw through the light in his eyes, which brightened as he described Annie, almost as if he allowed her to see his beautiful soul behind the brilliant blue.

He brushed a strand of her hair back from her cheek, this man who had witnessed so much pain and abuse, yet who had somehow retained a gentleness of spirit that pulled at her heart as no other.

She leaned over him and kissed the tip of his nose, lingering near his face briefly as an invitation for him to make the next move.

He pulled her over on top of him, and his body turned to passion as he confessed, "Last night I thought I'd go crazy without you. I almost went to your room, and it was all I could do to stop myself. I kept thinkin' you'd want me to be there with you, holdin' you, lovin' you." He rubbed her back rhythmically, unsnapping her bra, as he pressed his mouth against hers. Their lips met with a gentle pressure that filled her body with sexual longing. He continued kissing her neck, first one side and then the other.

"I had this fantasy of goin' to the foot of your bed and bendin' down to kiss your toes, which were like little pink pearls."

He was like steel beneath her and she pressed into him as he continued whispering and brushing her face and neck with his lips. "I moved slowly up until I kissed every part of your body before I reached these precious lips I'm kissin' right now." He continued to court her sexuality with amorous skill, a master of each move. "Then I would be inside of you and I would tease you until you could bear no more. I wanted to make love with you all night until dawn. That's why this mornin' I told you I didn't sleep so well last night."

His gentle hand lightly feathered up and down her inner thighs, encouraging her to surrender to the perfect fit of their bodies. Wanting, changing to needing warned her to roll off of him and lie beside him, reaching behind her back to re-snap her opened undergarment.

Frustration drove him to his feet, and he stretched his hand down to help Alyssa up. "OK, OK. You make me crazy, you know that? I just want to lie here all day and make love with you over and over again. I'm outa control, but it's got to happen soon, or I'll go nuts. You're unreal, Alyssa."

Alyssa was still dazed from his kisses. She wished she had just kept going with him, though she knew it would have changed everything between them, and the rest of the weekend would have been all about quenching their desire for each other.

But her moral guard cautioned her. It was too soon to have passion control her. Her thoughts soothed her desire until it retreated deeply inside of her, and she felt better.

They walked back toward the house.

Alyssa paused. "Matt, why do I get such a strange feeling about Peter? He's a nice guy, but something is wrong. Is he

OK?"

Matt studied the ground, and when he looked back at her, his eyes were wide and his mouth flattened. Red tinged his face. "Lena told me this mornin' that Peter is really makin' a mess of things right now." Anger filled his voice, which alarmed Alyssa. "He's trashin' the business and he's cheatin' on Amy. I swear, if I ever find out that he hurts my sister in any way, I'll kill him with my own bare hands."

"You don't mean that, do you?" Alyssa was taken back.

Matt's voice softened again. "Oh, it's just a figure of speech."

In the distance she heard a girl's voice calling, "Ollie, Ollie."

Ollie was a great big mutt, probably a combination of a Labrador, a collie, and some other breed, maybe a wheaten terrier. He was wonderful, and so funny looking, with one floppy ear and one erect ear. He had irregular markings and a long scraggly tail, just a great big bundle of furry love.

Matt crouched down and let the dog jump up to lick his face. "I found Ollie on a lonesome road not far from Charleston. I was tourin' old plantations and found this little starvin' puppy. He was skinny and hungry and sufferin', so I coaxed him into my car and brought him home for Annie."

He stood, and the dog bounded away, nose to the ground. Wiping off the slobber from his face he beamed with family pride. "All that opportunity I gave him and he only cares about my niece. He's somethin', crazy ole dog."

Alyssa's heart filled with a complex mix of admiration and tenderness at the thought of the successful businessman having a soft spot for this splendidly ridiculous animal.

A young girl came into view, running toward Matt with

that wide gait typical of children with Down syndrome, arms pumping as if he were the only person on earth. "Uncle Matt. I love you." She cheered, "I have missed you so much." Annie threw her arms around Matt with the power of a bull and the force of an angel all in one.

Matt exclaimed, "Hey, little darlin'. Uncle Matt has missed you, too. I want you to meet my new friend, Alyssa."

Annie glanced up at Alyssa. "She is real pretty. Do you love her like you love me?"

Matt laughed. "I'll never love anyone like I love my Annie." They all walked back to the house together. Matt held Annie's hand the whole way.

"I can't find Ollie, my dear Ollie. Did you see Ollie?" With that question Annie broke away and ran off. She continued calling Ollie's name in a desperate search for her furry friend.

When Alyssa and Matt arrived at the house, Amy and Lena were taking groceries out of the trunk of the car.

Lena struggled with the weight of a large sack, and Matt rushed to take it from her. "That's too heavy. Lena, let me help you."

Alyssa lifted a bag of beans out of the trunk.

Amy bubbled to Alyssa as they walked toward the house with arms full of groceries, "I am so proud that Annie introduced herself to you. Lena and I have worked hard with her at home to expand her manners. Her new school plays 'The Good Manner Game' with the students, and she brings the rules home with such pride to practice with us. Annie's very talkative. She's our family angel, but she's not always appropriate."

Alyssa reassured Amy. "Annie was wonderful just now.

She certainly behaved no differently than my own daughter, Lisa. You have every right to be proud of your lovely little girl."

The two ladies quietly continued bringing groceries in from the car. Alyssa remembered what Matt had said about his father, and his innuendos hinted that Amy had been sexually abused. Alyssa realized the drastic differences between Amy and her. Their childhoods, their marriages, and their daughters' probable futures were almost opposite from each other, yet she felt as if they were kindred spirits.

Confusion talked to her as she walked back and forth to the house, "It scares me to think of changing the perfect world Lisa and I have right now. Oh, my Lisa, how will you handle an outsider, a man, possibly coming into our family?"

Everyone was present except Peter, as usual. Annie asked several times where Daddy was and Amy just kept saying he was still working. They had a great evening barbecue with ribs, corn, baked beans, and salad. Everyone had a refreshing glass of iced tea, except Matt, who got himself a cold beer.

Alyssa choked back her physician's urge to warn Matt about the beer, reminding herself he'd cut back lately and was making a good effort to take care of himself.

The longer Matt thought about Amy, Annie, and Peter, the more certain he became that he couldn't just let matters stay as they were. Shortly after dinner he approached his sister. "I want you and Annie to come to Florida with me for a couple of weeks. We could even take my boat to Nassau for a few of days, and I could get us rooms at the Atlantis. It would really be good for Annie. I'm not very happy with what's goin' on here. Amy, you're too good for him. He's never been right."

They watched Annie, who was totally content and

oblivious to anything being wrong. She was home tonight with her family and her dog. Even if Daddy was working, she was content, though waiting impatiently for the hayride.

It was a great ride. The northern California air was fresh and the moon and stars were bright enough to light up the road even without the glow from the old lanterns that hung from the sides of the wagon. Everyone sang old folk songs, and Annie gave her own rendition of "Oh Susannah."

Matt watched Amy sit alone pretending to have a great time in order not to disturb the joy of the others. He saw his sister as a perfect Southern belle as she had been in her youth before she married Peter. She was quickly losing her shine and she looked old and tarnished, hurt and dull, as she sat quietly rocking back and forth with the unsteady wheels of the wagon. She needed to get away. She was long overdue for a vacation, and it must be painful for her to be around Peter anymore with his despicable behavior. Matt ruminated over Lena's morning information about Peter's habit of humiliating Amy and it was obvious that he didn't care who saw his insults and lack of respect. She had planned to go to Charleston and stay with her mother for a while, but her main concern was that Matt had loaned them the money for the business and she felt responsibility for that. "Amy, I want to put this whole balloon business behind us. I've had a few beers, and I know you'll think this isn't really me talkin', but it is.

"Matt, this is your third or fourth beer, and I know when your inhibitions begin to fade."

"I'm not drunk, OK? I would make this offer to you if this can was filled with lemonade, because you're my family and I love you. That jerk won't keep hurtin' you."

"Matt, stop."

"Hey, Sis. I have more money than I'll ever spend in five lifetimes. I don't care about the peanuts I've lost with those stupid balloons. I care about you. What do you say, Sis? Let Peter trash it all and take the repercussion by himself. He deserves nothing and he certainly doesn't deserve you and Annie. That settles it. You're comin' with us on the plane to Florida."

Amy showed no signs of resistance, only defeat. Matt moved over to her and put his arm around her, "C'mon. Amy, say yes."

The wagon drove on and Matt just hugged his sister. Alyssa watched him, the loving brother, care for his sister, and tears trailed down her cheeks. He gave Amy a gentle squeeze. She suddenly flinched and pulled away. Her hand darted to her right shoulder, then away again, but the motion gave her secret away. Matt removed his sister's blouse from her shoulder.

"Amy. He did this to you, didn't he?" Her shoulder was badly bruised and the black and blue spread to her back.

"No," she defended Peter. "I fell."

Matt didn't try to convince his sister to tell the truth. He knew where the bruises originated. That was the last straw. There was nothing else to do but end Amy's pain, and take her with him in the morning to Florida. She and Annie could stay with him forever. Nobody would ever hurt his sister and get away with it.

Amy bit her lip. "Matt," she pleaded, "Stay out of this, please. I'll leave California with you tomorrow, but let's promise to let Peter find his own suffering. Promise me, Matt?"

Matt didn't look at her, but he answered, "OK, OK."

Matt saw the disbelief and dumbfounded expression in Alyssa's eyes. He knew she'd seen Amy's shoulder. So much for the light and fun weekend he had planned with his new girlfriend.

"Alyssa, would you look at her shoulder when we get back?"

Alyssa nodded.

Matt remained stone faced and silent for the remainder of the hayride.

When they returned to the house Peter, as usual, was nowhere to be found. After the information Lena had shared that morning, Matt was confident that Peter was with his shack-up girlfriend. Matt wanted to protect his family. He wanted to fix all of their problems, and he would start by getting them all out of Calistoga. Remaining a businessman, he decided to ask Lena to find a buyer for the balloons in order to recoup some of his investment.

Alyssa examined Amy's shoulder. It wasn't broken, but badly bruised. It would heal much faster than her heart.

Matt decided to ask Lena to join them in Florida. He could use her brains in his own business, and Amy really needed her company during this transition. Matt took a walk alone with his cell phone, talking for about fifteen minutes before he returned to the living room and poured himself a stiff drink. The mood of the vacation weekend was now that of a rescue mission.

"Amy, the reservations are made for two more passengers to Florida, and Ollie will be on the plane, too."

He excused himself again from the room. "I'm goin' to walk in the vineyards for a while and get my head straight."

As he paced along the rows of grape-laden vines, he used

his cell phone several times. He called Italy and he changed dates of future appointments, making arrangements to have a few more free days before his next business meeting.

He stopped short when he arrived at his favorite spot near the pond. He sat on the grass and watched Annie's tire swing gently sway in the wind. The weight of the world had just landed on his shoulders as he buried his face in his hands only to feel the moisture of tears coming from his eyes.

Chapter Twelve

7he plane touched down in Menlo and the party of four got off. During the flight, Matt had watched Alyssa's charm and sincerity break through Amy's initial barriers; in fact the two women had begun to bond. Alyssa acted like she was falling head over heels for Matt, and he decided he was totally in love with her. He was comfortable in her presence and he was proud that he had been a gentleman and had resisted taking her to bed during their trip. His great fantasy crescendo was building to explosive levels and he believed he still was the oversexed fool he had always called himself.

Alyssa was like a child with her nose pressed against the window of the stretched limousine. "I can't wait to see Lisa. This was the longest time I've ever spent away from her." She had purchased a little glass tea set for Lisa in the airport. Annie picked it out because it was blue and she loved the blue sky.

The first stop was to take Alyssa home. They drove up to a gorgeous, gated ocean home. The driveway was lined with royal palm trees, and pillars adorned the front of the house, which was framed by a circular canvas canopy. The house and landscaping were meticulous.

Matt was impressed. "I really like your home."

"Thanks." Alyssa grinned as she got out of the limo. "It's not mine. It's my mother's house. She kept Lisa here for the weekend. I live next door. Do you want to meet my mother and Lisa?"

The driver opened her door, and Matt enthusiastically slid out of his seat beside her, "Of course I do. Alyssa, I've met your family. I've met your mother several times and I read books to Lisa. But I would love to see them tonight."

Alyssa giggled, "What's wrong with me? You've got me all dizzy in the head."

He squeezed his arm around her and then slid his hand behind her neck to rub it in approval while walking with her up the wide steps leading to the entrance.

Before Alyssa could touch the door, Lisa leaped out and jumped into her mother's arms. "Mommy, you're home!"

Alyssa's mother was right behind her with similar excitement. Behind her, a skinny, bug-eyed, fancy-looking foreigner appeared from nowhere like a leprechaun. Matt never liked the idea of leprechauns because they supposedly had powers that were beyond human control. They were sneaky and devious and they always seemed to ruin human plans. As a boy he had watched movies like Dance of the Leprechauns where their magic controlled all of Ireland, and it wasn't right. He hid his annoyance as he instantly recognized his foe.

Alyssa beamed. "Mother, you remember Matthew Hunter."

Matt reached out his hand to Dionna. "It's great to see you again."

Alyssa wasted no time in addressing the smirking man with the European features. "I'm so happy. When did you get back? I thought you were going to stay in Europe for longer. Matt, this is my best friend, my brother, Jean-Marc

Debussy."

"Hi, Jean-Marc. I've heard so much about you. It's great to meet you," Matt offered with a forced tone and a firm handshake.

"Likewise, it is a pleasure to meet you," Jean-Marc replied in a thick French accent.

Lisa skirted behind Jean-Marc and sneaked glances at Matthew.

"Lisa, remember me? I read the Bambi book to you in the office. How are you doin'?" When she didn't answer, and instead held tightly onto Jean-Marc's pant leg, Matt turned to Dionna. "This little girl's mommy missed her somethin' awful during our trip. Yep, her mommy missed her a lot."

Lisa studied his face and then faintly smiled in approval. She gazed up to her mother. "Mommy, I missed you, too."

Matt continued to address Dionna. "I want to thank you, Mrs. Tennison, for makin' it possible for Alyssa to join me in California. We had a wonderful time."

"You're very welcome." Dionna's face lit up. "Please call me Dionna."

Matt encouraged everyone to go to the limo and he introduced his sister and his niece.

Annie was delighted to see another child, and she quickly spoke up, "Uncle Matt, can Lisa come over and play with me?"

"Of course she can, but not tonight. Everyone's tired tonight." Matt got in the car and wished everyone a very good afternoon. "Alyssa, I'll call you later after you have time to rest up and visit your family."

Alyssa, as though caught in a dream, stood with her lips

curved in a soft smile as the limo pulled away from the drive. He settled into the luxury of the leather seat for the ride home. He'd rescued his sister and niece and would make sure his dog of a brother-in-law would never harm them again. Alyssa's little daughter had opened up to him. Alyssa herself seemed clearly ready for a serious involvement with him. Nothing stood between him and his dreams now.

Two hours passed and Alyssa had just finished a delightful tea party with Lisa when the phone rang. Dionna answered. With worried eyes, she held out the phone to Alyssa.

"Honey, it's Matthew and he sounds upset."

Alyssa took the phone. "Matt, are you OK? What's wrong?"

"Peter's been shot."

Alyssa's mouth dropped open. "What?"

"I guess it happened while we were on the plane this afternoon. Lena called me just after we left your mother's house. Apparently, Peter was caught in bed with another man's wife. They were both shot by the jealous husband."

"This is awful. Are they OK?"

Matt's voice shook on the other end of the line. "The woman's OK. She got away with minor injuries, but Peter took a bad bullet. He just got out a surgery, but he's bleedin', and they're on their way back in to stop it. It doesn't sound good."

Alyssa shuddered, holding the phone close to her ear. "I am so sorry. How is Amy taking this?"

"She's pretty shook up. I'm just relieved that she wasn't there alone when the news came."

Shivers continued up Alyssa's arms. "What can I do to

help? Matt, can I do something for her?"

"Well, maybe, 'cause you're a doctor and all, you could convince her not to jump on the next plane to California. I'll go with her if we can't convince her to stay for a while, but Peter might not even make it through the night. If you could come over and bring her somethin' to help her sleep, it would help." His words dropped to an almost inaudible whisper. She couldn't make out what he'd said.

"Matt, I'm sorry. I can't hear you."

His voice regained command. "I said, you knowin' about domestic violence and all, maybe you could help her."

Alyssa arrived at Dierdra II and Matt greeted her anxiously.

"Oh, baby. Thanks for comin' right away. Amy's a mess. I've never seen her like this. She's really broken up."

Matt was beside himself with concern. "I'm so fed up. It doesn't hurt me one bit that he got shot. I wonder how long he's been knockin' her around. Why does she still love him? She wants to go back to California to take care of him."

"She accepted those years of abuse. Now he might be dying and she's only thinking of that. It's a normal reaction. She's in shock."

Alyssa carried her black bag with her as he accompanied her down the stairs.

"But why would she let him do that to her? I got her out, and now she wants to go right back and let him pound on her again. It doesn't make sense."

"Matt, don't ask me why people get into abusive relationships and don't get out. There are a million excuses and reasons for not leaving. One of the common reasons is a denial of failed dreams. In Amy's case, it certainly wasn't just pride or nowhere to turn for protection and security."

Matt listened intently as he guided Alyssa to the bedroom where Amy lay, helplessly sobbing into her pillows.

Before entering the room, Alyssa turned to Matt and finished their conversation. "The battered woman's syndrome is sewn with one thread that never changes. Until it's over one way or the other, the battered person creates excuses to protect the abuser. Her situation is no different."

"Well, it's different to me. This is my sister we're talkin' about."

Amy agreed to take the injection, while Alyssa sat quietly watching Matt coddle his sister as he had on the wagon ride in Napa.

Matt's cell phone rang, and he quickly detached himself, got up, and left the room to answer it.

Amy continued, "I know he's been really hard on us, but I'm his wife. I just can't stop loving him overnight. He needs me right now."

Alyssa suspected that Peter had always been abusive to her, and perhaps, he blamed Amy for Annie's health problems and took it out on her. He never spoke a kind word to her the entire time Alyssa had visited their home, and the only real conversation Alyssa had overheard between them was the one that had ended with the sounds of Peter slamming his wife against the wall.

Alyssa put her arms around her new friend. "Maybe it would be good to wait for some information before trying to return to California? It's a long flight. There won't be a reasonable flight schedule tonight, and by morning you'll know more. Believe me, Peter's getting wonderful care and he wouldn't even be aware of your presence yet."

Amy hugged her back as though clinging for human support.

"He's my husband and he's Annie's father. I don't even know what life would be without him."

"I know it hurts. But you're strong and you have lots of love and support around you. I know how it is. I lost my husband a few years ago. It doesn't matter if he failed you in life. If you love him, it hurts."

Amy gazed at Alyssa with the lost expression of a child on her face, searching in Alyssa's eyes for answers and help. The injection had begun to work by now, and she'd be able to think and talk a little more clearly.

Alyssa continued, "Amy, I'm not an authority. I've never been abused. But I devote a lot of my time to helping people who have been mistreated. They all make excuses for their abusive mates and they keep going back to them for whatever reasons they each have."

"Death is very often the end result. You don't want that. Believe it when Matthew says you shouldn't return to California right now. He wants only the best for you."

She hoped she hadn't said too much too fast, but it was a shot at keeping Amy from frantically running back to Napa without thinking it through.

Amy looked around cautiously. Matthew's voice carried into the room as a low rumble; he was outside, pacing back and forth on the deck, and talking on his cell phone. "Alyssa," she whimpered. "I love my little brother very much and so do most people. Matthew is a powerful man and a very controlling one. He was a strong little boy and he usually got whatever he wanted. He would go anywhere or do anything he needed to do to make things go his way. He's worse now, because of all the power his money and business fame have brought him. I know you really like my brother, but don't let his love overtake you and smother you. He owns everything and everyone around him and he'll end up owning you. If you let him, he'll start making all of your decisions for you. He'd control my whole life if I'd let him. I'm not going to California tonight, but not because Matt says so. It's best for Annie and me to stay here, that's why." She bit her lower lip. "It's obvious that he's falling in love with you. He just loves totally and there is no compromise. I guess he gives it a hundred percent and he requires a hundred percent back. He's a very private and exclusive man, and he's worked hard for his position in life. Please, just don't let him take over and control you. You'll lose yourself if you do it."

Just then Matt returned to the room and he went directly to the bar to pour himself a drink. He flopped down on one of his white sofas, holding his glass of scotch out in front of him to avoid the swishing drink from spilling.

"I'm sorry I'm gettin' so many calls," he said. "It looks like I need to go to New York tomorrow night. At least I'll be here till then. Amy, why don't I have Mother to come down here for a few days? I'm really sorry, but I can't avoid this trip."

"No. I think Annie and I should go to Charleston until we know more. Alyssa has just put some temporary sense in my head." Her eyelids drooped. Now, the injection was working well. "Really, if he pulls through, some alone time might do him good. I doubt his girlfriend will show up at the hospital. And if he doesn't make it . . ." Amy mournfully buried her face in her hands.

Alyssa knew she'd helped Amy as much as she could for

now. "I guess I'd better get home. Amy, if you need anything at all, please call me, day or night, I can be here in just a few minutes. Matt, you would call me, right?"

"I'll call you if it's really important. You need sleep, too."

Carrying the black doctor's bag in one hand and reaching for Alyssa with the other, Matt struggled with confusion as they walked away from the dock. His mind flashed back to his past, scanning the long list of buttons he pushed to make things happen, usually in his favor. He briefly paused, remembering his rage in England the night he found his ex-wife with a lover. His behavior that night was totally uncalculated and so unexpected. Scanning back deeper into his past, the image of his father hitting his mother played through his mind in hideous memory of a childhood contaminated by violence. He knew that he had inherited some of his father's mean spirit, though he would never intentionally hurt a woman. Cold shivers ran through his bones. He let go of Alyssa's hand and slid his arm around her, as if protecting her from his thoughts. She was so pure and untouched by things that were painfully part of his character. He would be sure to protect her from his insufferable complexes. But could he ever really be sure he wouldn't hurt her? He had ruined most of the important relationships in his life. Squeezing her shoulder, he leaned his face down to kiss her cheek. She tilted her face toward his in the moonlight and smiled at him. Undeniable trust shone in the clear depths of her eyes. He promised himself that he would never let her down, no matter what.

They reached her car, which was parked in his private, covered, and secluded parking zone. He took her in his arms and tenderly drew her into him. He kissed her lips fully now, as if there were no hesitations. She was his and he was hers. The barriers between them were gone. He treasured her totally. No sexual passion was expressed right then, but a sweet and trusting tenderness of love between a man and woman had come alive.

Alyssa murmured, "I had such a good time with you this weekend."

"Me, too." He gently pressed his body against hers and kissed her deeply again. "I love you," he whispered. "I love you."

He slid his hand down her back and pulled her into him. Excitement rose between them and he knew making love with her was very soon to come. He visualized what it would be like to gently touch her as she lay nude in his arms.

"Matt," she whispered. "We're moving so fast. I felt like a lightning bolt hit me when we met. Nothing could have stopped me from this."

Their lips sought each other desperately now. He kissed her neck as his hands caressed her breasts and held them up for his lips to taste as if they were a succulent and sacred fruit near extinction.

Matthew's fondling was gentle and so passionate that ecstasy could have been minutes away. She wanted to tell him that she too had fallen in love. Instead, she invited him with body language.

He spoke with fervor, "I want you with me tonight. We've been through so much together these past few days. I don't want you to go. Let me just hold you all night until mornin'. I think we both need that."

She agreed.

Alyssa dialed her mother's number as Matt held her free arm up, brushing his lips up and down her smooth skin. Giggling from the sensation of goose bumps running up her spine, she found it difficult to speak. "Mother."

Dionna laughed, "I can read you so well. I just put Lisa to bed. She's fine. See you in the morning, my little daughter, good night. Just stay safe, Alyssa. You're all that Lisa and I have. We love you."

"I love you, too." She clicked the cover closed on her cell phone. "She's amazing," Alyssa thought to herself. "I didn't even have to ask. She always reads me so well."

By the confident look on Matt's face, she knew he was still as aroused like she was. They walked back up the gangway, now elegantly lit with guiding lights to the main entrance. He opened the door and held it for his princess in order that she could cross the threshold to a night in heaven with her king.

"Once again I enter your beautiful world." She sat on a plush couch and he, now stiff and awkward, moved toward the bar to pour two glasses of champagne.

He held his glass to her and said, "This is to you."

They relaxed, laughing about the silly and fun things that had happened between them since they met. They discussed the terrible situation Amy was in, and Alyssa suddenly felt the sting of lost love. "I never thought I'd want another relationship again. It's so strange. Time does fade pain."

"Alyssa," he said, "I've had a lot of women in my life. Men are funny that way. We're kind of like rats that just have one main drive. You know, I used to leave Carline and the children for weeks at a time on business trips. It can get pretty lonely on the road, and I'm not proud of some of the things I did. Carline and I had a really bad relationship durin' the last five years we were together. I've never told this to anyone."

Alyssa touched Matt's lips with her finger, "Shhh. You

don't have to tell me either." She didn't want him to feel the need to purify himself for her sake.

He continued, "No, I want to tell you. It would make me feel good to get this off my chest. I came home unexpectedly one night from a trip, and I found her with some friends in our livin' room havin' a party. My wife was with another man who was hangin' all over her. They had been drinkin' and havin' a great old time in my house. I found out later that she had been messin' around with this guy for a few months. I went off like a missile. I shattered glasses and broke all kinds of things." He leaned forward with his head in his hands and began to cry. "She always said I broke her nose. I loved her so much, and she trashed our marriage. I never forgave her. I guess it was partially my fault because I was gone so much. I knew she didn't ever want to move to America, but she agreed on the company gettin' started and she knew that most of the big contracts weren't in England. Anyway, what really killed me that night was that Matt Jr. saw me go crazy with his mother. He never forgave me for that. I cried like a baby afterward."

Alyssa understood his suffering, and compassion filled her heart. "Why wouldn't you have gone crazy? I'm so sorry."

He continued, "Anyway, none of that is an excuse for my womanizin'. I don't ever want you to be hurt by my past. I do have a reputation and it is worldwide. I never had a prostitute or anythin' like that. I never needed one. I guess I was kinda lucky with women, that's all. Don't you understand why I stopped havin' sex for a while? I want more than that now."

They sat quietly for a few minutes like two kids, one of whom had just confessed his biggest secrets.

"What if I pour us each another glass of champagne and

we get into my hot tub?"

"Matt, no more champagne, please. Let's check on Amy."

"Don't worry. I'm sure she's sleepin' pretty well after that shot."

Then they moved into the bedroom and Matt pushed the dimmers on all the lights. The only light left was a soft golden spray over the huge luxurious bed. Over the Jacuzzi were hundreds, maybe thousands, of tiny pinhole lights through the ceiling. Their glow created a gorgeous night sky with just enough light to see forms, but allowed a girl to be modest.

"How romantic." Alyssa once again wondered how many women had been in this tub with him before her. She wondered if all of his confessions could be part of his game to get her softened for sex. Then she thought that it couldn't be possible that he was a total player. After all, who would want to admit the things he'd just shared with her. She was intoxicated with desire for him. All of her fantasies and dreams about him were coming true, and after tonight she would be comfortable in his bedroom; hopefully, not with the same ending as all the others had.

"By the way, Alyssa. No other woman has ever been in this tub or on that bed. They're all yours."

She was not surprised that he read her mind.

"I told you that I haven't been with a woman for several months. After I met you, I had a new larger tub put in and I got a new bed. I knew this night would come, and I wanted everythin' new for you. My dear, you are the first to christen either one if you will give them the great honor."

He walked toward her and gently set down his glass. His magnetic body was touching her again and a soft set of lips were on hers as he kissed her mouth, and gently unbuttoned the front of her blouse, brushing himself against her. Knowing he was fully aroused gave her an overwhelming sense of feminine power. His shirt was open, too, and he shrugged it off his torso to the floor, simultaneously sliding the silky fabric from her shoulders.

She had on no bra, and she watched his gaze move downward.

"Oh, darlin', you're everythin', you're so gorgeous."

He once again cupped her breasts in his hands and with his index fingers he lovingly encircled her taut nipples, then lowering his face, he caressed one breast with his mouth. As his kisses became more amorous, she trailed her hands across the front of his chest and slid them down his firm abdomen. Ever so slowly, she unzipped him as he kissed her again and again. His pants easily dropped to the floor and she slipped her hands inside his underwear. His hands explored her soft, feminine body. He eased off her tiny panties.

Now they were two lovers, naked, touching, holding, discovering each other under the romantic stars of his hot tub. He held out his hand to help her into the water. As the warm bubbles covered them like a modest blanket, they rolled in their newfound joy. The water's slight suction between them encouraged total touching and hinting at the pleasures of internal intimacy. She was completely immersed in her love for him, in this most powerful and romantic love scene she had ever known.

"This time no movie of the past reminds me of now," he whispered, pulling her even closer. "You're my only leadin' lady. Baby, let's go over to the bed. Let me make love to you like nobody else ever has. Let me feel you like I've never felt anyone before. Oh, Alyssa. Please love me the way I want to love you."

She laid her head on his chest and sighed, "Matt, I do love you. I love you."

They floated up from the warm water together. Huge, luxurious towels awaited them, and they dried each other before they moved toward the bed. The soft sheets reached out to them, calling them. The perfect bed he'd provided for her awaited their arrival to join together with it underneath them. As they lowered each other down, their minds and bodies connected with harmony the greatest, most seasoned lovers would have envied, every motion a deeper expression of love. They shared each other, first one and then the other, cherishing their intimacy, tenderly kissing during a most private moment, and when he slid into her she was filled with a soothing relief that they were finally united as one.

Rhythmically they thrust their bodies together and kissed each other in every intimate way, until a surge of magic ecstasy filled their beings with the sweet nectar of each other. Their perfect mating dance had completed itself and it was good. They peacefully slept the rest of the night wrapped around each other as if they were long-lost lovers who had awaited this night for an eternity.

The next morning came too soon. Matt stirred beside her, rousing her from her peaceful sleep. He slowly slid the sheet down the front of her body just enough to uncover her torso, then carefully arranged a strand of her long chestnut hair over her shoulder, and draped it partially across her bare breast. She opened her eyes and smiled. He gazed into her face as if she were a field of wildflowers and he had been without eyesight until this moment.

"What are you doing, my darling?" she asked.

"I've just painted a beautiful portrait with your face, one of your breasts, and a strand of your hair. I wasn't quite finished with my masterpiece when you opened your eyes."

He then lay back down beside her, and held her for what was the most fulfilled moment of her life.

Eventually, he sat up.

"Do you think you could go to New York with me on Wednesday?"

"I have to work, and I have a child, not to mention my Thursday domestic violence class. I wish I could go, but I can't. I just took a long weekend, and I can't go away again for a while."

Matt frowned. "Well, what if we find someone to take care of your patients for three days, we take Lisa with us, and you skip your class just this week?"

Alyssa laughed. "Well, I wouldn't take Lisa out of school, but I might be able to arrange for someone to see my patients, and I could skip one class, I guess. Let me think about it. I'll see what I can do."

Matt broke into a huge smile. "Fine then, it's settled. You're goin' with me. I don't ever want to be separated from you again."

His assumption surprised her. Could Matt be happily taking control of her life, just as Amy had said he would? But then, who cared? They loved each other, and she desperately wanted to be with him.

Suddenly remembering Lisa and her promises of exchanging Napa for a kitten, she sat up and swung her legs over the edge of the bed. Her heart sank. "Matt, I can't take any more time away without preparing for it first. I promised Lisa I would get her a kitten this weekend because I went to Napa with you. I have an important class to teach on Thursday. It isn't easy to snap my fingers and cancel my patients for the week. I wish I could go with you, but I shouldn't."

Matt jokingly pouted like a little boy. He turned his bottom lip down and rubbed his eyes like a baby crying. "Honey," he pleaded in baby talk. "Pease twy to go wif Dada. He so sad."

He made her laugh, and she called the office.

"Susanna, I need to take another few days off. Could you see if you can move my patient appointments ahead?"

Susanna huffed. "You just took time off. Alyssa, you can't begin cancelling patient appointments whenever Matthew wants you to go away with him somewhere. Neither of you got where you are by doing this kind of thing. I know this is fun for you, but what about your responsibilities? This is medicine. Please listen to me. We've all worked so hard to make this office what it is today. The practice is already suffering financially. If you're going to start this, we should just close the doors now. Besides, what about the kitten? Lisa's counting the minutes before you take her to get one."

Alyssa ignored her. "Any emergent visits could be seen by Dr. Garbo next door, and I'll take Lisa for the kitten this afternoon before we leave."

Susanna grudgingly admitted that Dr. Garbo's office, coincidentally, had called to say he'd take call again anytime.

Dr. Garbo was every tired physician's dream. He loved Emergency Room call and he loved hospital admissions. He was burdened by school loan debt and the expenses of starting up a new practice. Young, hungry physicians were always welcomed relief to seasoned doctors, if they showed promise as future greats.

Alyssa called home and Lisa answered the phone. "Mommy, when are you coming home?"

"Mommy will be home this afternoon when you get out of school. Let's go find the kitty today."

Lisa was happy, Alyssa was relieved of her guilt, and Matt would have more time with her all to himself. Their unquenchable passion for each other had been unleashed. It was all too new to begin disappointing him, and her personal representative was still in control.

After all her effort, Matt reconsidered, "Honey, I'll make a deal with you. You don't have to go with me the day after tomorrow if you promise to go with me to Nassau when I get back. We'll take Dierdra II and stay in the Atlantis Hotel. They have a fabulous VIP suite that I'll reserve for us. You'll love it."

Irked and hurt, Alyssa wondered why anyone would want to leave this yacht to stay in a hotel. Where else but on Dierdra II could you make love in a huge hot tub under a perfectly simulated night sky studded with stars?

"I'll think about it," she answered.

Matt retorted, "I don't want you to think about it, I want you to say you'll do it."

"Well, I know what you want," she answered. "But I just made arrangements to go with you to New York."

She knew she would relent, but she really did want to go to New York. It appeared that Matt had decided to let the whole plan go, and he did just that.

"Oh, let's just forget the whole thing. You're right, you need to buy that cat this weekend, and you're a responsible doctor. I do love that about you, bein' a doctor and all.

He jumped up from bed and threw his arms back and forth, then up and down. "OK, I'm awake. Come on, baby, Let's go make breakfast on the deck. I'll teach you how to make the best biscuits and gravy you ever ate."

Amy and Annie arrived from the other side of the ship just in time for Matt's cooking. Annie sat by Alyssa at the table and gobbled down her biscuits and gravy.

"This is really, really good. Can we play with Lisa now?"

Matt liked the idea.

"Hey, Alyssa. Why don't we get Lisa and your mom, and all go to Charleston to meet my mother? I think our mothers would like each other. I could show you Charleston and take you around to all the hot spots where I grew up."

"I would really like that," Alyssa answered. "Let's do it when you get back from New York." She played a little cat and mouse, and waited for him to ask her again if she would go to New York, but he didn't.

Matt grinned at her and she grinned back with her tongue in her cheek.

He leaned forward to give her a teasing kiss. "You know, baby, you have an incredible way of flirting without doing much at all. It drives me crazy. OK, you win. We'll wait till I get back."

Magically, the tension between them melted away.

Whatever they had together could be sold for a fortune if only it could be captured and sealed in bottles.

Reluctantly, Alyssa departed from him that afternoon to meet Lisa after school.

This was better than Christmas morning for Lisa, who

excitedly bounced into the car before they drove to the Preppy Kitty Store. Lisa picked out a little female ball of orange fluff. She named her Mittens, because she had two white front paws. All of the typical kitty supplies were piled into the car. Lisa held her newfound joy snuggling in her lap during the drive home.

She repeated over and over again, "I can't believe you got me Mittens, Mommy."

"I'm so happy for you, honey. You must take really good care of her. I have an idea. Would you like to take a friend to Disney World this weekend?"

Lisa picked her school buddy, Caitlin. Alyssa called Caitlin's mom that night, and confirmed a trip to Orlando for Saturday and Sunday.

Alyssa weighed her life carefully. How had it been before Matthew Hunter? How was it now? Before she met him she was empty, and now she was full. Matt was going to take a bite out of Lisa's exclusivity with her. Alyssa knew Lisa would learn to like Matt, but she understood the careful conditioning it would require. The most important person in Alyssa's life was Lisa, and she would never let anything detract from that, but she would need to juggle a lot of things in order to make Matt feel that he was number one.

She had enough love to give everyone and she would make it work.

Lisa fell asleep that night with Mittens in her arms. Alyssa took the kitten away and closed it in Lisa's bathroom, where it cried most of the night. When Alyssa went into Lisa's room in the morning, Mittens was back in Lisa's arms in her bed. The three of them had breakfast together on the terrace overlooking the ocean. It was a warm, sunny morning in

Menlo.

The phone rang while they were eating.

"Hey, baby. I just wanted to say good mornin' to you. I love you more every time I think of you. Last night I couldn't sleep because you weren't lyin' beside me. I could taste you all over again. I just keep livin' it over and over again."

Alyssa replied with a quiet, soft voice, "Me, too." She watched Lisa feed the kitten a tiny bite of scrambled egg, and she smiled. She didn't remember ever being so full of joy.

Matt continued, "I'm takin' Amy and Annie to the airport this morning. Amy asked me to tell you she'd see you in Charleston in a few days if you can come. She really appreciates all you did for her. Listen. I drove to your house late last night and I put something on your front doorstep. Have a great day, baby. I love you. Gotta go."

Alyssa hung up the phone and went to the front door. Outside was a small bag, which she opened to find a little hand-painted Romeo. "The other half of the set," she said aloud.

She opened a note tied around Romeo's waist. It said, "Every Romeo needs his Juliet. Put them together, side by side, and think of me. I love you." She held the statue to her breast and found herself praying.

She went back into the house and stood in front of the fireplace. Carefully she placed Romeo beside Juliet, who had stood alone from the day Matthew pulled her out of the little bag from England. He was so earnest that morning. She convinced herself that she loved him at first sight. Maybe she did and maybe she didn't, but one thing was for certain. This man had taken a very short time to turn her hurting heart inside out. From the moment she met him she was more alive. Colors were more brilliant, flowers were more fragrant, and the skies told a story of love twenty-four hours a day. No matter what the future was, everything had changed forever.

She quietly spoke aloud as she so often did, wondering what he was doing at that very moment, "Romeo, Romeo, wherefore art thou, Romeo?"

When she arrived at the office, Dionna and Susanna anxiously greeted her with the news that Dr. Garbo had called twice and was finally ready to settle the purchase of the office. Susanna wanted to change gears, Dionna wanted freedom, and Alyssa was almost in financial ruin. Alyssa called Dr. Garbo, they arranged to meet at her lawyer's office, and she opened the door for her first patient of the morning. She plucked the chart from the door and saw there was no name on it. She opened the door to dozens of red roses. The rest of the staff pretended they knew nothing.

A note was strategically placed in the middle of the central bouquet. She read it silently.

> "Dearest Alyssa and Lisa, would you both be kind enough to rustle up somethin' to eat for us three tonight at your place? Call me if you can.
> Love,
> Matthew Romeo Hunter."

Romeo arrived for dinner in the crystal dining room at six o'clock that evening. Alyssa and Lisa had proudly prepared a lovely meal for him. They worked so well together in the kitchen, which was a special event they had cultivated together. Lisa was quite adept at setting the table, and she was very good at stirring anything that needed to be stirred. She liked to butter the garlic bread before it went into the oven, and she was great at choosing salad combinations from the crisper. The dinner was perfectly served.

Matt admired everything Alyssa had designed.

"Your home has real stars everywhere. We're air-conditioned, yet we're outside, yet we're inside. This is fabulous. I'm goin' to design a ship with a crystal dinin' room under the stars. This is definitely better than any ole hot tub with a bunch of pinholes in the ceilin'. Honey, you out did me."

Alyssa knew their home would excite him.

Matthew worked on befriending Lisa, and it helped his confidence that he could win her over. He felt at home with his two new girls. Lisa remained animated and even sang for him after dinner. He felt like he was a family man for the first time in years, and it was good. Lost in the dream of lying with Alyssa's beautiful body and smelling her aromatic scent, he luxuriated in his new world. Lisa had Alyssa's green eyes, two precious emeralds that money couldn't buy. He felt jealous, yet he didn't understand why. He was still an outsider, and Alyssa and Lisa were a bonded family. He wanted a wife, and he wanted a child to replace the ones he had lost. What could be better than to join their bond, as a family of three? They were wide open for him to take care of and to love.

The girls cleared the table and Matthew tried to help. Lisa told him he couldn't help because he was the guest. She was having a ball. This was a real live tea party. He allowed her to rule, and he knew she liked him for it.

Matt sat back and poured himself another wine. His thoughts deepened. He envied Alex. He wanted to be Lisa's father. For a moment he disliked Alex immensely because he was dead and dead people have no flaws in memory.

They become angels of eternity and that isn't fair. After all, who would be her greatest influence in life, Alex or him? His thoughts were beginning to get all mixed up with the extra wine, combined with the realization that this was everything he ever wanted to have in his life. He started to feel a loss of contact with reality, and everything looked distorted, almost psychedelic. He could almost jump from a building and fly, yet he would never do such a thing. He knew that another drink could turn him into someone he wouldn't want to remember in the morning. Yet, he still wanted another glass of wine. His mind began to race and his thoughts came at him with a million images a minute. He had to control himself from disconnecting reality. He put the wine down and struggled to control his mind. Why did this happen to him sometimes for no reason at all? It was almost as if a demon controlled his being after a certain amount of alcohol, but not always. He always controlled his behavior during business meetings, and he always was able to control himself with new relationships.

He once again found his faculties and he forced them back into control. Concentrating on the room and the present environment helped him snap his mind back as though it were a rubber band.

All this time Alyssa and Lisa had been clearing the table from the crystal room. Lisa was loading the dishwasher and Alyssa was cleaning the kitchen. They had missed Matt's minutes of reflective blackout. They were oblivious to his short imaginary struggle with love, jealousy, and psychotic insecurity. This was a struggle he had just completed by himself, as it had been many times before throughout his life.

Lisa comfortably returned to Matthew's side, and all three watched TV. It wasn't long before she fell asleep with his arm cuddled around her. Lovingly carrying the little girl to her room, he and Alyssa put her into her bed. They hugged each other while watching her snuggle into her pillow. Matt whispered, "Baby, I think she's startin' to like me a little."

"She's not only warming up to you, but she'll love you in no time. How could she help it? They say you can judge a man by the way dogs and children feel about him."

They returned to the living room and sat together quietly, until Matt broke the silence.

"Thank you for tonight, honey. You and Lisa really made a great dinner. She's such a sweet little thing. You're really lucky to have her. Alyssa, I want to be part of her life, too."

"Matthew, I love you so much," she whispered.

The next day as Matt left for New York. Alyssa was struggling with that phase of a new relationship when passion and love are so intermingled and confused that the only truth is perfection. The best was right then. There were no flaws. Matt was Alyssa's primary concentration, and she had no power to stop it or change her desires, nor did she want to.

It was Thursday morning, the 6:30 alarm played its soft jazz, the eastern sky outside of her window was breaking into color, and Alyssa was sick to her stomach from lack of sleep. Matthew Hunter's voice called to her all night long, as she tossed and turned, making love with him in her mind and lying in unfulfilled ecstasy until dawn.

This was an important day. Exhausted, Alyssa went to her lawyer's office to draw up the contracts to sell the practice to Dr. Garbo. A new Hope for Harmony House medical clinic was awaiting her employment with a very small salary, but she would be where she was needed and appreciated. Finally she could write a book that would leave an indelible message behind to the millions of women who were abused by their partners. She would teach them that it didn't need to be that way, and that true and healthy love was still out there. But they needed to make themselves healthy first in order to find it. She wasn't a victim of violence, but she was a victim of tragedy, and she spent years healing from Alex's death before Matt came into her life. Matt never would be with her now if she hadn't been able to grow and leave her own pain behind.

Chapter Thirteen

Southampton, Long Island was a second home for Antonio Capezzio, the notoriously known shipping magnate and owner of DeVinci Cruises, and son of Pascual Capezzio, one of the most powerful businessmen of his time. Pascual had been in direct competition with Onassis, and he never stopped trying to outdo the Greeks. His violent and untimely death left behind a tremendous and powerful name, money, bloodshed, and respect. Antonio was next in line to take over the family business, and now he, too, was beginning to smell the scent of bloodshed following closely behind him.

Matthew, his new image, was his cover, a connection to the legitimate world of luxury design. He was a logical choice: He was American, high profile, and he had a clean record. Matthew's connection would legitimize DeVinci Cruises, and his popular public profile would provide an effective smoke screen. Antonio had already shown his loyalty to Matthew with the Peter problem. He knew Matthew had no idea how indebted he was to the DeVinci dynasty at this point, and Antonio planned to help him rack up a few more favors along the way.

However, Antonio rarely collected on his favors. He took pride in building his human savings account, stacking favors next to each other in case of an emergency. Then when he needed to call on them, he could push them all at once like an army of powerful soldiers, a row of carefully placed dominoes, and watch them fall one by one. Antonio paced in his study, every few minutes checking the road to the house through his expansive bulletproof picture window.

He wondered why Matthew was late. Promptness was an important sign of respect. Very few people dared to keep Antonio Capezzio waiting.

Old man Capezzio had taught his son that fear was the first and foremost ingredient to Italian success, respect was next, and accumulating great wealth was last. With fear and respect, wealth was a natural phenomenon.

Antonio owned a small, expensive fleet of luxury ships that awaited guests from all over the world. Until now, DeVinci Cruises had been strictly for the wealthy. Each ship chartered parties of up to one hundred fifty people and the price tag was prohibitive for the working class. He wanted to move ahead and build a cruise line to accommodate thousands. This new family line would first sail around the ports of Europe and pass the Greek Islands to Turkey. Antonio Capezzio had a new urge to share his wealth with the common man, as he saw this opportunity as a business with no limitations. He wanted a little from many rather than a lot from a few. Many cruise lines were jam-packed with fun and adventure, but the most elegant vacations only belonged to the wealthy.

He had watched Matthew Hunter climb to the top of the food chain, never thinking he would offer him a key to the corporate offices of DeVinci Cruises. Matthew's thick Southern drawl brought international attention to a traditionally Italian world, and his vulnerability was exactly what Antonio wanted for this project.

Since Antonio's boyhood, his father had groomed him to take over the family business.

"Antonio, not all people need something immediately, in fact, most don't. Always remember that sooner or later everyone needs something. As you get older you will see how easy it is to figure out in the end who can be controlled."

Pulling his young son onto his lap, he continued to embed leadership in the little boy's mind, "A man with power always has enemies, and that's why he needs protection. When you play stick ball in the streets with your friends, you like to play with someone who is a little weaker in the game than you are, right?"

Antonio nodded his head, agreeing that winning the game was the best.

"Remember this, my son. A man who cannot keep his personal life together will never be able to be a true leader. Family is first. It's the most important thing you will ever have. If you have no family, you have nothing and you are weak. Now go along and play outside."

Matthew was definitely the right designer for the job. His work and his name would guarantee an incredible price tag for the first ship. His self-confidence could be manipulated, and he had no family to fall back on for inner strength. Matthew Hunter was an astute businessman who didn't appear to believe in trading character for money, and Antonio Capezzio admired that. He studied Matt's strategies that had made his fortune through brilliant creativity, hard work, and shrewd maneuvers. For the most part, his naive dedication to honesty was coupled with loyalty. Antonio reinforced loyalty, while teaching Matthew the value of his world of favors and punishments. Matthew's talents included sniffing out trouble before it happened, and he had no compunction about stamping out anything he felt was diseased. This would make a perfect game of cat and mouse, and Antonio planned to win it. The papers were signed in San Francisco contingent upon Matthew's producing a proposal within a deadline of three months.

New York was its usual exciting realm of confusion and business, but Matt was lonely in the Big Apple. His favorite spot, the beautiful Plaza Hotel across from Central Park, had been converted into private units. Matt hated things to change and decided to buy one of the apartments in order to secure a piece of his memories. But that night he settled for a room at the Four Seasons. He checked into the hotel and wasted no time in leaving for his meeting.

The traffic from the city was horrendous. Matthew dialed Capezzio's number from the limo phone.

"Hello, Antonio. I'm sorry, but the Long Island Expressway is backed up for miles. It'll probably be three or more hours before I get free of it."

"Don't worry, my friend. Why don't you go back to the city tonight, and come out here tomorrow. Pack a suitcase and stay with me for a few days. We'll get more done that way."

Matthew was glad for the reprieve. He had scheduled several technical meetings for the following week, and he could get some important details hammered out with Antonio more quickly by staying with him.

The first item on Matt's New York agenda was to purchase a condo at the Plaza with the best Central Park view. Staying in the city for the night would give him a chance to look at a few apartments, and hopefully, pick one and buy it. He found a penthouse. It had just the right features, including a private elevator that would excite Lisa and Annie, a balcony overlooking the park, a perfect view of the horse and buggies, and two master suites, one with separate closets and a huge bathroom for the girls to share. A grand master suite equipped with Jacuzzi and Swedish sauna promised secluded evenings for Alyssa and him, and a masculine library graced one side of the apartment. Its rich dark oak ceilings, recessed lighting, two walls of book shelving, and a huge built-in computer section with a thirty-six-inch screen were exactly what he would have custom ordered. A large safe hid behind a wall that opened with a button under the built-in desk. An oak bar accented with salmon-colored marble and a smoked mirror opened behind one of the bookshelves with the press of another button. He needed to entice Lisa with promises of fun and excitement. He'd be spending the majority of his time in New York during the next year, and wanted to start putting some get-to-know-you energy into the child. As he watched the horse-drawn carriages through his new living room window, he imagined her squealing for a ride through Central Park.

Alyssa could decorate, and choose every piece of furniture, filling the rooms with her own sensuality so it would feel like home to her. The apartment was over six thousand square feet of luxury, and no money had been spared in converting the space to total New York penthouse heaven. He was sure the two-story dream home would offer enough of everything for everyone with its seven bathrooms and its two master suites on the second floor, separated by a grand sitting area equipped with an open kitchen facing a large balcony overlooking the park. The two guest bedrooms, the library, formal dining room, huge gourmet kitchen, and even a movie theatre had been created in a separate area off the grand living room. Spacious servants' quarters were off one side of the kitchen and had been furnished in keeping with the rest of the apartment. Lisa and Annie could help decorate their room, and they'd order pizza and all eat together on the floor in a circle, picnic style, while they awaited the arrival of the new furniture.

His mind was going crazy with the fantasy of a real family, home life again, and this time a home life in New York City.

There was a great florist near the hotel that had satisfied Matt's courting needs for years. He wired twenty-four long-stemmed red roses to Alyssa's office with a short note, "I love you, and that's why I just bought us a wonderful place overlooking Central Park. You won't believe it. It's all for you, baby." He left the little flower shop and strolled to the hotel. His eye caught the view of a beautiful young lady who was followed by the bell captain with two large carts overladen with suitcases. He was proud that he had changed. At one time, he would have followed her, and he reassured himself that she could have been had for the night or for the week if he so chose. He courteously passed by her with a conviction to be above all that. Matt's yearning to be a family man reminded him that good family men were loyal to their betrothed. They came home to their children at night. He wished he could go home to Alyssa and Lisa that night. He loved his lady with all of his heart and he would do everything he could to give her a magic carpet ride for the rest of her life. He had deeply hurt too many other loves, and he repented. This was a chance to get it right, one more chance to wash away his sins of the past, and his heart burned with passion to settle down, this time, forever.

Passing the hotel doorman, he continued walking until he reached FAO Schwartz. He loved toy stores and no store had the variety and quality of toys one could find there. He bought a beautiful doll with long curls. She wore a gown reminiscent of the finery of a Charleston ball in the 1800s. He was lonely as he paid the clerk and took the package from her. He wanted Alyssa, and buying the doll drove his loneliness to new heights and magnified his desire for a family again.

Matt wished he could have had his daughter, Dierdra, with him right then. He'd have taken her shopping. Dierdra loved to shop because it was a girl thing. Most men shopped, as he had when purchasing the doll, just to get what they needed, and it reflected the way he approached all areas of his life. Women shopped to browse and enjoy the stimulus of the crowds and gaze at the pretty things in the store windows. As he walked down Fifth Avenue, he fantasized about having Dierdra, Alyssa, and Lisa together.

He thought about the night in the hot tub on his boat. "I've been to that place once in my life. It was that night, with her," he said to himself. "I love her and I want her. I'll ask her to marry me, and I don't want to be without her."

The next few days in Southampton left little time to think about anything except ship designs and learning about some of Antonio's idiosyncrasies. The two men spent long hours, late nights, and early mornings roughing through ideas for staterooms, ballrooms, and dining rooms with crystal ceilings that reminded Matt of Alyssa's home in Menlo. Antonio's hospitality was without limits. The technical engineers were invited to Southampton for the weekend, which sped the initial design work up a notch.

Four days had passed before Matthew returned to his hotel room in the city, exhausted, lonely, and already wanting to return to Florida. Amy was still in Charleston awaiting news of Peter's condition. Peter had been taken back to surgery two more times, he was doing very poorly, and in fact, he was now on full life support. Even the most optimistic prognosis didn't look good.

Matt decided to visit Alyssa for a couple of days, and then go to Charleston before continuing his new project. He ordered dinner in the room and watched TV, flipping the channels every few minutes, the climax of his evening being his anticipation of boarding the plane and returning to Florida. He pictured Alyssa's beautiful face and then briefly thought about DeVinci Cruises. He had just signed the business deal of his career, a deal that five years ago would have consumed him. Now he saw that deal as a final accomplishment, after which he would retire to be with Alyssa.

Maybe they could have a child, maybe two. He could make things right for the losses he'd racked up with Matthew, Jr., Robert, and Dierdra. Alyssa was part of his ticket to salvation. She had so many characteristics he admired, some of them he'd never considered important until now. Until now, he never had much interest in the spiritual side of life, though he knew right from wrong. Right and wrong were his tools to get what he wanted; and to go where he wanted to go with a clear conscience, a measure of his success and how he felt about the path he took to get there. Before Alyssa, it never had anything to do with being good for the sake of being good.

She was an angel sent to him to help him get back some of the old values his mother had worked so hard to instill in her children. Alyssa's very presence drove him to want to be a better man. She was like an addictive, sweet nectar. He wanted more of her or he would go crazy. He concluded that he had earned Alyssa's love. His celibacy before meeting her must have been an unconscious part of that preparation. The difficulty of giving up women was now paying off. The payoff was, most assuredly, going to be lots of sexual activity in the future.

The next morning he sat in the limo with a Bloody Mary in his hand. He made a quick pit stop at Tiffany's and chose a $32,000 diamond. As he rode through the tunnel toward La Guardia Airport, he was relieved to have gotten a direct flight to Orlando instead of going through Atlanta as Delta so often forced him to do.

Matt had a new decision to make and he needed major preparation to make it come true. He had the ring. Now he needed to dream up something even better than a hot air balloon proposal. He wanted it to be so perfect that she couldn't say no. There was only one way. Matthew, Alyssa, and Lisa would marry each other as a family. He would legally adopt Lisa and arrange for it to be official at the wedding. Alyssa and Lisa both would then belong to him from the beginning. How perfect. He decided to propose to them both at the same time. One would become his wife and the other would become his child.

The limousine ride back to Menlo was long. Matthew stopped at one of his favorite jewelry stores in Orlando, and he bought a beautiful little gold locket for Lisa. It had three little flowers engraved on it, each with a sparkling diamond in its center.

"Lisa will love this," he thought. "I'll have a picture of all of us together put inside."

He carefully placed the locket back in its velvet box, and continued holding it in his hand. He leaned his head back against the seat and closed his eyes. He was exhausted.

The cell phone rang. He was annoyed at the disruption of his short-lived silence and peacefulness.

It was Lena's voice. "Matt, it's Lena here. Are you in Florida?"

"Yes," he answered. "I have a proposition to make. But first off, what's gone on with the Peter thing?"

Lena was soft-spoken on the other end of the phone. "He died about an hour ago. Amy doesn't know yet. I've been the one keeping her informed of everything the hospital would share. Should I call her or should you?"

Matthew hesitated. "Lena, you've been a good girl. I'll be the one to tell her. She doesn't realize it right now, but she's better off without him. You've done everythin' just the way you should have done. Just close up the house and fly out here. I want you to work for me. I need your help. My deal with DeVinci is goin' to be great."

Her silence on the other end of the line was discomforting, especially because he wanted their communication to be on a higher note when he told her the news. "Lena, listen. I want you to know this first of everyone. I bought a ring for Alyssa. I'm goin' to marry her. I need you to help me keep everythin' goin' smoothly for me while all this is goin' on. I'll pay you very well."

"Congratulations, Matt." Lena's shock was obvious, and the break in her voice didn't help her hide it.

Matt felt relieved that it was out in the open. "Well, I haven't asked her just yet. I have to find the exact perfect time and place. I want the child there, too."

Lena's forced laughter was poignant. "You will make it unforgettable. I have no doubt."

Matt could have cut the ice through the phone. "Lena, about what happened back then. You've moved on from all that, right?"

Lena gave a soft, heart-wrenching gasp. "You're not asking me that. Matt, are you asking me if I'm over it? No

Matt, I'll never be over it. Am I still hurt? Yes. I lost a whole lot more than just you. I lost my chance at fulfillment. It eats at me and I'm still trying so hard to let it all go. Do I wish we were still together after all these years? No, Matt. The innocence we shared was smashed and destroyed. I love you, Matthew James Hunter, but I stopped crying for you alone in my bed a while ago. OK, we got that out in the open. It's funny. I envy her, but I pity her, too. I have to hang up now. Congratulations to you both. Good-bye."

An unfamiliar sensation of defeat settled on him. "Good-bye."

He felt his own great sadness in his chest. He didn't believe she loved him anymore, not really. How could she? If only he could turn it all around, he would, but he knew nothing could change what had happened that evening in the vineyard.

Matt thought about the past and the future and his fingers dialed Alyssa's number. It rang for what seemed like an eternity and then he hung up. He reached for the liquor cabinet and poured himself a Chivas Regal over ice. He was alone and lonely. He wondered what he could do to rid himself of his guilt over Lena's life. He had plucked her out of all that was good and pure and clean and threw her into all that was not fair. He would live with that awful reality forever. She turned to her Catholic world for repentance, strength and forgiveness and she found it there. The church was a world he could never join no matter how hard he might have tried. Religious devotion was too submissive for him.

Matthew slumped into his seat holding his cell phone and he dialed his mother's house in Charleston.

Amy answered the telephone and despite his effort to offer some light chitchat, she picked up immediately that something was terribly wrong. "Matt, don't sugarcoat anything. He's gone, isn't he?"

Matthew answered as gently as he could, "Yes."

There was silence on the other end of the phone and then his sister's quiet whimpering built into a slow crescendo to overt sobs.

"Oh," she said through her crying, "Everything is so terrible. How could it all come to this? Promise me that you had nothing to do with this."

Matthew gulped hard in hearing his sister's pain. "I swear, Amy. I would never have done such a thing to hurt you so. I didn't want you with him, but I wouldn't have done anythin' to hurt him, much less kill him."

In the background Annie's plaintive cries tore at his heart. "Mommy, Mommy, Mama, Mama, what's wrong? Don't cry, Mama, what's wrong?"

Matthew felt his throat catch, but not because Peter was dead. He had learned to despise Peter. Amy, his sister, was suffering and that broke his heart.

Amy cleared her throat. "Matt, I have to leave here and go to Calistoga. I need to go home."

Matthew answered with powerful control, "Just let me handle all of this. I'll make arrangements for his cremation and I'm goin' with you to Napa. Just stay close to Annie and wait for me. Tell Mother I'm comin' to Charleston. I'll be there as soon as I can get a plane. They leave for Charleston every couple of hours. I love you, Sis."

Matthew was sick inside. He hung up the phone, and he leaned forward, slid the glass open to his driver and said, "I'm sorry. Would you please turn the car back to the airport in Orlando. I need to catch a plane."

As the limo wheels turned back toward Orlando, he once again sank back in his seat and closed his eyes. He picked up his phone again and dialed Alyssa's cell phone. He needed to hear the reassurance of her soothing, velvet voice. Her phone was shut off.

This time his flight was not direct. He had to change planes in Atlanta. He hated Atlanta for its congestion. He never was one for long lines and long waits. Matt arrived in Charleston late that night, exhausted.

His mother greeted him at the door. "We were so worried about you. Why did it take so long for your plane to get in?"

He hugged her. "Stop fussin' over me." But she had such a sweet face and such a loving voice that no child of hers could ever be annoyed at her clinging spirit.

He walked into the house with his arm around her. "Mother," he said. "It's so good to be home."

Following his mother into the living room, he saw his brokenhearted sister cuddled up to her sleeping daughter on the couch, staring at the TV without really watching it.

Matt opened his arms and reached out for her to get up from the couch.

Amy jumped up and he hugged her tightly, offering strength and solace. "It's OK, Sis, we're goin' to get through this. You'll see. He turned his head to Annie. "Look at the little darlin'. How is she?" He reached down and kissed the petite bundle, asleep and wrapped in one of her grandmother's hand-crocheted lap throws.

"I gotta go to bed," he said when Amy didn't respond. "I hope you don't mind. Amy, are you and Annie doin' OK?"

Amy nodded that they were. He recognized it was a nod that simply meant she was worn out and didn't want to talk about it right then. Matt climbed the stairs to what had always been his room. He flopped down on the bed and once again he dialed Alyssa's home number.

Nobody was home and he left a message on the answering machine. "Honey. Where are you? I've been callin' and callin' you for hours. Peter died. I'm here in Charleston. In the mornin' I'm takin' Amy back to California. I'll call you later. I love you."

He clicked the phone off. Where could she possibly be? It wasn't like Alyssa to be out at this time of night. She should have let him know where she was.

The next morning Matthew and Amy flew to California without Annie and her grandmother. They were to follow in two days, after the funeral arrangements were settled. Matthew liked Amy's decision to send Peter's ashes to his family in Australia. He believed Amy's suffering might be partially vindicated when Peter's remains left American soil.

As they rode through Calistoga's winding roads and passed under its canopy of trees, Amy's nervousness at going home was apparent. She slipped her hand into her brother's, squeezed it tightly and sighed, "I don't know what I'd do without you. You're the best brother a sister could ever have."

Matthew lovingly looked at his sister who was squeezing his hand quite firmly now, and he said, "You're the best sister a brother could ever have. I love you. This is gonna be OK. I know it's hard, but it's gonna be OK. We're a strong family and we have each other. It's gonna be OK."

When they arrived at the house, nobody was there. Lena had left to see her father in Southern California for a couple of days to breathe the air of her own roots during this hideous time. Matthew suspected Emilio de la Cruz, the Mexican Migrant Labor Leader, her father, would offer the only true solace she could find.

The house had a very empty and lonely feeling as if it had been uninhabited for years. Amy prepared a pot of coffee, poured two cups, and gave one to Matthew. They sat quietly in the kitchen at the breakfast nook where there had been many mornings of laughter. Now there was only sadness.

Amy's misty eyes gazed at the wood grain in the table while she muttered, "Matt, I think we should have a small memorial service. It's only right and we need to do it for Annie and the rest of the community. He had a lot of friends. And then, I guess, we should just fly his ashes to his mother."

Matthew had already thought of this and had unofficially made those very same arrangements with the funeral home. He only needed Amy's approval and signature in order to carry out the plans.

The memorial service would be tasteful and short. It was so important for little Annie whose grief was overwhelming. Of course, she had no idea that anything out of place had happened. All she knew was that Daddy got sick and he died and that she would never see him again. Every few hours she clung to Amy or Matthew, her sturdy little body shaking with her tears.

Matt finally reached Alyssa on her cell phone.

"I am so sad to find out you've been going through all this while we were at Disney World. I can't believe you're back in California, and I didn't even know it.

"Well, baby, your phone didn't even have a message on it, your cell phone was off, and I had no way to reach you. I wish you wouldn't cut me off like that. I want to always be able to find you."

"I'm really sorry. I promised Lisa we'd go to Disney. I went with my mom and one of Lisa's friends. If it makes you feel any better, you were in my mind every second. I missed you the whole time. I wish I could be with you right now to support you through this ordeal."

"I can think of somethin' you could support. I'd like lots a sugar from you right now. Listen, baby, my cell phone is gettin' real hot on my ear." He chuckled and whispered, "You're a naughty little girl. It's all your fault that my phone is burnin' up."

Silence followed that statement as their hearts touched through the phone line.

Matt continued, "May I say somethin' serious to you right now? Alyssa, I love you so much. Bein' without you durin' these hard times just shows me how much I need you. I want you to be with me all the time. I don't know how we're goin' to put this together, but I don't want to be separated from you anymore. I don't want to be away from Lisa, either. When I come back to Florida, I want us to talk about it. That is, of course, if you think it would be OK to talk about it."

"Matthew, my ears are ringing, I've fallen so deeply in love with you. I not only dream about you when we're apart, but I dream about you even when I'm asleep in your arms." A new confidence rang in her voice, and it affirmed his certainty he'd captured her love. "My life began again after that first night with you at the Bistro. I couldn't imagine my life without your sharing it with me. I don't want to be away from you either."

"I'll be home sometime midweek. I'll call you later,

baby."

Alyssa caressed the phone, and softly whispered, "I love you." Only a dial tone answered. He'd already hung up before he realized she'd said something more.

Chapter Fourteen

$\mathcal{S}$ummer vacation was in full swing, and Lisa sleepily raised her head from under the covers to hear her mother.

"Lisa, it's time to get up and watch Rugrats. Come on, sweetheart, let's wake up." She stood at the foot of the bed and playfully pretended to pull on Lisa's feet. "Honey, let's get up so we can have breakfast." Continuing to bribe her, "I'll take you to Sandy's Café for pancakes with strawberries and whipped cream."

"Mommy?" Lisa yawned, stretching her little arms out and reaching for her mother. "Do you think Daddy is mad at us because we love Matthew, now and he has to be up in Heaven all by himself?"

"Now, whatever would make you think of that so early in the morning?"

"I was waking up, and I heard you in the hallway talking to Matthew on the phone. You told him you love him."

Alyssa gathered her daughter into arms and held her closely, marveling at the little girl's insight. "Lisa, do you really love Matt?"

Lisa nodded her head in approval.

"Daddy will never be mad at us, he'll always be with us, and he's happy we have someone here on Earth to love us and take care of us the way he can't right now. Just because we care about other people here on earth doesn't mean we'll ever forget Daddy. Heaven isn't a lonely place, it's a beautiful place. I'm sure Daddy isn't lonely."

Lisa wrinkled up her little nose. "Does Daddy love Matthew?"

"Well . . ." She struggled, beginning to stammer. "Yes. I'm sure Daddy loves Matthew in his own way." Alyssa knew very well that if Alex were living, he wouldn't love Matthew at all. They were very different types of men. One was a total humanist, centered in his life, at peace with himself. He was a highly trained doctor, a man who selflessly gave to others for the mere pleasure of wanting to make things better for them. The other was a self-motivated businessman, whose formal education had become secondary to his success. She learned early in their relationship that Matthew didn't feed on self-sacrifice as she and Alex had, but he fed on power, control, and the adoration that came from his handsome demeanor, his sexy personality, and his money. It wasn't even about his designing ability, she realized; it was about believing he alone was making the world go around. Though she knew her character was very different from his, she chose to accept that, loving him for the parts of him that she understood, and excited to learn about the parts that she didn't understand. She convinced herself that she would slowly help him change some of his outlook on life through love and loyalty, though she was willing to change for him, too.

"Mommy?" Lisa wrinkled up her nose and tugged her mother's sleeve to get back her attention. "If Daddy knows what we're doing, how come we don't know what he's doing?"

Lisa's questioning was more philosophical that it had been. She was really beginning to show some mature thinking.

Alyssa wished she had better answers. "I guess it's not

our turn to understand. Heaven is different than Earth. Right now, we just have to believe that things are a certain way. We don't always know why some things happen, like why Daddy died when he did. Some things happen for reasons that we can't explain."

Lisa crossed her arms in front of her. "But why did Daddy die?" She frowned as though it was all too complicated. "Mommy, I miss Matthew, don't you, Mommy?"

Lisa's questions were forcing Alyssa to think before answering. She had worked so long and so hard to stop wishing for a miracle to bring Alex back. Finally, she had found a whole life without him through new love. To say that she still missed him felt like a betrayal to Matt. Did she miss Alex now? She would always remember all that was good and wonderful about him, but she didn't want to miss him anymore. She was alive, and she wanted to live life to its fullest.

"Yes, I miss Matt, but he'll be back soon. Let's get up for breakfast."

"Let's take him to Disney World when he gets back, OK?"

Alyssa giggled. "OK."

Matthew reflected on what he was learning about true values. These were the values from which he had come, values that he had left behind years ago. He wanted to earn Alyssa's respect. His money was great, but character for the sake of spiritual growth was something else he wanted to learn. Maybe Alyssa, Lisa, and he could start going to church on Sunday mornings like he used to do with his mother and Amy when they were growing up. His girls would like that.

He heard the wind chimes on the porch blowing outside

as the front door opened, and he went to the hallway to see who was there. Lena walked in, her small leather overnight bag clutched in her hand, and brought back with her that incredible air of Latina elegance. As she came through the hallway, she didn't look like Lena, but rather, she looked like her full name, Marialena Vargas de la Cruz. Her mother was Rosalind Vargas de la Cruz; her culture perpetuated maternal value by passing down the name of the matriarchal heritage to her offspring.

Matthew was smitten with Marialena's beauty. Her silky long black hair was pulled to one side, draping over her sweater. Her flashing brown eyes danced, and her beautiful full-figured body fit perfectly into her tight designer jeans. Her elegance made her look hotter than a leading lady in a Zorro film. She was Matthew's symbol of total beauty, not only having been molded from innocence, but she was gorgeous and brilliant. She had come from a family of political sophistication, she was worldly, yet soft and feminine. She was educated, ran a business, and now had just finished writing her first politically based book. Lena was the magic behind the hot air balloon business. She had accomplished many things already. Now, at thirty-two years old, this beautiful lady was in the prime of her life. Matt knew he'd always be weak at the knees in her presence. She was the only woman he had ever known who completely controlled him sexually. His passion for her raged inside of him, and he knew his only hope to separate himself from desiring her was to stay away from her. Even with Alyssa beside him that morning on the terrace a couple of weeks earlier, he'd briefly felt her eyes dancing within his own.

He didn't forget how everyone had noticed them as a couple because of their physical beauty, charismatic spark, and fire together. During a several-month, passion-driven love affair, while basking in the ecstasy of their intimacy, Lena became pregnant. During a lovers' quarrel that got out of hand, she fell. Had Matthew known she was hurt, he never would have left her in the vineyard. He returned three days later to find that the baby he had fathered had been not one child but a set of twin boys, and the girl he had romanced was now incapable of ever being pregnant again.

Now, many years later, he watched one of his greatest angels come through the hallway toward him.

As though she read his thoughts, her eyes darkened with the pain they shared. "Matthew," she said, "How is Amy?"

"Hello, Marialena. Amy's doin' fine. She's hurtin' like you'd expect, but she'll be OK. She's in the bedroom."

Lena smiled at Matthew. "It's been years since you called me that." Her voice became husky and inviting.

Matthew grinned. "You look like Marialena tonight."

He took his half-full glass with him and turned toward the terrace overlooking the tiny vineyard from which Peter had personally plucked so many grapes through the years to create his personal vintage wine. Lena hurried into Amy's bedroom, and Matt's chest burned with old wounds of love that had never healed. His mistakes of the past might someday, surely, be forgiven. How many more emotional burials could he endure before he could be at peace? Alyssa had come into his life when he needed her most, she saved him from himself, literally saved his life. No man could ask for more than to have someone like her to love him and take care of him the way she would. He was wrought with confusion and despair.

He hated himself and he hated life. He put his drink on the porch rail, and he fervently drove his fingers threw his hair, almost pulling it as he paced back and forth. He wanted this whole ordeal to end. He wanted to go back to Florida. He wanted to see Alyssa. He wanted to get started on his project as designer of DeVinci Cruises' first ship. He wanted to erase what he had just felt for Lena when he saw her walk through the door. He wanted to leave Napa as soon as possible, and most of all, he wanted to forget everything that had ever happened there.

He briskly rubbed his face with his hands as if washing it with cold water, cleaning off the sweat and dirt of a hard day's labor in the sun. It seemed like he couldn't stop racking up more and more mistakes. He was sure that his kind of mistakes would never be forgiven in heaven. Then again, heaven in the afterlife was never something he took into consideration. His heaven was on Earth, and he saw himself as only one step less than a demigod. The thought lightened his mood a little.

Still, Matthew knew right from wrong, and could never resolve the burden of guilt for the night Lena lost their babies. That horrible time destroyed the magic that could have kept him with her forever. Not only did the quarrel have more venom than a rattlesnake bite, but Matthew had buried his mistakes deep inside despite his hard-won capacity to move onward. His lapse of control, and the eventual destruction of new life, was a ghost haunting those vineyards forever.

He turned around to reenter the house, stopping short when he saw Lena's silhouette in the kitchen.

He groaned under his breath. "Oh, baby, baby, baby. Do you still want me as much as I want you right now?"

Watching her through the window, her movements fanned his sexual arousal to an almost unbearable pressure. He knew how wrong it would be to ever hurt her again, and he also knew how wrong it would be to hurt Alyssa with unfaithfulness. But could any man ever truly be monogamous?

This was an opportunity he couldn't follow. He turned away from the window and hobbled down the stairs onto the grand veranda that led to the vineyard, and stumbled toward the pond near Annie's tire swing. He was drunker than he usually allowed himself to get; it didn't matter, because at least this way, by morning he wouldn't remember all he had just felt for Lena.

"Oh God, why can't I have her tonight? I want her. I belong to Alyssa, but I want Lena right now. I'm here all alone with Lena, and I'm lonely. Alyssa, this is all your fault, because you're not here. I even drank too much because you weren't here to stop me, Dr. Kippler. I blame you," he slurred, jabbing his index finger in the air, waving his arm around, intending to point it toward wherever Alyssa might be at that time. "Easy does it," he mumbled under his breath as he dropped to a sitting position, and then swayed back and forth until he painlessly landed on his back in the grass.

"Matt?" she called to him. "Are you OK?"

He turned his head toward Lena's voice, and first saw two angels, then focused them into one, then he recognized his beautiful evening fantasy curving her way toward him.

"Marialena, go away," he slurred. He shook his head. "I want you so bad. I'm outta control right now. I just bought a thirty-two-thousand-dollar ring for another woman. I want to be loyal, and I want to trust myself. Go away, please. I've worked so hard to change. Please, Lena, go back inside."

Lena's lips parted.

"Matt, let's talk a little."

He moved sideways to put distance between them as she approached him and sat beside him on the grass. "Why are you rushing into this marriage? Is it really what you want? You hardly know her."

His heart thundered. He couldn't look away from her. "What are you sayin'?" His voice hoarsened.

She leaned her torso over him in silent invitation.

Then his lips were pressing hers and his hands were undoing her jeans.

"I need you, Marialena. I crave you tonight. I've never stopped cravin' you. I don't care what happens. I need you, baby. I'm goin' to explode if I can't be inside you right now."

She offered no resistance, just complete submission. He held her tightly in his arms feeling that he had to, or she would change her mind. She rolled on top of him and moaned softly.

"Matt, I want you so much. You're so hard and big and beautiful, and I remember every natural detail about making love with you."

He pulled her closer. Many times he'd silently longed for this since he left her last. Her smell and her taste filled him with more desire than he had ever felt in his life. As they frantically unsnapped each other's clothes he lifted himself to help her slide his pants below his buttocks. He continued to move his body, teasing her, as he slid her jeans down with her help, and then impatiently shoved down his own. He rolled her over beside him, then as he lay on top of her, his fingers immediately found what he wanted. His mouth was all over her face and his kisses were desperate. He thrust himself inside of her warm, moist body and moaned with uncontrollable need. Sex was the perfect part of their past. His desire was unquenchable.

They moved with rhythm driven by passion until his explosion inside of her was met equally by her own, as it always had been in the past. "Marialena, baby, I'm there. Please tell me you were with me all the way."

She cried out, "Oh, yes. I love you. I'll love you forever. I don't want to, but I do."

Gradually, the pressure subsided, and Matthew lay in her arms. He stroked her face. "Oh, that was good, baby, it was just like old times."

Somewhere in the back of his mind, shameful thoughts of Alyssa whispered, but he pushed them back down as he sank into welcome oblivion.

For years Lena had longed to experience their simultaneous orgasm again, but not this way. This was the kind of mistake Matthew could turn his back on and walk away from. He could justify it as a moment of passion driven by alcohol and stress over this whole ordeal with Amy. She wished it could be more, and she resented him for that not being possible.

She lay on her back next to him under the stars as they used to do in that same location by the pond. Those were the days when they watched shooting stars and dreamed of life together.

Those were the days when they vowed to each other, that for the rest of their lives, every night before sleeping, they would say to each other, "Hey baby, I love you, and I'll always love you." He hadn't said it back to her tonight, and that omission drove home her fear that he no longer cared for her the way she did for him.

Those vows of always loving each other were part of a promise they made to each other that they would never let anger separate them while they slept side by side. Now, years later, he had returned to the pond alone to escape from her in order to hold himself loyal to someone else. But she'd known he wasn't strong enough. Matthew was a very passionate man with a sexual craving that had always controlled him. Lena knew him better than anyone ever had. She knew his secrets and she had chosen to love him long ago in spite of them all, knowing she would always be required to excuse his flaws, and adjust her own character in order to fit into his world.

That was, until his unforgivable behavior in the vineyard six years ago. She wished he had got help for his temper before the tragedy struck them all down. She longed for her sons, and she longed for their father. Again, she remembered the sensation of knives and sharp agony in her womb. Lena turned her head and watched Matthew quietly snoring, at peace, as he lay in the grass next to her. He was still so beautiful.

Her mind ran through the same questions she had asked herself thousands of times. What was missing inside of him? How could a brilliant and loving man be filled with such instant rage over something that to others wouldn't even mean a thing? What was going on inside of him when he imagined emotional exchanges, words, and interpreted things so incorrectly?

She remembered how he suddenly changed from a loving fiancé to a jealous madman in the vineyard. Usually his irrational behavior surfaced with alcohol. She thought about what had just happened between them and she knew it wouldn't have happened had he been sober. He must be very committed to Alyssa or he would have begged her to come back to him while making love. But he didn't. The emptiness of being alone hit her again mingled with the scent of the evening breeze in the vineyard, and Matt lying beside her brought back to life all that she had fought to forget. She closed her eyes and tried to rest beside him. Instead, like a movie, the nightmare replayed itself in her head.

It was a party in celebration of the grape harvest. There was lots of wine, food, and people from all over came for the gala affair. Lena was seventeen weeks pregnant, but hardly showing. She looked more beautiful than ever with a glow that was only for Matthew, as she gently pressed one hand on her abdomen to feel the gentle movement of new life inside. Nobody knew she was pregnant except Matt and Amy.

Other men couldn't stay away from her. Matthew accused her of flirting. He stumbled off into the vineyard, and she followed him in a desperate attempt to make him understand that he was wrong about her. She tried to convince him that she was only being polite to their guests, but under the influence of alcohol he was irrational. She reached for him; he grabbed her shoulders and shoved her away from him. She stumbled backward losing her balance, tripped sideways, and in trying to stop her fall slammed facedown onto the ground. He left her lying there alone and sobbing as he hurried in a frenzy deeper into the vineyard. She'd learned later he left the property and walked toward Calistoga in an angry and disconnected state of mind.

Not only had the accident been unbearable, he wasn't there for her when she needed his reassurance most of all. She had a broken heart, her faith in Matthew's judgment was shattered, devastated, and she called off their wedding. Matthew disappeared to Europe. She waited for his return, praying he would do something to help heal their pain. She was even willing to take the blame from him for the accident, because she should have known to leave him alone and not follow him. It was her fault as much as his. But he didn't come back and fight for her. She was never given the chance to make amends. She realized he never could face his own wrongdoings, though he held grudges for the wrongdoings of others. He always seemed to bury his own losses and mistakes, which is what he had obviously done this time.

She heard that he drowned himself in parties, liquor and other women, and he had moved on.

Lena lay gazing at him as he dozed. She stared at his facial lines that had deepened during those past six years. She took note of his eyelids with the same long lashes. She leaned over and gently kissed his lips as he moaned in approval, still keeping his eyes closed, though arousing slowly. He was that great guy who showered her with the perfect balance between good and evil. All of it, including her dead babies, was an indelible stain on their life together. She knew he could never change, nor would she, though the electric attraction between them had not changed.

She gently nudged Matthew to awaken him. "We should go inside."

They didn't make love again, though they shared his bed. He cuddled her throughout the night as if they belonged together. He slept soundly, because of the alcohol, she imagined. Alcohol seemed now to be a way of life for him, perhaps because of his business socializing, perhaps partially because it was an escape from some of the choices he had made.

Maybe now it had even become a physical dependence.

Chapter Fifteen

*T*he memorial service was at eleven o'clock the next morning. It was tasteful, short, and emotional, submerged in condolences from the more than one hundred neighboring families. Matthew's heart went out to Annie and Amy. Most dramatic was watching Annie, his little niece who had come into the world with Down syndrome. She had enough to deal with because of the physical handicaps, the mental retardation, and cardiac disease against which she fought so hard. Annie would probably never mentally or emotionally develop beyond the age of ten, and her total life expectancy was uncertain, even though she had received the best of medical care, including surgery for a congenital heart abnormality, all part of a chromosome defect. Now Annie was fatherless. This was just one more handicap she would never overcome. The super-stretched black limousine carried the family back to Calistoga in silence. Amy, Annie, Mother Hunter, Lena, and Matthew all sat across from each other and all quietly gazed out the window or just gazed forward. Lena and Matt caught each other's eyes and briefly touched, a whisper of the night before.

Lena turned away and quietly addressed Annie. "Are you OK, little angel?" Annie reached for Lena's hand and said nothing.

The next two days were sober and busy with preparations for Amy and Annie to move to Charleston. Matthew knew that Lena would never accept his offer to work with him on the DeVinci project, and he knew it wouldn't be fair to anyone if she followed him to Florida. She told the family that she would return to her father in San Diego, while she compiled the background material for her next book, a biography of her father. Matt avoided conversation with her while he watched her gathering Peter's personal belongings together, putting aside any things of sentiment and boxing them up.

Matthew stayed close to Amy and helped her pack Annie's toys and books. He had disappointed himself; having two lovers, loving them both, and betraying them both.

His discomfort needed resolution.

Should he confess to Lena that he still loved her? Should he admit to her that he had been lost for six years? Should he admit to Alyssa that he had tarnished his promises to her?

He wrestled with his sins, then realized that, actually, he had never promised anything to Alyssa. They weren't married, or even engaged yet. He'd bought her a ring that she didn't know about. Why should he feel guilty about making love with Lena, whom he had adored for years before he even met Alyssa?

He decided to move on from all of it and forget the whole thing. He would take one step at a time, and the right move would come to him. He believed it was in his favor that he and Alyssa had only known each other for a very short time. If he did leave her to return to Lena, Alyssa would get over it since the relationship had been short-lived. His first loyalty should be to Lena. Moving on from her wasn't easy after once again smelling her clean hair and devouring her sweet and sensuous body. He wanted her again. He was aroused again. He couldn't just let it go.

Lena was packing in her room and had sorted her folded clothes on the bed. She was squatting, reaching into a drawer as Matthew entered the doorway.

"Marialena, may I come in?" He eyed her lovely buttocks as she sprang up and turned around to face him.

"Sure," she answered.

Matthew walked over to her bed and carefully moved some clothes aside so he could sit down. "Come here, please." His soft please coaxed her toward him and she obeyed.

Lena sat down slowly as if she were waiting for a bomb to drop. He spoke to her with a quiet and loving voice in an attempt to remove her defenses.

He began carefully, "I understand how you feel about not wantin' to work with me. I agree with you. It was probably a bad idea. I wish I could say somethin' right for a change. I want to give you money to help you while you write your next book."

She held up her hand. "Matt."

He pushed it back down. "Please. Hear me out just this once. Marialena, drunk and all, bein' with you again brought it all back to me. I still love you. I would do anythin' in the world to put it back together and make it work. We could still be so good together. We could adopt children. We could open a whole orphanage if you want. I can't take back what happened to you and our sons. You know that I would never have hurt you on purpose. Sometimes I just get out of control, and I can't stop my anger until it just goes away. You've always understood that. I'll get help. I'll find a doctor, and get medicine to help me. Baby, I'm askin', let's put things right between us. I'll give my life to makin' it work. Marry me, Lena, please say you'll marry me. Let's put the ugly past behind us. I'll move to California if you want me to come back. I've never really been happy without you. I know you love me. Say you do."

Lena was numb. "Of course, I love you. My whole life was destroyed because of you. Matt, you just bought a thirty-two-thousand-dollar engagement ring for another woman, which you didn't hesitate to tell me about. What about her? Are you going to destroy her, too?"

Matthew came back quickly with, "Alyssa? I do love her. But it's all wrong if there's a chance with you. Don't you see? I never even would have met her in the first place, if you and I didn't go wrong. I'll break it off with her in order to make it right with you. We had babies that died because of me. You should come first. I've been thinkin' lately to start goin' to church on Sunday. I'll become Catholic for you. Baby, say somethin' to me, please."

Crying, Lena fell back on the bed, and her tears became sobs.

In between outbursts, she gurgled, "Don't you know what damage we've already caused the world? We are no good together, and we'll just keep hurting other people as we go along. We're like a bad drug that people shoot in their veins. It's an addiction. It's not a beautiful love anymore. Oh, how I wish it could have been one."

Matthew didn't want her to miss any part of the point. "Didn't I show you how much I love you? We're nothin' without each other. Did I satisfy you?"

He lay beside her and held her in his arms, stroking her hair and rocking her with all of his protective love. "Don't cry, little girl, please don't cry. Daddy's here now. I'll make all this up to you, you'll see."

He turned her face to his and kissed her, cupping her lips within his and then gently drawing back with a soft suction. It was part of his mating dance, which offered her physical separation from him, but only at his discretion.

He whispered onto her lips, "I wanted you the other night, not just for sex, but because I still love you and because you're still the most beautiful girl in the world. I want you now. I've never stopped wantin' you."

Because he had got no response, he backed a few inches away from her face. "Lena, doesn't all this mean somethin' to you? Say somethin' to me."

Lena said nothing. She lay in his arms for hours as they snuggled close together and gazed into each other's eyes, barely even blinking. No words were needed. Matt was content holding her because he was holding his soul mate again. He was head of the household. He held his home in his arms, and he wanted to continue doing that forever. They dozed off together while the temperature between them settled and equalized.

The afternoon sun was setting and they awakened from their nap still holding each other. Lena looked puzzled.

Matt was surprised and he asked, "What's wrong, baby?"

Lena answered, "I'm just trying to sort things out in my mind. My darling Matthew, let's try to do the right thing. We do love each other, but we made too many mistakes, even this is another mistake. Let's try to let go of the other night. This was a bonus that both of us wanted and maybe we needed it to heal our long-harbored pain."

Matt shook his head and held her tightly, afraid to let go, "No. You're not thinkin' straight. Don't ruin this for us. Let's start over again. All I want is to come home to you every day for the rest of our lives and be a good man to just you." He kissed her neck and held her cheeks, attempting to stir passion between them, though Lena didn't respond with kisses.

She displayed a moment of emotional clearing by chuckling, and answered him almost playfully, "Matt Hunter, you've never been faithful, not to Carline, not to me, and now not to Alyssa. Help me. I can't do this again. It's terminal for both of us. The only problem for me is that I have to start all over trying to forget you. Matthew, this isn't a rejection, it's just the end of a love gone wrong. Just don't go back to Florida now and marry Alyssa because we didn't work out. What happened between us should show you that you're not ready for that. You should go away somewhere and be alone for a while. Don't hurry to destroy her, too. Haven't you hurt enough people already? When does it stop? Why didn't this day happen years ago? We've grown so far apart."

Matthew continued holding her, kissing her wet cheeks as his own tears streamed down his face and blended with hers.

His agonized voice cracked as he whispered, "What did you think I should have done? You dumped me and I had to move on and find a life."

Lena pulled away from him and sat up, gathering all of her strength together. "You really see it that way, don't you? Why didn't you fight for me six years ago? I waited for you, because I thought you would come back, and try to make things right, but you never did anything but run away and hide."

Matthew sat up, put his feet on the floor, and stomped once to give himself a helpful boost to the ground. Feeling beaten, though, he lowered his head like a scolded schoolboy.

"I guess I was weak, or afraid, or hurt, but I had a dozen women since you, Lena, and not one of them could drown you out of my heart. I couldn't get you out of my mind, not for one day." He felt excitement fill his chest, and his energy heightened. "Then I decided to change. I went for months without even one date. I thought maybe, if I was good, maybe if there was a God, your God, he'd bring me back to you or he'd heal me from wantin' you. When I started healin', I got real sick. I was bleedin' inside and I went to the hospital. When I met Alyssa, I sorta took it as a sign that, maybe God, your God, was forgivin' me, 'cause it was the first time I felt somethin' special about anyone since I left Napa six years ago. She was beautiful, she was good to me, and she was a doctor who cared about makin' me healthy again. Lena, I almost died, for real. People can change when they almost die. I fell in love with her for those reasons. She's not like us, she's different. She doesn't understand how to fight for her rights. She's just good like an angel, and she makes things better for other people every day. That's how she lives her life. Can't you understand how it happened? I guess she gave me back some stuff I had lost, stuff I thought I'd never find again, like bein' with her made me want to start goin' to church." Matt welled up inside with pride, and his respect for Alyssa increased through every word as he described her to Lena. "She's really an incredible woman and she's the reason I'm a healthy man today. She literally saved my life."

He waited for Lena to respond, she didn't, so he calmed down his demeanor, lowered his voice, and continued, "But nobody is you. Now I gotta go heal all over again if I don't get you back. You don't need to worry about the ring thing. You must think I'm a heartless animal. Do you really think I'm so messed up that I'd just jump back to Alyssa and hurt her after all this? What am I supposed to tell her? 'I made love with Lena out in California. I tried to get her back, but she didn't want me, so I'm back here with you.' Do you think I'd do that to someone like her? She would never deserve that."

Matthew sat back down on the bed beside Lena, willing her to see the excruciating pain in his tearful eyes. "Please tell me. Help me. What should I do?" He tightened his fists in front of him, and opened them again spreading his fingers wide open several times as if he were trying to regain their circulation. He waited for her response, hoping she would fix all the confusion.

She didn't answer him, but continued to look down, staring at the bedspread, a sign of rejection.

"Oh, Lena, please." He paused, then stood up again and turned away from her, whispering under his breath, "Hey, baby. I love you and I'll always love you." He needed to say those words one last time out loud, even though he doubted she heard him as he left the room.

But Lena did hear him, and she fell back on her bed sobbing much as she had years ago in the vineyards. This time, her pelvis had no stabbing pain. The pain was in her chest and it pierced through her heart. He had just exposed more of his vulnerability to her than ever before. She had always believed that she loved him more than he had ever loved her. She tried to teach him to love better, but she couldn't. It was as if he had a hole deep inside that stopped him, though he always said he loved her as much as he could. His capacity to open up totally, surely was blocked by inferiority complexes, insecurity, anger, fear, and alcoholic, manic disease. Even with those thoughts of his shortcomings, her agony over losing him was possessive, leaving her in despair for the second time, with no hope for the future. Why had she broken down for just one more taste of him, after all these years, when she knew it would make things more difficult again? She was smothered by déjà vu. In the background, the radio tugged at her heart as it played a song sung by Taylor Dayne, "I'll Always Love You."

"I'll always love him for the rest of my days," she whispered to herself, burying her head in her pillow and continuing to weep.

Her broken heart had stood its lonely ground. Fool or not, she had let him leave the room without looking up at him. She knew it could never really work again once the thrill of being back together was over. As she listened to him describing her rival, it was obvious that the man inside the cocoon had metamorphosed. He was gaining a sense of spiritual understanding that had been missing in her own relationship with him. It was unbearable that he had begun to find peaceful solace in another woman's arms, but even more painful was that he said he wanted to protect Alyssa from what had happened in California, as if what they had shared were the sin. Matthew was temporarily caught in a web between two women, and no matter how much he begged her to come back, Lena knew she had lost.

This time it wasn't wrongdoing or weakness that would drive him from her. Goodness and new spiritual strength had now become something he needed, and Alyssa was his chosen vessel. Lena knew that, in Matthew's way, he believed he had made some long-overdue contact with God because of his relationship with Alyssa. He wasn't ready to surrender to God, he might never be, but he would surrender to a woman who made him feel that he had. Sexual betrayal was one thing, and it was bad enough, but matters of the heart were intangible. Lena knew that if she had agreed to marry him, he would have sooner or later been haunted by the loss of Alyssa's innocence. Though he truly loved her, having spent years wishing he could turn around the mistakes in the vineyard, he would never be able to relinquish his new chance of redemption.

It was obvious to Lena that Matthew would ultimately make the choice to return to Alyssa, believing that she was the more noble lady of the two.

Chapter Sixteen

*A*lyssa giggled as she hugged her mother, looking around at all that they had worked for and feeling the blessings of being able to let it go.

Dr. Garbo kidded with her, "Don't you want to buy my practice?"

"Sure I do. Hey, Susanna, let's buy a new medical practice." Alyssa reached for her best friend's arm and they joined together as they helped pour everyone's champagne.

Lisa dove into the chips and dip while she slurped down her Pepsi. She clicked her soda can against her mother's glass, and then bounced back to the buffet table for more goodies. Alyssa glanced at her watch. She knew Matt had been en route to Florida for most of the day. He could still surprise her and arrive at the office before the party ended. The gathering to celebrate the transfer of ownership from Dr. Kippler to Dr. Garbo lasted throughout the afternoon without any sign of Matthew. She tried to call him on his cell phone, but there was no answer.

Matt reached the airport with just enough time to catch his plane to Atlanta. He slept most of the flight as if he hadn't slept for days. There was an hour wait in Atlanta to switch planes to Orlando. He wasn't ready to return to Florida now. He decided to change his flight and go back to New York. He needed time alone. He needed to get his head straight. It was too soon after losing Lena again to go back and play the perfect lover to Alyssa. Though he knew he had fallen in love with a wonderful new girl, he didn't know how he should deal with the strong attraction he still harbored for Lena.

His past with Lena was shaded with sadness, but Alyssa had no bad memories of him. She adored him and her image of him was positive and respectful. She was beautiful and bright. She was loving and fun. She was great in bed. For a moment he wondered what it would be like to have them both at the same time. . . .

Matt had chosen to turn off his cell phone the night he made love with Lena in California. He knew that anyone who really needed to reach him could find him by calling Amy's home. He realized that he hadn't checked his messages for a couple of days. As he sat in the airport, he listened to them, one by one. A message from Alyssa, which had been left almost exactly at the same time he was making love with Lena at the pond, left him numb.

"Hello, my darling lover. I miss you so much tonight, you could not imagine. I was just thinking of the first time we made love in your new Jacuzzi and on the bed you had brought in just for me. Matt, I love you so much. I feel utterly blessed to have a man like you love me so totally as you tell me over and over that you do. Please call me when you get this message. I'm waiting for you."

He paused to digest her message, then he called Alyssa's cell phone. "Hello?" she answered. Her sweet velvet voice hadn't changed. In that instant, he was reminded that he could never do anything that would hurt her. Returning to New York City was the right decision He remembered telling Lena that he wouldn't jump back to Alyssa, and she didn't need to know about things that would only hurt her.

"Alyssa. Hi, it's Matt. Listen, honey, somethin' has come up and I need to go back to New York. I'm not sure when I'll be back in Florida. I've got a lot of work to do."

He pictured Alyssa's eyes dropping closed as she held the phone closely cradled to her ear, "Oh, I was so looking forward to seeing you. We've just finished celebrating the sale of my practice to Dr. Garbo. I was sure you'd surprise me and get here tonight."

"I know." He fiddled with the handle of his briefcase, which he had placed on the airport seat beside him. "It's just real important for me to go to New York right now. What with the funeral and all, I've lost a lot of time, and I need to get back on track with this project I've accepted."

She quickly added, "I'm sure it's been very difficult. I wish there were something I could do for Amy and Annie. I'll try to call Amy tonight to offer my help. Matt, speaking of business, Dr. Garbo doesn't need me to be here for the transition period. He feels comfortable to start out by himself, and I agree, he'll do well. I'll be free to travel and spend more time with you very soon. It's awful being away from you. I miss you so much."

"I miss you, too, honey. That's really great that your time will be freed up so soon. Maybe you could come up to New York in the next week or so. I'd like that." His voice was strained, and he knew she would guess something was wrong.

Alyssa asked, "Matt, is everything all right? You don't sound the same. Is everything OK between us?"

He wasn't the same. Nothing could be the same between them.

He rushed to fill the silence. "Nothin' is wrong, baby.

You're probably the only thing that I have in my life that is right. I just have a whole lot of thinkin' to do. I'm so behind in the project now and I'm pretty wiped out after this whole ordeal."

"I'm so sorry, darling. I wish I could be in New York with you tonight. I'd make love with you and lie beside you all night to help the pain go away. Do you want me to catch a plane tonight and meet you there? I could even be your secretary during the day."

Matt hesitated. "I'd like that, but I'll do better workin' without any distractions. I have a secretary who knows the details of this job, and if you were here I wouldn't want to work. Trust me, it wouldn't be fun for you to come up right now."

Just then a voice came over the loudspeaker, "American Airlines flight 9234 to La Guardia is now boarding at gate C47."

"I gotta go, honey, they're calling my flight. I'll call you later, OK?" They hung up. The flight call had saved him. He didn't want to explain himself to her right now. He was too confused, and his heart felt cold. Even her sexual offer didn't turn him on.

It was already dark when Matthew's driver pulled up to the Four Seasons. He was completely exhausted, and he felt like pouring a nice stiff drink and watching TV. He opened the liquor cabinet in his room, but for the first time in years nothing he saw appealed to him. Maybe it was time to stop drinking for a while. He decided to just take a shower and go to bed.

Morning came, and Matthew felt better about himself and his life. He felt clean and not poisoned by alcohol. His focus was clearer now. First he would call Rodolfo, his favorite interior designer, and have him work on the new apartment. Originally, he had wanted Alyssa to design everything, but really he needed it done now. After all, it was his apartment.

The thought cheered him, and he decided his children should be here with him to help fill this empty gap in his life. Stirring his coffee, he carried his cup to the balcony and sat at the breakfast table outside. He took a sip, breathed deeply, and felt good about this decision. He lifted the receiver from the phone cradle on the table and dialed London.

"Hello?" A soft, familiar English accent repeated, "Hello?"

"Hey, honey, it's Matt. How are you?"

"I'm very well, Matt. I didn't expect to hear from you so soon after our sour visit in California."

"Oh Carline, now you know that was just part of our ruminatin' old garbage."

"Whatever you say, and what may I do for you with this call?"

"How 'bout lettin' me visit with my kids for a couple of weeks here in New York? At least let me see Dierdra, and don't tell me they're all in school, or they're at camp or somethin' like that, please."

"No nothing like that. Didn't Amy tell you?"

"Tell me what?"

"Matt, I'm getting married. I didn't tell you in California, for obvious reasons."

"Well, that's great. Don't you think I have a right to know what man is livin' with my own kids?" Matt was smashed inside as if a bullet had shot him in the heart.

Ignoring his insignificant gesture of fatherhood, she continued, "The wedding is in ten days, and all three of them are taking part in the service."

Matthew's face felt hot, and his heart was pounding. He suddenly felt pressure, like a two-ton elephant was standing on his chest. "I hope you'll be happy, Carline. I'm really glad for you. Please talk to the kids and tell them Dad wants to see them. Maybe after the weddin' at least one of them could come."

He hung up the phone and sat back to relieve his chest pain. He reached for his coffee and tried to calm himself with good thoughts. She was actually a good girl and she deserved a good life. At the same time he felt he was being punished. Her new joy gave him chest pain. She was going to be happy and he was miserable. He couldn't even have the kids when he needed them. Even one of them, Dierdra, would really take the sting out of the bite right now. He leaned back farther in the chair and tried not to think of anything. The chest pressure subsided and left. Feeling a little better, he wanted some other input about this wedding thing. He took another sip of coffee, as he next dialed Napa.

Amy answered the phone.

"Hello?"

"Hey, Sis, how you doin?"

"Hi, Matt. I'm all right, and how are you?"

"I'm OK. I thought you'd be on your way to Charleston today."

"I was ready to leave, but then I decided to stay here for another day or two and tie up some loose ends. Mother and Annie are leaving for Charleston early in the morning."

"Listen. Did you know Carline was gettin' married?"

"She told me all about it when they came to visit us here. I assumed you knew and just didn't want to talk about it. That's why I never mentioned it to you."

He shrugged it off. "Oh, that's OK, I guess. I hope she's happy. Anyway, Amy, are you really doin' all right?"

"Yeah. I'll be fine," she answered. "After all your help, things have been a little easier to handle. Do you need to talk to Mama?"

Mother Hunter picked up the receiver, "Hi, Son. I'm glad you called. I guess you got to Florida OK. I'm glad you're OK. You sure helped your sister durin' hard times, I'll tell you that." She paused for several moments, then took a deep breath. "I love you, Matthew. Sometimes you are just like your father. He wasn't a bad man, Son, he was a troubled man. I hope someday you will forgive him, because I have."

Matt never heard her speak about his father like that. He wasn't sure how to answer her, so he didn't. He informed her that he'd been sidetracked on the way to Florida and went to New York instead.

"Mother, I'll be here for a few weeks to set up my apartment. I'll probably go back to Florida for a while after that to do some work on Dierdra II. I thought I'd stop by Charleston to see how things are on my way down there."

"Son," his mother answered without acknowledging his reference to the new apartment or his impressive yacht, "I heard you have a girlfriend. Amy said she's real pretty and she's nice, too. Bring her by, and I'll be good to her, you know that."

Matthew couldn't discuss his relationship with Alyssa right now. "Good idea, Mother. Is everythin' goin' well out there?"

"Oh yes," she answered. "Annie and I'll leave in the mornin', and I guess Amy wants to stay here for a few days. She says she has some things she wants to do, and she'd rather do them by herself. I remember how I felt when I lost your father. My heart hurts for her, and there's nothin' I can do to help her but just be there an' take care of Annie."

Matt tried to sound casual. "I know, Mother. Did Lena leave yet? She's always a real big help to Amy."

His heart raced a little as he anticipated his mother's answer.

"No, she's still here. She just got back from goin' into town to make sure the balloons are all safe in the warehouse. You want to talk to her?"

"Yes, Mother, I do."

After a long wait, his mother came back on the line to report Lena was outside watering the flowers and had asked that Matt call back a little later. He got the painful hint.

His mother added, "This whole thing hit her pretty hard, too. She's been cryin' off and on since you left. She's not real good at conversation right now. I guess your presence made everyone feel a little stronger. That girl sure did become part of our family."

Matthew knew why she was really crying. But he also knew deep in his heart that this time love gone wrong wasn't about to be made right. It just hurt and there was nothing anyone could do to fix it. His own carelessness had ripped apart a great thing. He felt a sigh of relief that she was still in Napa. It made him feel a little closer to her. It didn't really matter. Even if she loved him, he thought, she didn't want him. All he would do if he chased after her would be to lose his pride and dignity. At least this way, maybe she would always wonder if he still wanted her. He did want her. He wanted her more than he ever had. But he had lost. Time was the only healer here. It had helped last time and this time he would do everything he could to move on again and get a good life without her. He would use this loss as a lesson to never be careless with love again. If and when he continued his relationship with Alyssa, he would cherish her and never, ever hurt her the way he had hurt Lena.

That afternoon Matt took a long walk through Central Park. The park was beautiful year round. Each season gave it the magnificence that only nature deserved.

The thought of walking through nature in an almost pure form, something so beautiful in the middle of the hustling city, gave him a measure of hope for the turmoil at the center of his own life.

He walked until his feet hurt, yet he wouldn't allow himself to rest. Maybe some miracle would bring Lena back to him. Maybe she would appear on the street before him because she was going as crazy as he was. "Oh, Lena, I love you more than I love my own life. If there is a God, why won't he bring you back to me? I have changed, and I repent for what I did to you. Maybe now, I think I really could deserve you."

He wasn't even interested to know where he was, his senses were numb, and he realized that his life was stuck and his emotions were raw. He had chest pressure again, and his heart felt as if it had been stabbed by a thousand thorns. He stopped to catch his breath, then continued to walk, almost stumbling, blinded by his longing for Lena. His pseudo purity and his moral makeover before he met Alyssa had been intended to win Lena back. He just never had admitted it even to himself before he told her just a couple of days before in her bedroom. He wasn't a good man, he hadn't been a good man. He wanted to be one, but he didn't know how. His thoughts raced in circles from Carline to Lena to Alyssa and then back again. He kept walking, dazed by his whirlwind of memories and dead dreams. He ended up at Ground Zero. As he peered at what had been the fabulous Twin Towers, he realized that he was at ground zero in his own life. He finally had a breakthrough from his lost, tormented confusion.

He would place his heart on a back burner and pour himself into DeVinci Cruises. He was indebted to Capezzio, and he needed to make it right with him. Besides, work was the only area in his life that he had been good at and there were no major mistakes in that world to bring him down.

The two feminine representatives of his true youth, Marialena de la Cruz and Carline Winther-Hunter-Whoever, were both gone from him forever. All of the many games he played with himself regarding them were suddenly on the surface, and one by one, they were exposed to him as he slowly walked back to his hotel. He had wasted the most important times in his life with selfish ambition and carelessness, and his reward? Nothing.

By the time he reached the doorman it was late, he was exhausted, and he didn't want to think anymore. He no longer felt anything for anyone. He lay on the bed in his room, lost himself in the television, and fell asleep. His dreams were confused and exhausting and he didn't remember any of them upon awakening the next morning, though his sheet and his covers were twisted into a wet ball and his pillows were on the floor. He stayed in bed the entire day, hardly moving, though he knew he should make an effort to draft a plan for the cruise liner. Life was bleak enough to end it all. Matthew Hunter had too much respect for himself to do such a thing as cause personal bodily harm. Just remaining frozen in bed for a day without knowing which way to go, or to whom he could turn, was plenty misery enough.

Chapter Seventeen

 After two weeks without word from Matthew, Alyssa's gut feeling convinced her something had really been wrong between them the last time they talked, but at the time, she'd wanted to believe him when he told her he was just tired.

She gazed at the turquoise water of the ocean through her glass living room wall, as if it were a crystal ball guiding her next move.

"At this point, what do I have to lose if I call him and confront him? I'll call him and finish my hopes once and for all." She heard her own heartbeat so loudly that she feared he too would hear it in New York on the other end of the phone line.

His phone rang four times and then his voice mail picked up.

She left no message and hung up, her heart slowing down and then sinking. Something had changed. It had to be over. Maybe Amy could offer some news about Matt. She would just call Charleston to see how Amy was doing.

A woman answered the phone with a warm, almost raspy Southern accent, and as soon as Alyssa introduced herself, the woman—Matthew's mother—insisted she call her Mother Hunter. "Everyone in our family calls me Mother Hunter. When are you coming' to meet me? Amy says you're a real nice girl and you're real pretty. My Matthew always loved the pretty ones. Is he there with you in Florida? He said he was goin' to come to Charleston, and bring you with him last time I spoke to him, but that was two weeks ago."

Alyssa felt safe disclosing her own concerns now that she knew he hadn't called Charleston, either. "I'm concerned because that was the last time I heard from him, too. I was hoping you would know where he is."

"Well, he just probably is real busy workin' on that new ship he's buildin'," Mother Hunter spoke up with optimism. "I'm sure he'll resurface and call us all real soon. Matthew does that sometimes. He just disappears and you can't find him. Then he suddenly pops up again. He even did that when he was a little boy. Sometimes he was gone for hours and I'd go lookin' for him. I usually found him lookin' at the water and dreamin' about his future. That's probably what he's doin' somewhere right now."

"I just called his cell phone and he didn't answer," Alyssa confessed.

"Honey, would you like to come up to Charleston this weekend and spend a few days with Amy and me?"

Alyssa was surprised and flattered. "I'd love to come, but I can't right now. I'm in the middle of selling my medical practice and I need to be here for a while. But thank you very much. I hope I can come soon."

They ended the call with plans to meet soon. Alyssa found it strange that Matthew's family hadn't heard from him for such a long period and wasn't worried about him.

Seventeen days passed after that call and he still didn't call back. It had been over a month since she spoke to him. Alyssa was sick with disappointment. Her new dreams of a life with Matthew were crashing around her.

July rolled over Florida, hot and muggy. Dr. Garbo had made it abundantly clear he didn't need her hanging around her old practice. Everything she looked at reminded her of Matthew, and she needed to get out of Menlo.

She decided to take a Mexican holiday.

They could stay in the Las Brisas Hotel. It was there that she and her beloved Alex conceived Lisa, with the hopes and dreams of two young lovers, building their future as a family. Each bungalow at the Las Brisas had its own swimming pool with fresh flowers floating in the water. It was located on a hill, facing the water, and at night the lights of the mountain in front of it were breathtaking, like a chest of jewels spilling over the mountainside across the bay. They could watch the famous Acapulco divers and just relax far away from everything. Alyssa booked a package deal to fly to Acapulco that weekend. She made reservations for the three of them, Lisa, Dionna, and herself to stay in the same bungalow that she and Alex had occupied years ago. They would leave in three days, and be gone for a week.

"What a perfect summer vacation." Dionna was thrilled and helped Alyssa shop for Lisa.

Alyssa's spirits improved a little just because she was getting away.

Thirty-three days had passed and Matthew still hadn't called.

Alyssa resigned herself to the possibility that it was over. Maybe he'd changed his mind and he decided she wasn't for him, or maybe he'd met someone else. She flashed on Lena. She couldn't help being haunted by, and a little jealous of Lena's beauty with its obvious power over Matthew. For a moment she was convinced that he was in Napa with Lena. Maybe he was really in love with her. It seemed like there was an undercurrent of tension between the two of them.... She stopped herself from imagining. It really didn't matter what he was doing or what female he was with, because he was gone. She decided to do everything she could to wipe him out of her mind. If one good thing had come of this, it was that she'd handled the relationship responsibly; Lisa wouldn't be hurt by the breakup.

Alyssa went to the office on the morning of her flight. She left all of her travel information with Susanna. "If anything goes wrong, just call me. I can always come back."

Susanna chuckled. "Alyssa, what could possibly happen to bring you back? This practice will survive long after we all leave. And don't worry. I'll call you immediately if Romeo shows up."

The flight on Aero Mexicana was quiet. Alyssa tried to be cheerful, but how could she, really? She actually snapped at Lisa who was complaining because they didn't serve Mexican food. She wanted a tortilla. "Stop fussing, Lisa. You can have all the tortillas you want when we get to Mexico."

After Lisa settled for a sandwich and eventually drifted off to sleep, Alyssa talked to her mother about her broken heart. "Mother, I'm going to have a great vacation with you and Lisa. I'm just so sad that Matt isn't with us. Things seemed like they would be so different. He really had me believing that we had a future together. Maybe he got cold feet after Napa Valley."

Dionna reached over to her little girl seated next to her and hugged her tightly, "Sweetheart, let's just wait and see what happens. "Maybe he just was really brokenhearted after the funeral. After all, you really haven't known him that long to be so sure of how he handles his own stress," she added. "Give it a little more time."

Alyssa sighed, "I don't know. I just want to forget it right now."

She decided to accept a mango margarita, compliments of the airline.

They arrived in Acapulco mid-afternoon. The airport was tiny, but clean and attractive. Acapulco was a little pocket of glamour and fun, lush and green and raw and romantic. It sprawled out from the embrace of a tropical jungle to quench its hot thirst in the wonders of the Pacific Ocean.

As their car drove away from the tiny airport, Lisa's nose was pressed to the glass window.

"Mommy, Grandmother, look," she exclaimed with excitement. "They have a Costco and they have McDonald's."

It was weird to see that even Acapulco had such places. Hooter's Restaurant and Planet Hollywood enjoyed popularity on the main strip, which was filled with tourist attractions, sports bars, and nightclubs. But most of the town was still authentic Mexico, unspoiled and traditional. As they rode toward the hotel, the cab driver pointed out a house. "Sylvester Stallone made a film there several years ago. All the cab drivers still talk about it to the tourists. They often point to that gorgeous mansion overlooking the water and claim it was his house. Other rumors claim that he had never purchased the house at all, but only rented it during the filming."

Alyssa had heard of how important it was for the Mexican people to please. They would tell any story they needed to in order not to disappoint their listener. They would give wrong directions rather than to show they didn't know the right ones. The people of Acapulco were like laughing children. She couldn't help but to flash upon Lena, who was Mexican. She wondered if Lena would lie to her about Matthew in order to please. That would be doubtful for any woman to do.

As they drove up to the Las Brisas Hotel they were greeted by several hotel employees. They were helped out of their car and ushered to the inside where cool drinks were awaiting them, and charge cards were imprinted. Alyssa rented one of their pink jeeps and they were escorted up the winding road to their bungalow. It was very clean and quaint. Lisa couldn't wait to jump into the lovely swimming pool, which was shared by another bungalow. Alyssa had tried to get a room with a completely private pool, but there were no vacancies to satisfy her reservation. The concierge apologized, "I am so sorry, Señora, but there are several famous dignitaries here right now, and our rooms try to accommodate everyone's needs. I am sure you will be very happy with your bungalow, please trust me."

"Never mind," she said. "We're going to spend most of our time at the main pool down below."

The main pool was actually at a country club setting a few minutes away from the hotel. It was on the water and quite lovely with a bar right in the pool. Several people were usually sitting in their bathing suits on cement stools in the water, sipping delightful drinks served in fresh pineapples. A five-star restaurant was within a few feet of the pool, and they decided to have dinner there on the first night. It had been a long trip and everyone was a tired. Tomorrow would shed a whole new light on the trip.

When the trio arrived back at the bungalow, everyone took turns getting ready for bed. There was a bottle of cold champagne on the table awaiting them.

"This is great. The hotel is welcoming us with champagne." Alyssa pointed to the bottle lying in an ice bucket. "Mother, let's open it and toast to our vacation in Acapulco."

Alyssa felt more cheerful since their arrival. She loved being away from everything that was familiar. As she reached for the bottle, she spotted a welcome note in one of the glasses. Alyssa smiled as she read it aloud. "Would you three lovely ladies join me by the pool for a glass of champagne?"

Lisa ran to the window and exclaimed, "There's a man sitting by our pool. It looks like . . ."

Before she could finish her statement, Alyssa finished for her. "Matt."

She felt her face light up like a Christmas tree.

Sliding open the door and looking down from her balcony. She paused with a sexy grin. "Hello, stranger. What brings you to Acapulco?"

Matt looked up at her with that gorgeous broad smile of his. "You."

Lisa began to bolt through the door and her grandmother stopped her. "Lisa, no. Let Mama go down to see him first. We'll wait here for a few minutes."

Alyssa left the balcony and walked down the stairs in her robe.

Matthew stood up and took her in his arms, "I missed you. I called Susanna when I couldn't find you. She told me you were here. I'm sorry for the inconvenience of two bungalows and one pool. I changed your reservation to surprise you."

Alyssa retorted with indifference, almost as if she were speaking to the air rather than to a man, her man. "Well, I am surprised after not hearing from you for thirty-seven days, but who's counting? Where have you been?"

She could feel the hurt in his voice. He was so sorry. Tears began to fall onto his cheeks and she saw his remorse. "I've been thinkin' a lot. I needed some space. I guess I shoulda called you and told you, but I'm here now. I came all the way to Acapulco because this is where I want to be. I'll tell you what happened, I promise. I got all caught up in my work, and I just had to work out some issues of my own before I could take us to the next step. Let's just not talk about it now, OK?"

Alyssa could only look into his beautiful blue eyes and grin.

He held her closer. "Oh baby, you feel so good."

Alyssa's heart, once again, melted in his arms.

Dionna and Lisa came down the stairs. Dionna made a grand entrance carrying the bottle of champagne. "You guys forgot the champagne. Let's celebrate."

They drank the champagne and Lisa had a coke. She swam in the pool and the adults watched her while they enjoyed one of the most beautiful scenes in all of Mexico. Acapulco at night, the lights across the bay and the perfect warm and fragrant air, was paradise. Especially when Matthew was here to share it with.

Alyssa gazed at the lights across the bay. "They're the most beautiful night lights I've ever seen."

Matthew laughed, agreeing with her. She couldn't imagine a more perfect night.

It was a clear night, the moon was bright, and she was in Acapulco with the people she loved most, enjoying the view of the horseshoe-shaped natural bay. The city of Acapulco and its beach life was directly in front of them and all of it was within that bay. Alyssa watched Matt from across the table. He was irresistible, not because of his wealth and fame, but because of that beautiful combination of sophisticate and child. His sexuality was powerful, yet innocent. Nobody could ever be bored if he was near. He was exciting and crazy, romantic and not at all predictable. He'd surprised her this time, for sure.

Matthew stood. "I just happen to have another bottle of champagne in my bungalow. I'll be back in a jiffy."

As soon as he was out of earshot, Alyssa was anxious to tell her mother, "He said he missed me. He just needed some space, but he came all the way here to make it up to me. He changed our bungalow to one that shared a pool with him in order to surprise us and be near us."

Dionna yawned, not seeming to share her excitement. "Honey, we just drank an entire bottle of champagne. I need to take Lisa to bed. I don't want any more to drink. You kids stay up together if you want to, but let us go to bed."

Matthew came into view carrying the champagne and a large sack. He called for Lisa to come out of the pool. "I have a surprise for you."

Lisa scrambled out of the water and excitedly opened the bag. She pulled a box out of the bag and laid it on the ground to open. She took the lid off and squealed with delight as she held up a beautiful doll with a ball gown like the ones women used to wear in Charleston.

"Oh, thank you, Matt." Lisa wrapped her arms around Matt and gave him a big, soaking-wet hug.

Matt gently took the doll from Lisa to show her something special.

"See what happens to her?"

He turned the doll upside down. Instead of panties, there were the head and torso of a black slave girl. The doll's gown turned inside out and converted to a ragged and tattered old dress.

Matt began a story in his soft Southern drawl. "This is called a topsy-turvy doll. In the days of slavery in the South, the slave children weren't allowed to play with white dolls or with white children for the most part. The slave mamas made their children dolls that were white on one side and black on the other side. When the slave masters came into view, the slave children turned their dollies to the black side so nobody would find out that they were playin' with a white doll dressed in a gown of wealth and fantasy."

Alyssa spoke up, "What a great piece of history. Lisa, isn't that an interesting story? Matt, you were really sweet to do that."

Lisa nodded, carefully handed her new doll to her grandmother, and headed back into the pool with a huge splash.

Matt smiled. "Lisa is a sweet girl."

After the second bottle was emptied, Dionna yawned again. "I think that champagne will help me have a perfectly sound sleep. I'm really tired. Would you two lovebirds mind if we go to bed? Lisa, come on with me. Let's finish getting ready for bed and look at your new dolly."

Lisa reluctantly climbed out of the pool. "Aw, do I have to?"

One look at Dionna and she knew there was no bargaining. She wrapped her towel around herself and gave both Alyssa and Matt another wet hug. Alyssa got a kiss to go with it.

Matt quickly caught the extra touch that Alyssa got. "Hey, where's my kiss?"

Lisa giggled as she ran toward the stairs. "Mommy will give you your kiss."

Matt called back at her, "Hey, darlin'. You want to go to CiCi Water Park tomorrow? You can play with dolphins there and they have lots of rides and fun things to do."

Lisa was already in the bungalow with the sliding door closed behind her, squealing with delight, "I love Acapulco!"

Matthew watched her disappear. "She's really somethin', isn't she? She's goin' to be just like her mother."

They sat alone together quietly gazing at the lights across the bay. The Acapulco night clouds were beginning to fade the jewels resting on the mountain behind them.

Matthew broke the silence. "It's hard to believe that this world is here every single day and we're not. This lifestyle goes on for these people like it's a natural thing. We're so caught up in the rat race . . ." He stopped talking. Then he added, "Are you happy I'm here?"

Alyssa leaned forward, intentionally placing a serious hand on the table. "What do you think, Romeo? I'm a bit bewildered, and I'd like to know where you've been for more than a month without even calling once. I can't pretend I'm OK about everything."

"Honey, I've had a whole bunch on my mind with the funeral and all. It just stirred a whole lot of questions up in my head about my life and about my past. If you really need to talk about it right now, we will. But I'd rather not put a damper on such a great night. All I can say is, nobody can rightfully move on to the future until the past is cleared up. I have done that now."

Alyssa couldn't contain her curiosity. "Is there someone else?"

Matt looked down. "There's always been someone else at one time or another. Is there someone else right now? No."

She wasn't satisfied with his evasive answers, but she agreed, this was not the time to push the subject further.

Alyssa was dissatisfied that Matthew was obviously, satisfied with his responses to her.

She had no idea where he had really been or what he had been doing. Was it that he didn't want to hurt her, or was it that he had a right to keep secrets if he wanted to do so? She wanted to believe that his mysterious behavior was a thing of the past. Whatever was his reason for disappearing must have been a good one. She wanted to make love with him and hold him all night. She wanted to build their life again and not nag him for needing personal time and space.

Matthew stretched toward her, reaching his hands across the table. "Let's take Dionna to Avenida Costera Miguel Aleman tomorrow to shop and browse. We have to show her the town square. It's such a beautiful, peaceful place shaded by rubber and mango trees. Have you been shoppin' there before?"

"You question me as if you've been there many times."

"Well of course I have, baby, which is why I can show it all to you guys."

"I don't remember if I've been there," she answered. "I came here several years ago with Alex. We did go see the La Quebrada cliff divers. I want Mother to see them while we're here."

Matthew scowled, obviously picking up the scent of some interference.

"Now, Alyssa, let's make this trip about us, OK? If you don't want to do something because it reminds you of Alex, then let's just forget it. There's plenty to do here." He didn't really give her a chance to respond. It was as if he had the entire trip planned out ahead of time.

"We'll all have lunch at the Plaza Las Glorias Mirador Hotel and watch the divers over the hotel's wonderful food. After that, we'll take Lisa to CiCi Water Park."

Alyssa liked the fact that Matthew never forgot to add something special for Lisa.

"Let's go to my bungalow for a while. I want to hold you and kiss you and taste everything about you. I've missed you, baby, I've really missed you."

She looked up at the balcony of her own bungalow. The lights were out, and obviously Dionna had coaxed Lisa to go to sleep. Getting up from her chair, Alyssa reached for Matt's arm.

They were hardly in the room when Matt began kissing and fondling her. He slowly stepped forward, and she responded to his teasing her to the bed. She moved in his rhythm very comfortably and with almost no foreplay. Matthew seemed particularly tender that night, as if he were making up for something. Alyssa was particularly submissive that night, as if she had to prove she had forgiven him for something.

"I love you, Alyssa. I can't bear to think that you have ever been with anyone else but me. I want you to bond so tightly to me that we can't breathe without each other. I want to be so tight with you that nothin' could ever tear us apart."

She luxuriated with the feeling of his warm, satisfied, limp body against her and wrapped herself around him as if to protect him from tomorrow and hide herself from yesterday.

Alyssa awakened about eight o'clock and hoped that Lisa was still sleeping. Matthew soundly slept as she quietly left his bed and hurried back to her own bungalow, where Dionna and Lisa were asleep in the same bed. Dionna had pulled Alyssa's covers down for her in anticipation of her late return.

Lisa awakened, jumped out of bed, and bounced to the bathroom, "I'm ready for Mexico, Mommy and Grandmother. Let's go get Matthew." Alyssa pretended to be alert. She needed toothpicks to hold her eyelids open, though she felt she could go days with sleepless nights if they could all be like last night. That painful emptiness of losing in love was gone.

The Las Brisas was famous for its private swimming pools, its spectacular views, its pink jeeps and its morning breakfast, which was slipped through a cubbyhole in each bungalow. The breakfast consisted of hot coffee, hot cocoa, sweet rolls and fruit. Matt brought his breakfast out to the terrace by the pool to share with everyone else. They combined their fruits and rolls and they shared quite a morning feast.

Matthew seemed content that Alyssa had forgotten the more than one-month disappearance act he had pulled.

But she hadn't forgotten it at all. She continued to feel waves of hurt and anger that needed to be expressed and relieved. Turning to her mother, she stiffened her back and straightened her arms on the sides of her chair, preparing to stand. "Mother, would it be OK if Matt and I take a walk while you and Lisa get dressed? We'll come back in about an hour and pick you up."

"That's fine. Come on Lisa, let's go get all cleaned up so we can ride in the pink jeep."

Lisa grabbed another sweet roll for the road and skipped toward the stairs leading to their bungalow.

"Matt," Alyssa encouraged, "Let's go back to your bungalow to talk." Sitting on the bed, she was all business. She had changed from a kitten to a lioness, and she was fighting for her pride.

"Matt, I want to let your disappearing act go. I don't even care what happened, but I think something went on that you're not telling me. It's just a hunch. Is there another woman, or several, or what?"

Matthew chuckled, and she realized he thought he was exonerated. It was obvious that he had no intention of opening up to her about where he was or what he had done during the past month.

"Hey. What do you think? Maybe I was involved with some big espionage thing or somethin'? If anythin' so important went on, it wasn't enough to keep me from you. I had to do a lot of things. I needed to clean out my closet to make room for everythin' good and fine about you and Lisa. Trust me, baby, please trust me. I've never been dishonest with you. I've been pretty open from the beginnin'. I even told you all about the thing with Carline. I never told that to anyone before."

She felt like she was reading his thoughts, and she was desperate to ask him the fatal question.

"Matt, tell me. Did you and Lena ever have a thing?"

Tears filled her beautiful, pained, searching eyes, and he reached to comfort her.

"Oh, baby. I love you. You know I like to watch you when

you're all riled up like now. It's sexy."

"Stop it."

Matthew tried to wiggle away from his discomfort as he reached for her.

Alyssa rose from the bed and crossed her arms in front of her.

"This is serious. I need to know what kind of life I'm going to have loving you. Are you going to answer my question? I need to know. If it's over, it doesn't matter, but if it happened and it's not over, I need to know."

The tears streaming down her cheeks forced him to get serious.

"Honey. There was a time, but it's gone. I don't ask you about stuff that doesn't matter anymore, do I?" He was thinking, "I needed to do what I needed to do, and say what I needed to say in order to fix everything. I deserved closure with Lena in Napa. I had to know if it was really over with her in order to move on. Now Lena was history. She doesn't want me, and I couldn't have her back, of that I'm convinced. Sometimes, a man has to do what a man has to do, and the last thing I wanted to do was to hurt Alyssa." Furthermore, at this point, he had made his final choice, and he didn't feel guilty, not even one little bit.

"I want you and only you — and Lisa. The past is dead. It's like a foreign country. Did you ever think about how different foreign cultures are to us? We don't understand them because we're so different. It's the same with the past. It's hard to understand it because it's so different from now. Nothin' stays like it was. That's why there are generation gaps in families. I don't want to waste time tryin' to figure out the past, not yours and not mine. We need to move on. Yesterday's gone, five minutes ago is gone. It's too far away. Let's not let that happen to us, OK?"

"Oh, stop it. Just stop it."

Matt didn't want to deal with all this serious and heavy conversation. He saw her, just for that quick moment, as an intruder rather than his invited lover. Her voice wasn't soft, but rather piercing to his ears.

She walked into the bathroom to get a tissue, talking nonstop from the door. "I'm trying really hard to move on, as you like to put it."

Returning to the bed, she plopped down and looked at him eye to eye. "I need some answers. We're different that way."

Leaning forward, she rested her elbows on her knees and looked down at the floor. "Maybe you don't care what I did before I met you, but I do care what you did before we met, and I can't help it."

He hadn't heard a word after her remark about moving on, as he liked to put it. "Now, wait a minute, Alyssa. Move on from what? The fact that I'm a private man? I've always been that way, and I'm not goin' to change, not for you and not for anyone." Stopping conversation for a few seconds helped him get a new grip. He got up and walked to the window, glancing down at the pool, and then turned around facing her. "Alyssa." The soft sound of her name coming through his voice helped him even more. "You just have to trust me that I would never do anythin' to hurt you or Lisa. I'm not goin' to cheat on you or break your heart." He didn't like the way she was still staring at the floor. "Baby, are you hearin' me?"

She kept staring at the floor and he couldn't tell if she was in a trance or listening to him. "You're my exclusive lover and friend, and I'm never leavin' you again, not unless you make me go away. Alyssa, please look at me and say somethin'. This is where I need you to respond to me."

She looked up at him and then stood facing him. "Matthew, something isn't right. I can't put my finger on it, or maybe I don't want to. I've been very open with you about Alex and me. I've shared things with you about me that I hardly could admit to myself. You're close one minute, and then I feel a distant wind rushing through you that blows you far away from me. I hate it."

Matt stepped close to her, wrapped his arms around her body, feeling her tremble with submission, and he loved it. "Just trust me, baby. I love you. I'm not hidin' anythin' important from you. I want to bond so close. You know as time passes we'll mesh more and more. We've got exclusive rights to each other, yes?"

He lifted her beautiful chin up close and gently pecked her lips with his. Looking into her eyes, he knew that there would never be a need to mention Marialena to her again. The ring thing was not far away.

Chapter Eighteen

$\mathcal{J}$uly and August passed without incident. Matt flew to Florida from New York every weekend. He called Alyssa several times daily and filled her and Lisa's computers with adorable e-mails. The three of them grew closer and closer until Matthew was secure with his plan.

He held the phone close to his ear as it stopped ringing.

"Hello?"

"Mama? How are you?"

"I'm just fine, Son. I wish you wouldn't make yourself so scarce the way you do. You're not so young anymore. When I don't hear from you I get worried. It's been over three weeks since you called me this time. Last time, your girlfriend called because you disappeared. Why do you do that to the people who care about you, Son?"

"Mama I'm sorry I've been a little shy of callin' you. I got so much on my mind."

"Matthew James Hunter, this is your mama talkin'. Is this new girlfriend keepin' you from doin' your business? I'd like to meet her if you're really serious about her. What about her child? Are you wantin' to take on that kinda baggage? This girl looks to me like she's got a tail on her."

"Now, look. I'm not makin' any plans about anythin' until I see fit. If I decide to marry her, please, Mama, be nice."

Matt could hear Amy in the background coaxing their mother to back off.

"OK, I'll be supportin' anythin' you choose. I guess I always had a dream for you to get back with Carlene and your children, that's all."

"Mama, Carlene got married this summer, and my kids are grown. Trust me on this one, you'll love her, and her little girl will win your heart, too. You know, it's kinda excitin'. We never had a doctor in our family, wouldn't that be somethin'? I gotta go. Give my love to Amy and Annie."

Alyssa's pulse quickened as she held Lisa's hand in the airport. Matt had made arrangements for them to join him in New York for a weekend. They arrived at the JFK terminal, which was a longer ride to Manhattan than from La Guardia, but the limousine was stocked with goodies, as usual. Alyssa and Lisa were so excited to see Matthew and to be in New York that the ride was a pleasure. Lisa enjoyed sipping her coca-cola, and her eyes bubbled wide open as the city lights began turning on to compete against the setting sun. The car phone rang.

"Hey, baby, I'm so sorry I couldn't pick you up at the airport tonight. I'm still hung up on the Long Island Expressway. I got caught up workin' on this architectural snag we got here."

Breaking into a full smile, Alyssa gushed, "Oh, don't you worry. We're so excited to be here, we'll just wait at the apartment for you. What time do you think you'll be home? Do you want me to make us a little dinner?"

"Actually, that would be great. Why don't the three of us just rest at home together tonight? I've missed you so much all day long," he sighed.

They had a lovely dinner catered in from a local Mexican restaurant because Alyssa couldn't find anything in the cupboards to prepare.

Lisa stood like a grown-up lady at the dinner table, and raised her glass of milk.

"I want to make a toast. Mommy and I wanted to take you back to Acapulco tonight." As soon as she said it, a fit of giggles popped up and her other hand clenched her knuckles over her mouth. She plopped back into her chair and tried not to wiggle too much as she wondered what Mommy's handsome prince might say.

Matthew raised his glass to her. "That was so nice. This is to the sweetest little girl in the whole world." He turned to Mommy. "Oh, honey. This is the best we'll ever have. I'm so happy."

After dinner, Lisa carefully pulled on her new nightie and climbed into the wonderful white canopy bed that Matt had picked out for her. Her room looked like Macy's department store, and she was mesmerized with all of the new stuffed animals around her. "Mommy, Matthew, would you tuck me in?" Lisa was content, and she wanted her mother and Matthew to feel as happy as she did on this glorious night. Beaming, she gazed at her mom and the man who might be her daddy one day standing over her bed. She smiled and said, "I feel like we're a family."

After she received her hugs and kisses, she turned her face to her new stuffed bear, wrapped her arms around his soft, furry body, and closed her eyes.

Despite the wonderful fun they had all day, New York City felt very big and very far away from home. A crawly feeling spread through Lisa's tummy when she thought about actually having a real daddy. Suddenly she missed her grandmother, and she wished she could be home again. She squeezed her new teddy tightly as if he could make it all not so scary.

The next morning, Alyssa served breakfast for them all on the terrace overlooking Central Park. Matt pointed to the horse and buggy teams lined up along the street, awaiting passengers.

Lisa pleaded, "Oh Matt, could we go for a ride?"

Matt was thrilled that everything fell into place so easily. "Why it's funny you should ask." He smiled at Lisa. "Do you see that pretty buggy with the red bows on it and the roses lyin' on the seat?" Lisa craned her neck over the balcony and nodded. "Well, little darlin', that's ours for the day if you and Mama want it."

"Oh Matt, that's wonderful." Alyssa stood up and moved to the back of Matthew's chair. Wrapping her arms around his neck, she whispered in his ear, "I love you so much."

Lisa had already run to her room to get dressed for the excitement ahead. They all got ready and took the elevator downstairs. The doorman held the door for them and the horse and buggy with the red ribbons was waiting for them in front of the building. Matthew took the bouquets of long-stemmed roses off the seat and set them on the side of the buggy. One was red and one was pink. He reached for Lisa's hand and helped her onto the buggy. Picking up the pink bouquet, he turned to her and said, "These flowers are for my little girl." After placing them in her arms, he lifted Alyssa's hand as she gracefully stepped up onto the buggy. Picking up the red roses, he leaned toward her. "Mommy, these red roses are for you, because I love you, baby, I'll always love you."

The horse turned toward Central Park and before long they were moving through beautiful woods that seemed to be miles away from New York City. They were in the country.

After about an hour, the buggy halted. The driver got off and gathered a large red and white checkered blanket, a huge picnic basket, and champagne in an ice bucket from his driver's seat. Matt took the picnic basket and the blanket, walked to a small cozy area under a tree and spread the blanket down. "Ladies, please, join me." They sat down, watching Matt take pride in opening the picnic basket and spreading out an incredible array of prepared gourmet foods. Seconds later he energetically popped the champagne open and popped a bottle of sparkling apple juice for Lisa.

"Now," he said with that broad grin, "I just happen to have three champagne glasses in my pocket."

He skillfully pulled out three glasses from inside of his coat, never taking his eyes off of Lisa's response. She clapped her hands and reached for her glass. After pouring Lisa's apple juice, he poured two glasses of champagne.

"Let's toast," he said, "to the best trio in the whole world."

The champagne was Matt's favorite Crystal. They emptied the bottle, and the buggy driver was summoned to bring one more. Matt opened the new bottle of bubbles, and despite Alyssa's gentle protest, poured two new glasses.

"Hear ye, hear ye, I have something to say to my court."

Alyssa laughed. "Speech, speech."

Matthew began his speech with a half-cocked twinkle in his eye. "Lisa, I have a present for you."

He pulled the golden locket out of his pocket and handed it to Lisa.

"Oh, I love this." She held it up. "It's the prettiest necklace I've ever seen." Matt helped her fasten it, then reached into his pocket and pulled out a tiny little black velvet Tiffany's box. The bubbles in Alyssa's light head almost made this moment unreal to her. The warm glow she felt turned to a full blush rushing to her cheeks as she anticipated what she had been waiting for since she first met him. With a sheepish expression, he leaned toward Alyssa.

"I almost forgot." He opened the box and handed it to Alyssa. The most gorgeous and biggest diamond she had ever seen sat gracefully on a golden band.

"Matt, it's unbelievably beautiful." Her voice cracked.

"Alyssa and Lisa, I want to ask you both to spend the rest of your lives with me. Will you marry me?"

"Oh, yes," squealed Lisa, as she threw her head back and laughed." Matt and Alyssa burst out laughing at Lisa's comical response. Matt turned to Alyssa. "Well, that's one down. May I take that engagement ring out of the box and slip it on your finger?"

His watery blue eyes would have melted an iceberg. "Yes, Matthew James Hunter, yes."

With her encouragement, he took Alyssa in his arms and kissed her. Reaching for Lisa, he commanded, "Come over here and hug your new daddy. I can't wait until we're a real family."

They finished the champagne and Lisa had a second glass of apple juice. The picnic was over, but the party had just begun.

As the horse and buggy ride continued, a beautiful antique carousel appeared. Lisa lost control as she begged, "Oh, may I please have a ride?" She got two rides.

Exhausted, they returned to the apartment in the late afternoon. This was a day never to be forgotten by any of the three. It was a perfect day.

Alyssa sparkled as she bubbled over, "Matt, let's call my mother and tell her the news."

"Honey, let's wait a little while and just share this tonight with the three of us. I don't want to scatter the energy of all this around yet. I just want to be alone with us, OK?"

Alyssa was taken aback by the exclusivity of Matt's response. At the same rate, she was overwhelmed at his loving desire to seal their connection together with the intimacy of a threesome. She wondered what Amy would say when she heard that her brother was getting married. Alex's parents had died before she met him. This would be her first experience in combining her small family with another family, all trying to be one. She flashed on holidays together, and visits with in-laws. There would be so much time ahead to share everything together.

"OK, if that's important to you. We'll call my mom tomorrow. It's actually right that we just hang out together tonight." She brushed her fingers through her hair and twisted it back into one of her famous messy buns, her voice dropping just enough to show disappointment, "I'm just so excited to tell her. She'll be so happy."

He reached forward with outstretched arms, calling her to him. "Well, baby, if it really is that important to you, go ahead and call her now."

Moving slowly toward him with her head down, she answered, "No. You're right. We'll wait until tomorrow."

Matt placed his hands on her shoulders, then comfortably slid them around her back, holding her in a bear lock.

"That's my little girl. I'm glad you see it my way, baby. Let's take our time together." Kissing her forehead, he continued, "I think I'll wait to tell my mother until after we go to Charleston to meet her. I know she's goin' to love you both, and I want her to see how lucky I am before she hears that we're gettin' married." His flirtatious hands began wandering playfully, and he gave her a little gentle squeeze and slap on her buttock, "Hmm, that's really nice what you got there."

Morning came too early for Matt and Alyssa, who had been awake most of the night talking, planning, and dreaming of their family union soon to come.

"Mommy, Matt, wake up." Lisa jumped onto the bed and playfully shook two very tired people. Pinching Matt's cheeks and squeezing them together, she begged, "Aw, come on. Please, wake up. I'm so hungry!"

Matt cocked one eye open, lying very still, then suddenly he grasped her shoulders, "Boo!"

Giggling and throwing her head back, she gasped, "Oh, Matt. You scared me."

"I'm hungry, too. I'm as hungry as a big ole bear. Alyssa, wake up. We have a starving daughter here." He let go of Lisa, and he turned to Alyssa, who was quite awake. He began tickling her, which invited Lisa to join in the fun.

"Hey, guys," Alyssa giggled. "Two against one isn't fair."

The playful moment started a perfect morning before the threesome sat on the balcony for their newly traditional New York City family breakfast.

Matthew flashed on his mother, and felt his nerves rattle slightly, as he really jumped for only one person in his whole life — her. He needed to get on with the next step, which was to call her and tell her he was bringing Alyssa and Lisa to Charleston to meet her. His deep Southern tradition dictated parental respect, though he'd never credited his father with the title of parent. His mother was his only true parent, a perfect angel, a queen, and his symbol of all that could be good.

However, he never forgot the fresh switch she often picked off the old willow tree out back when he was bad. She made him dance in a circle to avoid the sting of the thin green branch, its leaves whipping his legs over and over again while she gave him a good ole Southern lecture about bein' a good little boy. Even as an adult, he feared getting her upset, almost as if he anticipated the stinging again.

"Honey, I need to call my mother and tell her we're comin' to Charleston. I'm goin' into the bedroom where the street noise isn't in the way. She has some trouble hearin' when the background is loud." He got up from the table and carried the phone with him into the next room. He was suddenly stirred by his Southern roots haunting him, calling him back to the battery. His mother hadn't been happy when he married Carline, because she wasn't Southern. Now he had proposed to another very Northern girl, even if she was from Florida. Matthew dialed his mother's number and paced back and forth in the bedroom until she picked up the on the other end.

"Hello?"

"Mother, it's Matt. How you doin?"

Alyssa heard him from the porch. She tried to catch his every word, though she caught something much stronger than words. She'd never picked up until this moment how very deeply he was rooted in the old South. She had led a sophisticated childhood, traveling around the world with her parents, knowing only the best of everything money could buy, studying foreign languages and learning to understand many diversities of life that only world travel offers. She was very broadly groomed as a child, and she realized how Matthew was really very different. His Southern accent became so pronounced while he talked on the phone, she could hardly decipher what he was saying. He laughed frequently, but she couldn't hear what he was laughing about. A lonely sense of estrangement overcame her as she felt like she was on the outside looking in. She felt that same uncomfortable energy that she'd experienced when she first arrived in Napa. It was as if there were a country called the United States of America, and another country called the South. She imagined that Matt's mother was unhappy about her and Lisa's new position in Matt's life. Maybe Mrs. Hunter was still fighting the Civil War, as many Southerners were.

Matt returned to the porch after a few minutes. "OK. Mother is excited to have us come to Charleston. How 'bout if we go tomorrow?"

Alyssa felt a tightening in her chest, and she suddenly felt like a lioness in nature, backing away from a would-be lion that had taken his place as head of the pride without having won his ritual rights. Holding the sides of her face with both hands, she contemplated the abrupt travel plans. Then she turned her head toward Matt. Suddenly, she needed to be blunt, even if it meant she risked offending him. "Did you tell her about our engagement?"

He sat back down at the table and poured himself another cup of coffee. "No. I thought we should spend some time with her first. It's better that way. Mama's sorta traditional, and I need to do this just right."

"Are you worried she won't be happy about us?"

"Don't be silly, I didn't say any such thing. Southerners just do things differently from other people. I bet she's already pullin' the greens from the garden and plannin' tomorrow night's dinner. She's a very good Southern cook. Everythin' is authentic just like before the Civil War."

Alyssa's mouth dropped almost to her lap. "I can't believe this. Did you tell her that, for sure, we're going tomorrow?"

Matt's face turned pale. "Baby, don't you want to go?" His tone changed to submissive innocence.

"Of course I want to meet your mother." Looking toward the streets below, she tried hiding the tears blurring her vision. "I just thought we could have decided together when we'd go before plans were solidified. You met my mother under no pressure at all. I'm a little nervous meeting yours."

"Honey, is somethin' wrong?" He got up and reached for her. "You're cryin'. What's wrong?"

"Nothing." She wiped her tears with her napkin and tried to cheer up. "Lisa, I want you to go brush your teeth and take your shower. Then we'll do something fun."

Lisa moaned, "Aw, Mommy. I want to watch the Rugrats first, OK?"

Alyssa nodded and stood to begin clearing the breakfast dishes from the table. "Now that you've made arrangements for us to go to Charleston, do you mind if I call my mother and tell her our news?

"Of course not. Let's call her together right now."

The flight to Charleston was uneventful. Lisa slept, Matt read the newspaper, and Alyssa just rested in her seat beside them.

Matt's mother was waiting at the door for them as they drove up to the house. She was a round little woman with soft eyes and silver hair, very different from Alyssa's mental picture of her. She wore an elegant beige suit, a string of pearls round her neck, very little makeup. She was beautiful.

"Well, so this is your pretty new girlfriend." She hugged Alyssa and spotted Lisa at the same time. "And who is this little girl? This must be Lisa." Reaching down for Lisa, she grasped her up into her arms and squeezed her tightly. "My, my, you are a heavy, big healthy girl."

Helping Lisa back to the ground, Matt's mother beamed at her son. "Well, Matthew," she said. "It's about time you threw away that tattered old black book of yours. I think you've found two keepers."

She meant no harm, but Alyssa frowned. She didn't want to know he'd had an actual black book.

Amy rushed out of the house to greet everyone. She hugged Matthew and then folded Alyssa into her arms. "Oh, it's so good to see you all."

Alyssa was surprised at how frail and gaunt Amy had become. She seemed to have aged twenty years, and for sure, it was all part of finally coming face-to-face with her abusive past. Often the classes in the Harmony House culminated in one of the ladies realizing that, since she escaped her husband's clutches, she wasn't ducking anymore every time someone moved a hand close to her. Amy was probably losing sleep and certainly losing inner peace right now as she had been sifting through her pain and the injustice done to her. Domestic abuse had taken its physical toll after the fact when she finally could be safe in letting down her defenses and began hashing out the past years within her mind.

"Amy, we're so glad to be here. It's great seeing you and Annie, and meeting your mother has been one of my greatest anticipations."

Annie followed her mother. "Hi." She appeared much more subdued than the little girl who ran for her uncle in the vineyards not that long ago. The sparkle was missing in her eyes, and Alyssa deduced that she was picking up on the pain of her mother's defeated and broken heart, and ingesting it as her own. Alyssa hoped Amy could begin reaching for the light again before it ruined the future for both of them. Maybe she would have to opportunity to help sort out some of those issues with Amy during this visit.

Annie went directly to Lisa, pretty much avoiding contact with everyone else, even her uncle. She took Lisa by the hand. "Come on Lisa, let's go play."

She led her to the yard to play. "Lisa. I have a new tire swing. Want to see it? Come on, where is Ollie? Ollie! Lisa is here." Lisa cheerfully followed Annie's lead, making it easy on herself to get away from the adults. The two girls got along famously as they played with Ollie out by Annie's new tire swing. Lisa was in awe of the Spanish moss that hung from the branches like locks of hair.

Mrs. Hunter and Amy retreated to the kitchen to prepare Southern sweet tea for everyone, and take the fresh biscuits out of the oven, and Alyssa and Matt sat on the couch, gazing through the living room window watching the two girls playing. The welcoming party immediately erased all the apprehensive pre-introduction jitters. Alyssa felt instantly at home, and now she agreed that Matt's decision to come to Charleston today was the right decision.

"Honey, smell those fresh-baked biscuits? I grew up with that smell always hittin' the house just before breakfast and dinner. Mother makes 'em from scratch. I'm gettin' hungry right now."

"Yes, they smell great."

Alyssa was mesmerized by the huge sprays of Spanish moss hanging from the trees. "Matt, isn't the moss incredible? It seems to hang strategically from the trees like soft scarves, providing privacy and a kind of protection for us all from the outside world. It's almost like we're in a safe fortress, the Hunter Fortress."

Matt rubbed her back lovingly. "I never thought of it like that before. See, honey? I told you everythin' would be fine. Please don't doubt me, baby, I'll always do my best to make the right decisions for our family, I promise. My mother already heard such good things about you from Amy, how could she help but love you from the start?"

Alyssa turned her head toward him. She reached behind her back and grasped onto his massaging hand. She pulled his arm around to the front of her and cuddled his hand within both of hers, lifting it to her lips, and while kissing it with several tender pecks, she continued staring at the girls.

"I don't know, Matt, everything seems too perfect to be true. I'm almost afraid to admit my joy for fear it'll be taken away."

Alyssa couldn't wait to see downtown Charleston. The closest to this romantic city she had ever been was in following Rhett Butler through his adventures with Scarlet.

Matt whistled his way to the kitchen, where Alyssa was waiting for him and talking to Amy while drinking a glass of sweet tea.

She took in his boyish T-shirt and shorts and the baseball cap on his head, and felt her eyes double in size. "Matt, I've never seen you dressed so casually. You look like a young Southern boy."

"I am a young Southern boy." He dashed up behind her, leaned down, and grasped her around her shoulders, playfully wrestling with her.

"And when I take one look at you, I feel very much like a Southern boy. See? That's why I love you like a little dumplin', and sometimes I just want to eat you all up." He planted several breathy, fervent kisses while pretending to bite the side of her neck.

"Stop." She shrugged her shoulders trying to push his face from her neck, laughing as goose bumps traveled up her spine. "That kind of kissing reminds me of a fingernail going across a blackboard."

Matt continued his playful teasing, now on the other side of her neck.

"What? You mean like this?"

He stopped his game abruptly, stood straight up, and reached for her hand.

"Come on, darlin', Daddy's goin' to show you the sexiest town in the South."

Alyssa got up from her chair, following Matthew's command, and turned to Amy.

"Don't you want to come with us? It would be good for you to get out. Come on, Amy, please?"

Amy turned her head toward the window, and avoided any eye contact. "I don't feel like socializing today, besides, I have a lot to do here at home." She reached for a napkin from the napkin holder on the table and gently blotted her eyes. "I'll help Mama watch the girls, and then rustle up some dinner for us all to eat when you get home. You two lovers go have fun." Obviously avoiding Matthew, she turned directly around and faced Alyssa. "Alyssa, thank you for the pep talk. That's the kind of help I need right now. I wish you lived near us so we could spend more time together." Amy looked away again, covered her face with her napkin, and began to cry.

Alyssa glanced at Matt, encouraging him to help.

"OK, you're comin' with us, you hear?"

"Thanks, Matt, but no." Amy got up and slowly turned toward the hallway. "I'm going to lie down. You guys go along now."

Walking to the car, Alyssa focused her eyes on the driveway. "I feel guilty going out to have fun, and leaving Amy this way. We were talking about her depression when you walked in. She needs to start fighting for her own survival, or it'll take a huge toll on both her and Annie."

"Oh, honey, you're readin' too much into this. I think she's doin' great. Y'all can't expect her to be jumpin' for joy just yet. But I agree that Annie does seem a little more distant this visit than I'd like her to be."

Matt stopped in front of the passenger door and opened it. "She is too serious right now. I've never seen her like this."

"She may become even more serious if Amy doesn't start trying to snap out of some of her own pain. It rubs off on Annie. I think she needs to consider taking an antidepressant for a while, just to help her climb out of the hole."

"Maybe you're right. You should talk to her about that when we get back. She wouldn't ever listen to me right now."

Alyssa slid onto the seat, and Matt closed the door. She sat alone for those few seconds before the driver's door opened on the other side. Her gut feeling was that something wasn't quite right with the whole Napa situation. She couldn't put her finger on it, but it was far from settling. The palpable resistance Amy displayed against her brother's attempt at consolation was out of character, and chilling. It was almost as if she were taking her anger about Peter's death out on him. Alyssa decided to hold off on the pursuit of answers to any of this until the timing was just right. She was learning to read Matt's moods, and she was getting better at communicating with him on his terms in order to keep the peace.

As Matt got in the car, he looked over at her with squinting eyes. "Are you sure you want to go? We don't have to go, ya know."

"This is exciting to me, to see Charleston. I feel I'll understand you better after I see everything here through your eyes."

Alyssa reached over and rubbed Matt's shoulder as he turned the key and started the car.

"It must have been so much fun growing up here."

"It was fun. It's a great little world here. I missed out on some. My father kept me pretty busy pickin' cotton after school, and punishin' me as much as he could for things I didn't do."

As he turned the car out of the drive and glanced at her, he grinned.

"But I had plenty of time to go off by myself and fish and hunt for oysters in the battery. I had some great friends, and we used to swim in the water hole behind the Weaver Mansion with a couple of real cute girls."

He briefly took his eyes off the road and threw his head

back laughing.

"I managed to take in culture whenever I could, and those two girls had a lot a culture."

"Matt, I don't want to hear about your wild oats."

"Well, honey, you gotta understand. Money was tight back then, and we spent a lot of time survivin' the best we could. That little water hole was free."

"So you've said. Free in more ways than one."

Matt slapped the steering wheel with both of his hands, "You're jealous of my past."

Alyssa broke into a giggle. "Kind of, I guess. Isn't that silly?"

"Anyway, I'm takin' you to see some of my stompin' grounds in town where I had the best times."

They parked near the marketplace, which was a great strip of individual stalls, each with a proprietor selling his or her arts and crafts. Matt pointed at a row of horses being hitched to large, multi-passenger carriages.

"Let's take a horse and buggy tour. You'll see the hot spots of the city, plus the drivers always teach some interesting stuff about old architecture and the Civil War."

They enjoyed the ride through Charleston as Matthew helped the driver point out the historical points of interest.

"Alyssa," Matt instructed, "the architectures of these homes are fashioned from England, France, and Italy. And what's most amazin' is the fact that the houses were built with only two rooms per floor. They were very narrow and long. Huge six-thousand-square-foot homes were three stories high and only had six rooms. This was all part of their air-conditionin' system. The breeze easily passed through one window and out the other on the opposite side of the room. Isn't that cool, baby?"

Alyssa beamed and snuggled up to Matt. "Is there any subject you don't have some knowledge about?"

The driver slowed the buggy to a stop and broke in on Matt's dissertation. "You may know your stuff, but I bet you don't know how much just one of these slave quarters goes for today." He pointed to a tiny building behind an immaculate mansion on one side of the buggy.

"Yes I do." Matt leaned back in the buggy's seat and grinned at Alyssa, winked, and leaned forward to continue his discussion with the driver. "They're mostly valued at over one million dollars, and that's just for the slave quarters in back. Forget the prices of the main houses."

"OK, you got that one."

A light tap of the whip on the side of the buggy encouraged the horse to move forward. It pulled to a stop in front of the marketplace, and Matt stepped down, helped Alyssa down, and tipped the driver.

Reaching for Alyssa's hand, Matt stopped short on the sidewalk. She understood his deep pride in being from Charleston. He released his hand from hers and rested them on his hips, lifted his face to the sun, and sighed.

"Honey. Can you imagine how beautiful all this was before General Sherman destroyed it? How could anyone be so destructive? Destroy somethin' so pure and fine? I hate what the Civil War did."

"Matt, seeing all this has left me with such a powerful respect for your past. My childhood was so different from yours. Maybe all this is why you exude such power and tradition. It's in the way you move, the way you grin, it's even in the way you sit in a crowd of people. I'm in love with the South."

He reached for her hand again and they began walking.

"It better be in the way I make love with you, too."

"Yes, that, too."

He picked up their pace and charged forward.

"I'm hungry. Let's go to Bubba Gump's for lunch. It's a grand tribute to Forest Gump and Bubba. Every kind of prepared shrimp is available just like Bubba said it could be cooked. There's a little souvenir shop there where you can buy somethin' nice for Lisa, too."

"Oh, I'd love that. This feels like we're in some kind of movie."

Matt suddenly slowed down and dropped her hand from his. His mouth twisted in disapproval.

"Honey, I think you love the fact that I'm Southern more than you love me for bein' me. It's startin' to kinda bug me."

Her mouth dropped open, her gait came to a standstill, and disappointment and hurt over his statement washed over her in waves.

"What are you talking about? You have it the wrong way around. I love Southern because it's you. I'm just so excited to be here. I'm sorry if you think I'm too bubbly about it all, but I can't help it. This is all more foreign to me than Europe is."

Matt didn't answer her, she assumed he understood what she was trying to say, and they finished the walk to Bubba Gump's in silence.

At the restaurant, they sat in the garden and shared a

barrel of beer shrimp. Alyssa drank sweet tea and Matt drank two beers.

Noticing the little shop across the courtyard, Alyssa broke the silence. "I'm going to look in the shop for something I can bring home to Lisa and Annie. Do you want to come?"

Matt shook his head.

"It'll take just a few minutes, and I'll be right back."

Alyssa left the table and walked toward the door of the tiny souvenir shop. She could feel Matthew watching her walk from the back. Aware that her natural wiggle through the crowd would get his attention, she turned it on a little more for him.

Sifting through the T-shirts in the shop, she found a pile of children's shirts with words of wisdom written on them. She picked out a shirt for each of the girls with "Life's a box of chocolates. You never know what you're gonna get" written on them.

As she handed her purchases to the clerk, she smiled.

"Life is a box of chocolates, and I'm so lucky that my box of chocolates turned out to be so wonderful."

The clerk, a happy-go-lucky fellow, was anxious to make conversation.

"You have one of the prettiest smiles I've ever seen."

"Well, thank you very much for saying so." The short, innocent exchange added unexpected sweetness to Alyssa's day. She thanked the friendly young man again and turned to make her way back to Matthew.

He was standing just inside the entrance to the shop, a scowl marring his handsome features. He held the door open for her as they left the shop, and began scolding her with harsh annoyance as they walked away from the courtyard.

"Why did you flirt with that guy? You were gushin' all over him." His voice picked up volume, and Alyssa noticed people turning their heads and looking at Matt. Heat prickled up from her neck.

"Please don't be so loud. I wasn't flirting with anyone. I just thanked him for saying he liked my smile. He was just a boy, for goodness sake. Don't be so silly."

Matt became quiet again. As they walked along, passing shop windows dressed in artifact décor, he offered no comments, and she watched him ignore his surroundings. She felt his cold shoulder for several hours. He wasn't mean, and he didn't berate or attack her further, but remained smug. She was confused as to how he could distance himself from her for nothing. She couldn't believe how he got it in his head she had flirted with the cashier in the souvenir shop. Really, she just paid for a shirt.

Suddenly, her romantic excitement of her first visit to Charleston faded. She had never seen Matthew display such inappropriate behavior. Something wasn't right. Maybe he was feeling difficulty showing his hometown to her, but she couldn't understand why, when he was the one who wanted her to be there. He'd orchestrated the whole trip without even consulting her.

She took note of his slowly warming up to her and his making a point for her to understand that he wouldn't tolerate what she had done. He broke the ice by pointing to a wooden soldier he could see through the door of one of the shops.

"Honey, I want to see how much that statue is. I almost bought one kinda' like it about a year ago, and I've kicked myself for not gettin' it ever since."

She felt a new type of distance between them, a combination of hurt, annoyance, and confusion.

"Sure. You look at the statue, and I'm going into the shop next door."

"Don't you want to see the statue with me?"

"Not really."

"OK."

Hoping he would see she had emotionally pulled back from him, she moved toward the door of the next shop. As the seconds passed, her emotions began centering on confusion. "Maybe it was my fault," she whispered to herself.

She found a chair near the door outside and sat down and just gazed forward, dazed.

Matt came out of the shop empty-handed.

"It was a reproduction. That's not what I wanted. Hey. What's wrong? Are you OK?"

Alyssa's looked up as Matt as he neared, her bewilderment growing as her eyes locked onto his.

"I really feel upset at how mad you got at Bubba Gump's. You gave me the cold shoulder for more than two hours, do you realize that? I didn't flirt with anyone. I was just being friendly, because I was happy."

He shook his head, "Well, I may have overreacted. But a woman can't even smile at a man, but what he'll think she wants him. That's how men are. You should know that, bein' you're so pretty and all."

"First of all, if that's true, so what? And second of all, is that really what you think? If a woman smiles at you, you think she wants you?"

Matthew lifted his shoulders and stretched out his arms.

"Oh come on, you know I don't think that. But that's what they say. Men are animals."

Alyssa stood up and turned toward the direction of the car.

"Matt, it's not right to blow up over something you were imagining — something that wasn't even happening."

Matt followed her as she led the way on the sidewalk toward the marketplace.

"Let's just drop it. Let's move on. This just is bein' made too much of."

As they walked to the car she tried to be fair in her mind.

Maybe she was feeling a little frisky, even the wiggle she'd put in her walk was a bit much, though she'd done it with only him in her mind. Feeling a little embarrassed at her own behavior, she decided to put the whole restaurant ordeal behind her in order to keep the peace, though her outing had been ruined.

By the time their car rolled up the driveway to the house, Matt was refreshed.

"Here we are, baby. Home again, and I wonder what Amy has cooked up for supper. Let's go see what they've all been up to since we left. Don't forget the presents for the girls."

As he opened her door and tried to help her out of the car, she pulled her hand away from him.

"I'm still a little offended, Matt. I don't just move on as easily as you do."

She swung her feet out of the car and got out without his ceremonial assistance.

Having heard the car drive up, Matthew's mother stood at the door waiting for them.

"It's about time you two got back here. These girls are a handful without their parents controllin' 'em."

Reaching for Alyssa's hand, Matt sped up his pace toward the porch. Alyssa reached back and grasped his hand in return, the sign of unity, as they neared his mother.

"Mother, where's Amy? I thought she was goin' to help watch the girls."

"Amy has helped some. But she's not feelin' so good today. She cooked for a while, and now she's sleepin' in her room."

Alyssa tripped over one of the steps and Matt caught her as she fell.

"Honey, be careful."

She glanced at him and smiled, "Thank you. That could have been a bad fall."

Matt's mother, aghast, rushed forward. "Alyssa, are you OK?"

"I'm fine, thanks. I think I caught my shoe on the step. Where are the girls now? I'm so sorry if our leaving made it hard on you today."

Mother Hunter smiled. "Oh, don't worry. I was just havin' a little fun with y'all. They're in the livin' room watchin' TV."

Alyssa's iceberg had melted with her near fall and Matt's rescue. They entered the house in search of the girls, and reaching the living room, she stopped short. "Matt, look— how sweet."

Lisa and Annie had fallen asleep, sharing a pillow on the carpet. The TV continued blasting out cartoons as the children dozed comfortably, head to head, in front of it.

Matt answered, "They're two little angels. I want us to have a baby someday."

Alyssa giggled. "You're silly, you know that?"

He shrugged. "I don't think that's silly at all. You're still young, why can't we have a child together, maybe two? There's still time. Honey, walk in the gardens with me for a few minutes, please?"

She followed Matt outside, passing the sleeping girls quietly in order to not awaken them.

"Aren't you tired after such a hectic day?"

"No. There's somethin' I gotta say. I shouldn'ta behaved that way. I know it was wrong, but I can't stand it when another man looks at you. I want you to be just mine."

He walked on, clasping his hand in hers, and not a word spoken, until they reached the old willow tree on the south side of the house.

"Alyssa." He put his arms around her. "Let's make our weddin' plans while we're here. Would you like to get married on Dierdra II in early spring?"

"Of course I would. That would be incredible."

"We could turn the livin' room into a chapel and we could get married at sea off the coast of Florida. What do you think?"

"I think it's a great idea."

He finished a dream kiss with a whisper, "You're sayin' you're not gonna hold the Bubba Gump thing against me?"

"I'm saying that I still want to be Mrs. Matthew James Hunter." She felt the blood rush to her head as romance once again erased all doubts.

"Good. Let's go tell my mother."

Chapter Nineteen

*T*he plane to Orlando was delayed, as usual, and the exhausted, screaming infant being held in the next aisle didn't make the takeoff any more enjoyable.

Lisa sat in the window seat, Alyssa sat next to her, and Matthew took the aisle spot.

"I just gotta be able to stretch out these ole legs." He put his head back and covered his ears with his hands. "If that kid'll stop cryin', once we're airborne, I'm goin' to order me a teeny-weeny drink and relax."

Alyssa pulled some crayons and a pad of paper from her purse and handed them to Lisa. Then she turned back to Matt, her hands reaching for the back of his neck.

"You're so tight, honey. I'll give you a good massage when we get home."

He rhythmically rolled his neck, responding to her, feeling the cracking of tension release.

"Ah, that feels better. I know there's nothin' we can do about a wasted day in the airport; I just have so many deadlines, it makes me crazy. My goodness, why did I ever take on this shippin' deal?"

Alyssa pulled her hand back, reached for Lisa's, and looked out the window together with her daughter as the plane picked up momentum along the runway.

"Mommy, you always do nice things for everyone. These are pretty crayons." Lisa opened the box and took out a red crayon. She wrote across first page on the pad, "I love Mommy," ripped it off, and handed it over.

Alyssa took the cherished gift from her daughter's little hand.

"I love you, too. Lisa, you've been so good on this trip, and I'm very proud of you."

The baby whimpered and exchanged his tears for a bottle. Matt leaned back again and closed his eyes as they lifted off the ground. Recent events began replaying in Technicolor before his tired, closed eyes, and his first visual stop was Bubba Gump's. He once again watched Alyssa wiggling her way through the crowd as she moved toward the gift shop. He felt the anger rush to his head as he saw other men's sexual arousal follow her across the courtyard. Allowing his anger to intensify, he flashed on her flirting and gushing over the clerk's gawking grin.

"It's just not right," he muttered.

"What's not right?" Alyssa stroked his shoulder.

"Oh, nothin'. I was just dreamin', I guess."

Returning to his memories, he thought about how furious he was at her for what she did in the store. Now that it was over, he was able to step back a little. He knew she didn't do anything wrong. He just couldn't control his possessive jealousy, but if only she weren't so darned beautiful, it would be easier. Out of the blue, his visualization adventure took him to Napa, where he once again saw lovely young Lena lying on the ground in the vineyard. That was jealousy, too. He felt so sorry about that, but at least his distortions hadn't hurt Alyssa, not physically, anyway.

Leaning toward her ear, he whispered, "I love you, and I always will. I don't ever want to do anythin' to hurt you."

"Where did that come from?" She pecked his nose with a kiss.

"Honey, do you have any of my Tums on you?"

Coming from nowhere, those elephants of indigestion began sitting on his chest again.

She grasped her purse and moved things around in it, searching for the six-pack at the bottom.

"I bought some at the airport. Here they are."

She fumbled to open the pack and pull out one roll.

"Are you all right?"

"Yes. It's just nerves."

The flight attendant pulled the beverage cart backward coming down the aisle in front of Matt. He looked her up and down, undressed her, redressed her, and spoke up as a gentleman.

"Miss, may I have some water?"

"Of course, sir. Would you also like juice, soda, or a cocktail?"

"No thanks. Just water."

The elephants slowly disappeared, and Matt invited a brief doze.

As the plane touched down in Orlando, Alyssa grabbed a free hand on each side of her.

"Getting home to Florida will be the beginning of a new adventure for us all. We have so many things to plan, and we have so much to look forward to. Aren't you guys excited?"

Lisa didn't respond, but stared out the window as the

plane taxied to the terminal.

Matthew leaned over toward his bride-to-be and whispered, "I love you."

"Good, because I love you, too."

"Good, because I love you more. Now give me some sugar."

Their lips briefly met, but then Lisa pulled on her mother's arm. "Mommy, Matt. You guys stop all that smooching on the airplane. Mommy says teenagers don't look good doing that in public. Anyway, I'm thinking, and kissing bothers me when I'm thinking."

"Now Lisa, mind your manners. Your mama and your daddy need a little love. You want to kiss me instead?" Matt leaned past Alyssa with his lips pursed, offering his cheek to Lisa, only to burst out laughing.

"No way. That's gross." She playfully pushed his head away. "I changed my mind. You can keep kissing Mommy."

"Well, I will. That is, if you'll tell us what you're thinkin'.

"Actually, you know how the movie stars put their names together? Like Brangelina?

"How 'bout if we call you guys Malyssa? That has my name in there, too."

Matt reached across the seat to tickle her tummy.

"Lisa, you surprise me more every day. Alyssa, what do you think? Let's become Malyssa."

Alyssa had a better idea.

"Maybe it would be a bit more masculine if we could be called Mattlysa."

Lisa widened her eyes and opened her mouth as she reached toward Matt for a high five.

"Yes."

Their palms met in midair.

"High five to you, too." The union of names changed his half grin to a full smile.

They picked up their luggage at the baggage claim and followed the porter outside to the curb where the car Matt had rented was waiting for them.

Lisa pouted as she dragged her little Barbie suitcase on wheels behind her. "Awe, I wanted a limo with Cokes in the backseat."

Matt reached for her free hand, "I'm the limo driver today, and I'll buy you a soda to drink in the backseat. How about that?"

"OK." She looked downtrodden, struggling dramatically, while pulling her suitcase behind her.

Matt reached for the suitcase with his free hand. "Hey, punkin', give me that heavy load. I can handle it."

He dropped his girls at their house, and he drove off to check on Dierdra II. "I'll call you guys later. Let's all get some rest tonight."

"I'm ready for that," Alyssa yawned. As they entered the house it was obvious that Lisa had one thing on her mind. "Mittens, here kitty, kitty, kitty."

Alyssa passed by the suitcases and drew the curtains open in the living room, viewing her luscious Atlantic Ocean. She still felt the numbness of everything that had transpired during the past few days.

"Mrs. Matthew James Hunter," she sighed as she crossed

one arm in front of her chest supporting the other, and rested her chin on her hand. "Pinch me, because this isn't real."

She glanced around the room, decided Lisa would be OK for a few minutes on her own, and then turned toward the door, threw off her shoes, and with the sprint of an athlete, she raced to the shore. When she stopped, the water lapped at her feet, refreshing her and washing away the residual fatigue from the trip.

"I'm going to start spending more time with myself."

Automatically she began slowly moving, picking up speed along the sand as the surf splashed against her shins. Though the warm water felt soothing and inviting, she resisted jumping in and broke into a jog instead. As the fresh air cleared her mind, she flashed back to the Bubba Gump episode, which she had put out of her mind for later.

"Now seems to be later. That was really bizarre, but I haven't seen any other signs of instability in him except those few jealous minutes. I wonder how hard it'll be for him to work in New York while we're here in Florida for most of that time."

She luxuriated in fragmenting her thoughts and turned to the memory of how she'd felt when she sold the practice. She wanted more time away from professional responsibilities. Why then had she transferred all of that to the Harmony House, and its horrific fight against domestic violence?

"Matt and I are in the same boat," she told herself. "We both need to stop and smell the roses before they wilt. I'll start by walking on the beach every day. Jean-Marc would do that with me, if only he were here."

The thought of Jean-Marc was enough to make her turn around and go back to the house.

A few minutes later, she held the telephone receiver, anxiously awaiting the sound of his voice on the other end of the line.

"Jean-Marc, it's Alyssa. I miss you. We just got in from Charleston and I have so much to tell you. Please call me back."

She slowly put the phone back and began unbuttoning her clothes as she dragged her body up the stairs to turn on her jet tub. She put on some light music, poured herself a small glass of wine from the Jacuzzi bar, and dropped her clothes to the floor. Her bare skin felt dry and rough to the touch as she rinsed off in the shower, and she worried which texture Matthew had found. Was her skin soft or rough? He had never said one way or another. Dropping the towel from her shoulders, she stepped into the warm fragrance of lavender essence. Nothing was more glorious than an oil bath after exercise. She lay back in the water and floated as every muscle relaxed, relishing this moment of total tranquility.

The phone by the tub rang.

Reaching for the receiver and reluctantly holding it to her ear, she answered.

"Hello?"

"Hey, baby, what you doin'?"

"Oh, Matt, it's you. I was dreading the phone."

"Well. I can always call back later."

"Oh, no. I'm lying in the tub with a glass of wine and relaxing. It feels so good to just relax and do nothing."

"I'd love to be in that tub with you, baby." His voice took on a gravelly sex appeal, as he whispered, "Oh boy, would I ever."

Her body moved spontaneously to the top of the water, and then sank back down to the bottom of the tub, as she held the phone against her lips and whispered back, "Get in your car and come over, Mattlysa. I'll turn the hot water back on and it'll be all fresh and warm for us. I'm lying in lavender oil. Just think how slippery it would be hugging me right now."

"I'll slippery you right now." His voice abruptly stopped playing. "Honey, I've been thinkin'. I'm goin' to push myself to finish this DeVinci project before the weddin'. I never woulda taken the contract if I knew then that I'd be marryin' you within the next few months. I don't need this project. I just want to get all the stress over with before we get married. This'll mean I won't see you much until I'm done. It'll be worth it if I can stand stayin' away from you for that long."

Alyssa stiffened her body, and sat up in the tub. "Matt, I worry so about your health. You do need to slow down and take some deep breaths. I've been thinking about this very subject since I got home. Please don't think I'm nagging. Matthew, you need to slow down and think about nutrition. And you know alcohol isn't healthy. We went through this already when I first met you. You could have died so easily, and I never would have you now. I don't want to lose you."

"As usual, you're readin' my mind, 'cause I don't want to ever lose you, either," he replied easily.

"Matt, stop making everything so light. This isn't funny. After we're married, let's promise to relax more, and exercise and start paying a lot of attention to our nutrition. Promise me you'll stop drinking."

"I agree with you. Let's make these years ahead the best we ever had. We have more money than we'll ever spend. I just want to take it easy and play with you for the rest of my life. I'm the man who planned to slow down, and instead, I'm goin' to need to speed up for a while like I never did before. But just for a little while, I promise. Honey, if I get grumpy or tired, just support me, baby, 'cause it's goin' to be gruelin'. I gotta hang up and make my reservations for New York. I'll call you later. I love you."

"I love you, too."

She hung up the phone and relaxed back down in the water, only to float back up again, touching the faucet handle with her toe and turning the hot water back on.

The phone rang again.

"I might as well forget this bath," she grumbled as she sat up and turned the faucet off with her hand.

"Hello?"

"Alyssa, it's Jean-Marc. You sound so annoyed. Did I call at a bad time?"

"Oh, no." She stretched her body back down into the water.

"I'm so glad to hear your voice. Can you hold the line for a minute? I'm just getting out of the tub."

She put the phone down, reached for her towel, and stepped onto the floor. Wrapping it around her waist, she reached for the phone again.

"I have missed you so much. I'm so happy you called. We just got back from Charleston, and I was thinking about you."

"Maybe you should go to Charleston more often, because you obviously don't think about me very much anymore. If Dionna didn't keep me posted, I wouldn't be able to guess how you are doing."

"Then you know, right?"

She reached for a second towel off the rack, and with one hand began rubbing her hair dry. The silence on the other end of the line was heart wrenching.

"Jean-Marc?"

"I'm here. Alyssa, I wish you would wait a little longer before you take such a big step. I know you love him, but you haven't known him long enough. Please."

Alyssa walked to her closet, dropped her towel and reached for a silk robe. She tucked the phone in her neck as she slid her arms into the sleeves and tied the sash around her waist.

"Let's not waste our talk on all this. Tell me, what's going on in France? I still want to come with Lisa for a week this Christmas holiday."

"That would be marvelous. Do you think Matthew would agree with that?"

As she neared the vanity, she stopped in her tracks. Her voice trembled, as the peach fuzz stood up on the back of her neck.

"Of course he would. He's not the ogre you think he is. I wouldn't be marrying him if he was."

Alyssa sat down at her vanity, dropped the phone in its cradle and pushed on the speaker button, and picked up a silver comb, looking at herself in the mirror.

"I don't think he's an ogre, I just think he's very controlling, and very jealous."

She tilted her head and began gently combing her hair.

"Well, you're wrong about him. Besides, he's going to be working very hard for the next few months, and he won't mind at all if Lisa and I go to Europe for a week."

"Great. We'll plan it, then."

"I'll talk to you later."

"Ciao."

But as she hung up the phone a restless uneasiness overtook her, and she was reluctant to discuss the trip with her fiancé. Anyway, no need to worry about it now, as Christmas vacation for Lisa was several weeks away.

Still sitting in front of the mirror, she gazed at her face. She saw a very young-looking, quite beautiful, thirty-something lady. Pleasure overtook her senses. She truly had found new joy and had become reacquainted with the girl she left behind when she lost Alex. That girl was back because she'd fallen in love with Matt. Maybe she wasn't even that much older looking. Could it be? She took another hard gaze into the mirror. A trip to France with her was just what she needed. It would give her a chance to build some one-on-one time that they had most recently missed out on together. France was gorgeous in the winter. The Debussys and the Tennisons had spent many Christmas holidays together in Europe. She remembered the hours she and Jean-Marc had played in the snow as children, and how much fun they'd had together sled racing, ice skating, building snowmen, and having snowball fights in the Alps. Thinking of Jean-Marc brought back memories that money could never buy.

Matthew returned to New York with sheer dread. Two weeks passed, and he hadn't taken himself away from his work for more than quick meals, short sleep sessions, and a few late-night cocktails. He called Alyssa a few times every day, and he whined about his misery during seconds of time he took away from work.

"Honey, all I do in my spare time is fantasize about the weekends I can steal from Capezzio and escape to Florida to be with you. I don't know how to hold on here. It's like I'm gonna crack up or somethin'. I haven't seen you in almost two weeks."

"It seems like months."

"I'm gonna be strong and hold off comin' to Menlo until next month. Besides, December is a great time to get you up here."

He hung up the phone time after time with the same promises of a future together getting closer and closer.

He knew she was worried about him, and that was comforting, because he, too, was worried about himself. One night he got out of the shower and looked at himself in the mirror. He saw a very old and very gray-looking man. His face was drawn, and he was shocked to see that he had lost so much weight. Matthew James Hunter never forgot a meal in his life, at least not until now. He immediately made one of his desperate calls to Alyssa, his lover, his doctor, his best friend, his soul mate, and his future wife.

"Honey. Somethin's wrong. I just saw myself in the mirror. I've lost a lot a weight. I'm takin' a few days and comin' home. Would you pick me up tomorrow afternoon at the airport? We gotta talk."

"Of course I will."

Florida was where they could forget responsibility and love each other without stopping for a couple of precious days. Then the cycle would begin again. He knew that, but right now he had to take one step at a time. He put the phone down and returned to work.

By morning he was rested again, so he cancelled his

flight to Florida and went back to the drawing board. The ship would be registered to Italy. Antonio Capezzio had put together his personal group of the finest engineers and crew that money could buy. This was his biggest baby and there was no limit to the expense he was willing to incur in order to please himself. Matthew plodded on, day after day, night after night. He had to get this thing finished.

Alyssa's absence did nothing for the many lonely moments of his unfulfilled male desire. He was sick with exhaustion and the demands of his work. He drank heavily at night, never quite able to completely drown his misery in Scotch. He resented Alyssa's responsibilities to the life she had created before she met him. He begged her to come to him. She promised she would come soon while he threw temper tantrums on the phone during his desperate pleas for her love. He even threatened her that if she didn't make it right somehow, he would consider walking away. Often his speech was slurred and he feared she could smell the alcohol through the phone.

He frequently heard her pleading before they hung up, "Matt, I wish you wouldn't drink so much every night. I'm so worried about your health."

Alyssa believed that this was the behavior of an exhausted and sad man. He was desperate and lonely. She decided not to take Lisa to France for Christmas after all. When she could slow down with the Harmony House, and when his project was completed, she would marry Matt and she and Lisa would follow him wherever he needed to be. He wouldn't need to drink because she would fill his life with what really counted. He would be complete with all that she would give him.

"Hold on, darling," she prayed, "We'll have it all soon."

Chapter Twenty

Matt had always dreamed of the luxury of monogamy, but he tended to awaken from his dreams often, tossing and turning, and realized that the drive to procreate was a man's privilege. For Matthew, that drive was part of the much-needed orgasms that helped him center his genius. Masturbation did wonders in relieving his pressure valve, but it did nothing to fulfill him as a man. The pressure of need built up quickly inside of him until he thought he would explode. That need demanded a warm, soft body. It demanded the scents and juices of real life in its raw form. Sex and love could go together, and that was the best. But sex and love were not necessarily synonymous. His desire for escapades didn't interfere with his desire for love. In fact, being with someone he didn't love only made the love experience more powerful. It was an almost therapeutic chain of events. Still, he remained loyal to Alyssa and stood his ground against his natural instincts of desire. What he thought in the privacy of his mind was his own business, and that was never going to change.

Matthew had never known such work stress. One by one his designs were rejected by Capezzio. The demands put on him required long hours of agonizing over revised creations with loss of sleep and little reward. Matthew Hunter, a man of fortune and fame, had taken on a contract that made him feel like an apprentice. Maybe Antonio Capezzio was a big shot in his world of sin and favors, but Matthew James Hunter was the creator and owner of one of the largest luxury yacht corporations in the world. He may have climbed to fortune and fame from a little Southern American family, but there was one medal he wore. His climb was through education, fortitude, and talent. Antonio couldn't claim his title with the same dignity. Antonio had a title because of money and fear, which were powers he inherited from his father. The only thing Matthew believed he had inherited from his own father was an ingrained low self-esteem, which in an odd way, drove him to succeed.

Finally, after six long weeks, he created a feasible partial design.

His driver picked him up for the tedious ride to Long Island, and Matthew sat the whole way never uncrossing his fingers except to dial Alyssa's phone number. "Honey, I think he's goin' to love this one." He spread the plans on the seat beside him, scanning them carefully. "I just finished the grand dinin' room, and I fashioned it after your dinin' room in Florida. The ceiling is clear glass under the stars. The huge center chandelier looks like it just hangs from eternity and the glass cuts make it sparkle like diamond-cut prisms. I'm tellin' you, it's magical. He has to love this one."

"You're amazing." She moaned through the phone, and he imagined her touching it with her lips. "It's unbelievable to hear you like this again. Your energy is back."

"Yeah, and it's back in more ways than one. I wish I could show you how much it's all back right now."

He pictured her squirming on the other side of the receiver. "I want to make love with you right now."

Ignoring her comment, he carefully rolled up his plans

and rubber banded them together.

"I'm a country boy at heart, Alyssa, and I'm startin' to miss my roots in South Carolina for the first time in my life. I was thinkin'. Maybe we should buy a big ole house near the Battery, and we could stay there sometimes on holidays and stuff."

"I'd like that, and you know that Lisa would love any chance she could get to be with Annie."

"Honey, I really don't know why I ever woulda wanted to become part of a new cruise line, I musta been nuts. I must sound like a broken record to you."

"I feel the same way you do. It's almost over, Matt. But what would happen if you quit before you finished?"

Matt shuddered. "I can't do that." He looked through the window, hoping to dissipate his uneasiness in just thinking of what could happen if he quit before finishing.

"Matt, are you there?"

"Yeah, honey. I'm here. Look, I gotta go and tighten up some of this presentation before I get there. Anyway, it's gettin' cold here in New York. Can you come up here this weekend? I need to cuddle with you to keep warm."

It was early December, Christmas was in the air, and the wedding was three months away. Alyssa flew to New York, and combined Matthew time with adding a few feminine touches to the apartment's decor and shopping while he was working. Snow and rain had been active together, and the streets were slushy with dirty melting ice. Looking out the window, she realized how depressing the gloomy weather was.

"I wish we could take a drive to Vermont and stay in a cabin in the snow for the weekend. It's so beautiful there with the trees blanketed in white."

He was obviously deeply in thought, his hand racing across the large piece of paper on his drawing board as he sketched out a balcony for DeVinci.

"Honey, you know I don't have time for any of that. Be sensitive, please. I'm busy here, can't you see that?"

"Oh, chill. I'm just commenting, I'm not asking. Actually, you've been quite grumpy for the past couple of days."

"Well. Maybe I've been stressed with this last major piece of the project."

He placed one hand on the middle of his chest and rubbed his sternum with his fingers. "By the way, I'm havin' a lot a indigestion. Would you run out and get me some Tums? And don't start doin' your doctor thing with me. I just want some Tums."

"If I've developed a tendency to harp about your health, it's because I love you. My medical training means nothing to you, and I'm helpless in trying to convince you to take care of yourself. You've cancelled two different appointments I made for you with the cardiologist." She realized she was barking up the wrong tree. It would take more than a ton of bricks to fall on him before he realized what he was doing to himself and to her.

"Well. You shoulda asked me if I had time to go. Honey, you can't just be makin' appointments for me when I'm workin' with deadlines here."

"I think we have a deadline to get that indigestion checked out." She reached to touch his back. "Matt, it could be more serious than simple indigestion. It could be your heart or an ulcer or something else. Remember when we first met how you wanted me to take care of you? Let's use my knowledge for something in this relationship. You used to listen to my medical advice."

He twisted his shoulders around and jerked forward, avoiding her contact. "Well, you're not my doctor anymore, you're gonna be my wife. I told you to let up on all that. You're makin' more stress here than it's worth. I'll be fine."

He got up from his drawing board, slid open the glass doors, and stepped out onto the terrace. Pacing back and forth, and craning his neck over the balcony, he mumbled, "Actually, you're right about it outside down there. All that dirty slush on the streets is pretty disgustin' to look at."

Alyssa had gone into the bedroom and didn't hear what he was saying, though she knew he was talking. Then she flashed back to her father lying in his hospital bed, dying from leukemia. He always tried to do the right thing for himself and for everyone else around him. She couldn't think of one thing he abused in life.

He was so pale and so frail as he lay there, yet even in that physical weakness, he asked, "Alyssa, you're a doctor. I never drank, I never smoked, I always ate well, watched my weight, exercised, and I tried to respect the Good Book. I never lied, and I always tried to be fair. I never cheated on your mother, and I loved you both with all of my heart. Why then, why me?"

She couldn't answer that question. "Why, Daddy, why?"

Back in the present, she realized the self-inflicted neglect Matthew dumped upon himself was unbearable. Yes, the writing was on the wall, and she was frightened by it. She compared her father and her childhood to his. Southern people seemed to eat so carelessly as compared to the Mediterranean lifestyle she had known. She imagined the insides of his arteries clogged, though his cholesterol, happily, had never really been high.

"I just need to get this phase of the project completed and then we'll take a few days, OK? Let's go to Vittorio's tonight for dinner." He entered the bedroom and moved toward her. "I love you, you know that."

Flashing back to her father again, she threw her arms out in front of her, blocking his advances. "I know. It's all right. I understand a lot more than you realize."

That evening they caught a cab across town to Matt's favorite restaurant where the finest Italian cuisine was prepared. Alyssa tried to cheer him up in the cab, but when she playfully reached for him, he pushed her hand away.

"I just don't want to be touched right now, I'm sorry." He snapped at her, "Just let me chill for a few minutes." He glared out the window. "You need to learn to read my cue cards. It's called body language, Alyssa. Why don't you read my body language?"

A huge lump filled Alyssa's throat as her eyes welled up. "What's going on? Do you want me to go back to Florida? Your annoyance is pretty palpable, and I don't seem to be wanted here, which makes me want to leave and go home."

"Oh, don't be ridiculous."

"You know, Matt, you never even one time bothered to read my body language when you felt playful!"

"Alyssa, just stop it, OK?" He covered his face with his hands, and rubbed firmly as if washing his stress away with his palms. "Let's just have a quiet dinner and go home to hit the sack early, OK? I don't feel well tonight."

They sat quietly together in the restaurant, sipping wine and taking in the ambiance.

Alyssa watched Matt's face tighten as he chewed his food. He twisted in his chair, contorting his body, visibly struggling to get comfortable.

She leaned forward. "Are you feeling OK? You look pale, honey."

Matt answered her without much enthusiasm, "I'm just tired."

He had nothing else to say during dinner as he picked at his food and appeared more and more ashen.

"Matt, I'm worried about you," Alyssa sighed. "You really need to get some rest. Let's go home. I'm going to make an appointment to get you checked out tomorrow, and this time you're going."

She raised her arm to call for the waiter. "May we please have the bill?"

Matt sat quietly, not even resisting Alyssa's leadership.

"Thanks. I don't feel well, honey. I need to go outside and get some air. You don't mind if I leave you here to finish up and meet you outside?"

She stood to help him.

He got up by himself and made a beeline for the door. She watched him intently as she signed the check, grabbed her coat, and hurried after him. They left the restaurant, and stood outside for a few seconds.

"Alyssa, I need to walk for a while, and get some air." But, after a few steps in the cold, he leaned against the brick wall of the restaurant.

Sweat dripped from his forehead. "I'm dizzy, baby. I feel so weak. It's like I can't get enough air."

He was as white as a ghost as he grasped his chest. Alyssa

called out, "Please, someone help us." She struggled, trying to support his weight, as one of the waiters came out and helped her move him inside out of the cold.

She held onto him for dear life, "Please, call 911."

The paramedics arrived, and within seconds, a cardiac rhythm strip was run, an IV was started, and he was given medication to slow down the attack from progressing.

One of the paramedics turned to Alyssa, "Ma'am, it looks like he's having a heart attack. We need to get him movin' pretty quick here."

"Please, I'm a doctor. Let me ride with you." She jumped into the front of the ambulance with the driver and turned to the back as they slid his gurney in and secured it in place. The ambulance sped off with sirens and lights, forcing a parking lot of traffic to miraculously clear for them in the most noble way. The EMT working beside Matt in the back was a pretty young girl. She was starting a second IV site in his other arm, while watching the cardiac rhythm strip for any changes.

"You just rest easy, sir. You're doin' fine."

Her accent was transparent.

He lifted his mask from his face and gasped, "Are you Southern?"

"Yes."

"Where you from?"

"I'm from Mississippi."

"Good."

He tried to lift his arm, but he seemed too weak to follow through with his gesture of approval.

"Now please, sir, leave your oxygen on, and just relax. Don't talk right now, OK?"

He nodded while she helped him replace the mask over his face as the ambulance neared the emergency room driveway.

The ER staff was waiting for them, and Matthew was rushed inside to continue receiving life-saving care. Those familiar elephants were sitting heavily on his chest, now seeming to weigh more than they ever had in the past. He was moved briefly behind a curtain while the nurses drew blood, chest x-rays were taken at bedside, and Alyssa was asked questions about his insurance. She finished the financial information, moved near him, and gave them the welcomed medical information they needed about his past and his history of this present episode. The cardiologist entered the ER.

"Hello, Mr. Hunter, is it?"

Matt nodded, his painful distress too great to allow any apprehension or fear.

Alyssa stood close by. "I'm his fiancée and I am a physician. I can give you any pertinent information you need.

"Good. Would you mind stepping out from behind the curtain with me for a few seconds?"

The attending physician opened the curtain and signaled to Alyssa to join him.

They walked out of Matt's earshot before the physician spoke to Alyssa. "He's having a pretty substantial attack in the inferior wall, as you've seen on the monitor. I'd like to take him into the cath lab and see if we can open that vessel up. I don't know how much muscle we can save, but it's worth a try. When exactly did the actual pain begin?"

Alyssa retraced his behavior changes. "I think it's been about an hour and a half since he showed signs of pain. I can't be sure, but I think we're still in a pretty good window."

Moving toward the nurse's station, he signaled for one of the nurses to call the catheterization laboratory and get it ready. Shortly afterward, Matthew was moved from the emergency cubby to the hallway. He appeared calm, quiet, and his pain had been slowed with medication. He didn't speak with the oxygen mask over his face, though he turned his head and gazed at Alyssa walking beside him.

She knew he was afraid, but so was she.

"Don't worry, darling. You're going to be fine. I'm right here with you."

Her journey beside him ended at the end of the hall when the wide doors swung open and the medical team took him into the laboratory.

"I wish I could have just kissed him for reassurance," she whispered through fresh tears.

Alyssa sat in the family waiting room with her eyes closed, praying that she wasn't losing another love.

"It isn't fair. He's only in his early forties." She knew how his family history, his weight, his hypertension, and his drinking habits were all risk factors for his heart disease. This DeVinci project was too much stress for him, which only aggravated his mental, emotional, and physical frailties.

She didn't pester the staff for information; when they knew something either way, they'd let her know. Instead, she tried to block from her mind images of his heart muscle falling still, the cardiac monitor flatlining, the surgeon calling for the crash cart, and a cardiac arrest code going into progress. An hour passed without any word of Matthew's condition. She paced back and forth, trying to make sense of anything that was happening. Another hour passed, and a nurse came through the swinging door.

"Miss, I'm with Mr. Hunter. Are they almost finished? Is he OK?"

The nurse smiled sweetly. "Are you Mrs. Hunter?"

"Yes. I mean I will be, I'm his fiancée."

"The doctor will be out in a minute to talk with you. He's done well. He's a lucky man."

A few minutes later, the cardiologist came through the same swinging doors.

"Dr. Kippler?"

"Yes." She swallowed hard.

"He had a little damage to the inferior wall, and his left anterior descending artery was narrowed, but we were able to balloon it open. I did stent a diagonal vessel. He was lucky that it was closed off just shy of the bifurcation. We had a hard time placing it, but I think we'll be OK. We'll be moving him into the cardiac unit in a few minutes. As soon as they get him settled down, you can sit with him. It'll probably help him rest better if he sees you. That weight will need to stay on his groin throughout the night, and we don't want him to move."

Matthew lay in the Intensive Cardiac Care Unit, and Alyssa quietly sat beside him as he struggled with discomfort throughout the night. She watched the monitors and the IVs flowing in awful anticipation that something would go wrong, but it didn't. It seemed like yesterday that she'd watched him fight for his life in Menlo. Now she was that sweetheart she wished she had been back then.

Sitting close to the side of his bed, she leaned her head on the sheet and rested it there, touching his side. Tears streamed down her face as he reached for her hand, and his warm, manicured fingers slipped into hers.

"See? I told you I'd be OK."

Two days later she had made preparations for Matt to fly by private plane back to Florida. He insisted on returning to Charleston, not Dierdra II, not Menlo, and not Alyssa's home.

Alyssa called home healthcare for twenty-four-hour nurses to be with him for the next week. She stayed with him most of the time and joined his mother with the worry of his recovery. Alyssa knew very well that this was the beginning of a potentially difficult road. Matt's father had died at around Matt's age. The catheter results were not terrific. Matt had two clogged vessels. To make his condition worse, he was young to have a heart attack. She counted on this incident to help him stop his excessive drinking and personal neglect. He had become so thin, a far cry from the overweight hunk he was when they met. She would do anything to help him stay alive and improve his health. He was just so stubborn and impossible to budge.

Alyssa called Jean-Marc, who was still in France. She cried, "You're the only one I can talk to right now. I feel so desperate. I never needed you more than right now. Mother told me she called you and told you about Matt. I've made so many mistakes."

Jean-Marc made a gentle sound of sympathy. It encouraged her to further uncover her mental anguish.

"I blame myself because I knew what he was doing to himself. I tried to help him, but I was afraid to push him. Great doctor, huh?"

"Alyssa, do you want me to come home?"

Grief turned to dread. Not dread of Matt's future so much as dread of his behavior if Jean-Marc returned right now.

"No. It's better that I work through this with him alone. You know how jealous he is. You marked it from the beginning."

"I hope you handle that."

"I always seem to say or do the wrong thing."

She sighed through the phone, and somehow the simple action relieved a little of her sadness.

"I need to work on how to help him instead of getting in his way. He's been under so much stress. I'm afraid I'm not a very good partner for him. What good is a doctor if she can't even help her own family?"

Jean-Marc broke in, "I can't believe your lack of confidence. What's happening to your sense of self-worth, Alyssa?"

I'm just so depressed. I haven't felt this terrible for years. I don't know if I can handle it if he doesn't make it."

"Alyssa, stop that kind of talk. What's going on? You've helped more people in a day than most people help in a lifetime. I can't bear to hear you talk like that. What can I do to help you? You don't want me there, I'm no good to you here, so what can I do?"

"I don't know," she answered. "I just need to hear your voice for strength, but thank you for wanting to come. Matt wants to stay in Charleston with his mother for a while. I'll be going back and forth until he's well. He needs me now more than he ever did."

Chapter Twenty-One

*A*lyssa stepped behind the wheelchair, following the volunteer who was inching her beloved Matthew past the nursing station toward the elevator. She was tormented by the memory of how she'd felt when Matthew passed by the nursing station in Menlo, exuberant to have a second chance, and a new lease on life. She never then would have believed the scenario of today. That day she saw celebration for him, and she longed to be the one taking him home. Today was more like a funeral procession. Matt was frail and quiet, and she was sad and lonely. Today they were leaving the hospital together, no longer the sparkling taste of new and hopeful love, because Matthew had lost his effervescence, and his invincible creative spirit was gone.

After she helped him into the limo, she stepped back from the curb. A very attractive young lady bounced by the car, and Alyssa glanced at Matt through the window. She hoped to see some sign of his old healthy self, peering through the glass, checking out the swiveling hips and shapely legs. He didn't. She remembered herself passing his car and feeling his eyes burn through her like a magnifying glass on paper in the sunlight.

The car window opened. "Honey, can we go?" When she didn't immediately get in the car, Matt's grumpy impatience continued, "What's the holdup?"

"Please Matt, I was just getting my bearings for a

moment."

"Well, honey, please let's go. I got the willies, and I just wanna get out of this place."

He pushed the button and the window rolled up again.

DeVinci Cruises was put on hold, and everyone around Matt became a servant to His Highness. Even Antonio Capezzio called Matthew. "Matt, don't worry about anything. We're so close to the end here that it isn't a problem. All of the major designs are in, and the ship will, for sure, sail because of you. Get well, my good friend."

Matt hung up the phone. "Alyssa, wait till you hear this. The once vibrant lover, creator and inspiration of DeVinci Cruise Lines, is no longer needed."

Alyssa came running to the bedroom from the kitchen. "Darling, what do you mean? Antonio is worried about you. He isn't dumping you, he's worried."

Matt sank his back into his pillow. "I hate life, and I hate the ugly head of poor health and illness."

She wiped her hands on the dish towel she was carrying. "Matt, darling, tomorrow you're going to Charleston to be with your mother and Amy and Annie. You've got to pull out of this depression. It isn't you."

"Right. I'm goin' to South Carolina, and you're headed back to Florida. What am I supposed to do without you under my tree for Christmas?"

She grinned and moved in close to him. "I see a little spark comin' back, darlin'."

He looked up at her with those clear blue eyes that she loved so deeply. "Don't try to tempt me with Southern talk, 'cause I'm a poor, sick, dyin' man."

"Oh, Matthew James Hunter, you're about as dead as a dogwood in full bloom." Leaning over the bed, she touched her soft lips to his.

"I think I'm feeling a little life here."

"Honey, you're makin' fun a me."

"Oh, stop. I'm having some fun. I love you, Matthew Hunter."

Alyssa hadn't even opened her eyes, dawn was barely breaking in Menlo Beach, and the phone rang. She fumbled for the receiver, and groggily dragged it in front of her, looking at the caller ID. Resting it against her ear, she closed her eyes again.

"Matt?"

"It's me, all right. Alyssa, let's get married. We don't need a big weddin'. Let's do a small weddin' here in Charleston. I can call in the troops and have heaven built here in a day for the ceremony. I'll fly a bunch a designer gowns in from Italy, you can choose one, and we'll go for it. What do you say? I just want to be with you. I want to spend every second I have left with you. Oh, I forgot. Merry Christmas, baby."

"Merry Christmas. What time is it? It's still dark." She reached over and pulled the blinds open. "Oh, it's beautiful. There's a thin orange line separating the ocean from the sky. It's the crack of dawn."

"It's the crack of dawn, all right, and we're gettin' married immediately, OK?"

"Immediately?" She gasped, feeling as if she had just stepped out of a cold shower. "It's impossible. What about all of our plans?"

"The only plan I have is to be with you."

She groped for words. "I don't care about a big wedding. I just want to be with you, too. But Matt, we need to think of other people involved with our lives. Let's slow down just a tiny bit and let you get back to your old self first. I know you've had some serious health issues, but we're going to have a long and normal life together in spite of this setback."

Matthew snapped "You don't care about me. You only care about yourself and your lifestyle. I am sick now, don't you know that? What kind of doctor are you, anyway?"

He hung up the phone in his frenzy.

She dialed Charleston back, and he answered the phone.

She played it cool, knowing that he had hung up, but giving him another chance to redeem himself. "Matt, did we get disconnected?"

"No, I hung up on you. I think you need to go find someone else who is healthy like you are. Maybe you can go run with your good sweetie pie, Jean-Marc. Leave me alone. This was all stupid, anyway." He hung up again.

Alyssa, a physician, knew very well about Matthew's health problems. She also knew that he was becoming, and could remain, a cardiac cripple, which would destroy him faster than anything.

This time she didn't call him back. "He is so damaged," she told herself as tears rolled down the sides of her cheeks. She lay in bed and absorbed the spiritual strength from the brilliant colors bursting through the dawn and up into the sky.

The bedroom door opened. "Mommy, Santa came. Hurry." Lisa ran through the room and jumped on the bed. Alyssa reached over and grabbed her, holding her tightly. Lisa had been her life for several years before she had ever even heard of Matthew James Hunter. This was Lisa's morning.

"Well give me a Merry Christmas kiss first. Boy, do you smell good. Have you been into Mommy's perfume again?"

Lisa placed her neck against her mother's nose, and like a Parisian Lady she tilted her head back. "Grandmother sprayed me. She's downstairs waiting for you to get up. Come on, Mommy, all those presents are going to get moldy."

Dionna was in the living room with a great grin across her face, as she spotted her daughter and granddaughter at the bottom of the stairs.

"Merry Christmas."

Alyssa's silk robe untied. As she moved forward, she retied it, and then reached for the loving arms of her mother. "Merry Christmas, Mama."

One by one, Lisa opened her Christmas stash. A huge box sat conspicuously near the front door. In large letters, "Lisa" was written on the wrapping paper in gold glitter. She hadn't even noticed it while she handed out presents and opened her own.

"Here, Grandmother, this one is yours."

Dionna opened a tiny silver hand-tooled box, and in it was a diamond tennis bracelet, the beauty of which Alyssa had never seen in her life. An attached note read, "Merry Christmas, Dionna. These diamonds are clean and beautiful just like you. They have a good history, and they're not blood diamonds. I made sure of that. My love to you, Matt.

"Alyssa, look at this bracelet."

Alyssa beamed. "It's beautiful, like he said, just like you."

Lisa noticed the gift in the foyer and squealed, "Wow,

wow, wow, wow!"

Jumping up and down, she clapped her hands as she circled the huge box.

"This is for me."

It took no time to carelessly rip off the wrapping paper.

"A real live Barbie motorcycle!"

The real live Barbie motorcycle was a Barbie bike with a small electric scooter motor, the governor set to run a maximum of five miles per hour. There was a card with a button to push. Lisa pushed it and Matt's voice came on.

"Merry Christmas, darlin'. This is for you to ride around the driveway. Stay safe on it, and when you get really good at drivin' we can take it to Central Park. I love you, Matt."

She began jumping up and down again, "Mommy, could we take it outside and let me ride it?"

Alyssa helped clear away the wrappers, and she wheeled the bike toward the front.

Lisa turned the lock and pulled open the heavy wooden door. "Mommy!"

Alyssa turned the handlebars toward the porch and stopped in her tracks. "What is that?"

Parked in the driveway was a shiny, black Porsche. A giant red bow tied to the top had a long red streamer running down the front hood with, "Merry Christmas, Alyssa," written on it in gold glitter.

"I guess gold glitter is our thing today."

Matthew's gifts were the center of attention all morning. Lisa drove her new motorcycle until the battery needed to be recharged, and then Alyssa, Dionna, and Lisa drove along Ocean Boulevard in the Porsche with the top down. The rich new car smell, combined with new leather, was enhanced by the breeze moving through the seats as they cruised along the beach road. Dionna looked down at the diamonds sparkling on her wrist, turned one side of her mouth up and nodded her head in approval as she began running her other hand across the exquisitely lit dashboard.

"Alyssa, you hooked quite a guy."

Keeping her eyes on the road, Alyssa turned both sides of her mouth up for a second, then her face tightened.

"I really love him, Mama, but he's having a hard time with this heart thing. He's really not a very strong person in a lot of ways. I worry about losing him to something awful. I don't even want to say it, because I don't want it in the air. But he's not so stable as we all think."

Dionna grasped the back of her seat, helping herself twist her torso toward her daughter. "Honey, he wouldn't try to hurt himself, would he?"

Alyssa shook her head, "No, I don't mean that. It's like he loses personal control, and he says things he doesn't mean, and he does things he doesn't mean to do. I've got pretty good at reading him. He can't handle confrontation. Sometimes, it's just his confronting himself that's too much for him. There's a lot of childhood damage control he's weathering, and I'm not so sure he's got a handle on much of it."

"That's a mouthful of information, and I'm not sure I'm following you."

"That's OK, 'cause I'm still figuring it out. Anyway, it's a beautiful car. I just don't know if I can drive it very often. I've never wanted the image of wearing the profits from other people's sickness on my back. Could you imagine my driving up to the Hope for Harmony House in this?"

Dionna agreed. "Unfortunately, that's the reputation of most doctors. All doctors are rich."

"Well, that's not why I went into medicine."

Two days passed and there was no word from Matt. Alyssa decided to leave him alone and let him stew. Then Matthew called. He didn't mention their last conversation, or the presents, but he asked her to come to Charleston. He had just finished his first session with cardiac rehabilitation at the medical center, he was feeling better, and he wanted to talk about the wedding plans.

Most important were the words, "Honey, I love you."

Alyssa also said nothing about their last conversation. She understood his despair.

"Your Christmas presents were over the top, Matt."

"You guys are over the top," he answered.

Alyssa knew Matt was a handful. She often felt like she was taming a huge black stallion like Beauty. There were tough and rough places inside of him that she couldn't reach yet, but he was beginning to trust her and love her more than anything in the world. Something about that dark and wild side of horses excited her, though their unpredictable power and physical strength frightened her, too, quite like Matthew's.

She flew to Charleston the next day. Matt picked her up at the airport in a limousine. They sat in the usual romantic atmosphere on the way home, Matthew style. He handed her a champagne glass of the sparkling stuff.

"Now, don't get all high on this stuff, it's just Perrier."

Alyssa was so relieved to see his progress that she dropped her defenses. She had never known real love until she met him, she realized that now.

Clicking their glasses together, gulping their heavenly water, and losing the world around them, their lips met and melted together. Again they were glued to the universe of physical compatibility. They were lost in that magical kingdom of lust and love that shapes much of life's direction, both good and bad. Matt pulled his lips away from hers with a soft suction. He raised his arms and cupped her shoulder with tenderness.

"I love you. I was just thinkin' about your name. Alyssa Kippler-Hunter, MD."

Alyssa giggled. Matthew pulled her into his arms with one of his famous come-hither attacks. "Baby, I want you."

Alyssa admonished, "Matt, we'll make the best love we ever have made, but just wait a few weeks. You've really been sick. You'll be OK, but we need to give it a little more time."

Matt pulled away from her, and in a mimicking tone, he answered, "Yeah, yeah, yeah.

Just promise me that you'll be with me on New Year's Eve in Charleston."

That night Matthew was remarkably normal and friendly. Alyssa felt lassoed in for New Year's Eve. But she believed in his roots, and wanted to celebrate in Charleston, away from the rest of the world. She agreed.

Matthew had additional plans. "I want your mother and Lisa here. I want to marry you on New Year's Day."

Alyssa was convinced that weddings should have been created for Charleston, in Matthew's mother's house, on this New Year's day. A perfect ceremony was performed in the Hunter living room, which Matt had converted into a sacred garden chapel, studded with white roses, gardenias, and blooming dogwood trees glistening with tiny white lights winding through their delicate branches. Alyssa directed the floral displays to be placed, enormous orchids and white roses shipped in from different parts of the world. Violins played, champagne was passed, and the gourmet foods were endless. She wore a slinky pearl-studded gown and Matt wore a black tuxedo. Lisa wore a full, white Southern gown with a little pearl-studded tiara on her head, and Matt's locket around her neck, making her the most beautiful flower girl in the world. Matt insisted portraits be made of her after the wedding and said, "We're blowin' these up life-size."

The wedding was intimate with only immediate family invited, though Matt had personally called Jean-Marc, who arrived without hesitation.

Matthew's children even came for a very brief visit just to attend the wedding ceremony and greet everyone. He was so proud.

Grasping Alyssa by the arm, he turned her toward his three English memories.

"Alyssa, y'all must admit. They're like British royalty."

She clung to her new beloved husband. "And they all love you very much."

"Oh, baby. I hope so." Exhaling, he repeated almost as a whisper, "I hope so."

Changing his attention, he swirled his Perrier, grinned and gazed into his bride's eyes, and swooned at her while pursing his lips. "And, I love you more than anythin' in this world, Alyssa Kippler-Hunter. Ya know, I never thought I'd let my wife carry any name but mine. But that Kippler part doesn't even bother me. I guess it's because of the doctor thing."

Antonio Capezzio sent twenty cases of fine champagne as part of his wedding gift to the bride and groom. Alyssa wondered why all the champagne had arrived wrapped in bows right after Matt had a heart attack.

She felt the gift was a little thoughtless.

Matt expressed joy while verbalizing where they might store the new cases of delectable spirits that he had stopped drinking. Alyssa hoped he would notice her frown that she exaggerated just for him.

"We'll have the rest of our lives to slowly drink it," he laughed. "Lighten up, baby. It's our weddin' day."

On their first night as husband and wife, six weeks since Matt's heart attack, he was unable to achieve an erection. . Alyssa's assurance did nothing for his confidence. He knew he had a problem in the bedroom. He hoped it was just fear in combination with the medication he was obligated to take.

Her comforting him didn't help.

She annoyed him as her Pollyanna philosophy started, "I love you, Matthew Hunter. I don't care about anything except that you are alive and we are together."

Matthew retorted, "What's wrong with you? I can't even please my wife on our weddin' night. If you really loved me, you would need to have sex with me. You never really have loved me, have you? You have only loved medicine and Lisa. Don't you get it? Marriage is nothin' without sex, at least not for a man. If I didn't need intimacy, I'd just hang out with the guys. I don't know what your problem is. Are you sick or somethin'? You're not right. I don't want a wife who doesn't know about love."

He knew she would begin her lamentation, and she did. "A woman doesn't measure love by sex. Sex is wonderful with love, but love can be wonderful without sex. I would love you and care for you if you were a vegetable," she whimpered. "I love you and I need you. I don't care about anything except that you're alive. Besides," she continued, "We do have savior medications like Viagra. You can take it now that you're off the nitroglycerin. I'll call your cardiologist tomorrow."

"I don't want Viagra. I want myself back. I want to be the vibrant man, the lover, the excitin' male who picked you out of the crowd of thousands because you were the best. I want to tease you and please you so that you can have it all, because you deserve it. Can't you see that, baby?"

But in reality, he saw himself as a man who would probably die while making love. An orgasm could be his worst enemy. He was frightened to die, but he was even more frightened to live, because living with the love he had always required could be fatal.

The famous cliché, "cardiac cripple," was real. Matthew knew he had the disease.

Things got better when he passed his first cardiac stress test after the attack. His cardiologist gave him an encouraging bill of health, praise for his twenty-pound weight loss, and an excellent blood pressure reading.

He handed Matt a prescription for Cialis with a grin. "Don't spend this all in one place."

The next several months were eventful only for Matthew's personality changes and his several trips to New York, most of them with Alyssa by his side. He finally accepted the aid of antidepressants to help him pull out of the doldrums. He returned to his DeVinci project, and finished it with less dedication than he had before his health setback. Antonio tried to pressure him into continuing as a partner, but Matt wanted to retire. He still owed Antonio for a few things, and he refused the last paycheck draw of more than five hundred thousand dollars.

"Antonio Capezzio, I know money cannot buy things we do for each other for love and friendship. But I ask you, please, let's even the score. What more can I do, but give you part of this ship without cost?"

They hugged and patted each other on the back. Antonio playfully tweaked Matt's cheek with his thumb and index finger.

"Forget it, my brother. You're a good man. We're more than even."

"Antonio. Are you happy? I mean really happy, deep down inside?

Antonio's face flushed. "What kind of question is that? Of course I'm happy. I have everything."

Matt sought eye contact with his Italian counterpart. "Antonio. Are you happy?"

Antonio fidgeted. "What do you want me to say?"

Matt lowered his tone and froze his gaze. "I guess I want you to say no."

"OK, no."

"Me neither."

Antonio turned away, walked forward, and disappeared through the doorway.

Alyssa knew she could convince Matt to use an occasional Viagra or Cialis. In fact, they were incredible drugs. It wouldn't be difficult to make him realize that his sexuality, which had always been so great, could be as good as ever. He did have nasty periodic mood swings, which Alyssa tolerated in view of his health concerns, but the antidepressants he was taking helped. All in all, their marriage was a stable one. They moved from Alyssa's neighborhood near her mother and Jean-Marc and built a gated home about five miles away on the intra-coastal waterway, complete with a climate-controlled wine cellar. Dierdra II was anchored at their new two-hundred-foot dock, and she was easily seen from the palatial pillared living room. Alyssa made sure that the sunrises were unobstructed.

It was a Thursday night, Alyssa had a class at the Harmony House, and Lisa had a ballet class and needed to be dropped off at Dionna's. Alyssa was in a hurry, but Matt stopped her before she got out the door.

"Alyssa, please don't go tonight." His tone was desperate.

"I have to go. The Harmony House has several new ladies and my lecture is important tonight. Besides, they're delivering two new exam tables while I'm there. I need to open the clinic for the movers. I'm so sorry. I have to take Lisa to Mother's now."

Matthew grabbed Alyssa's arm. He held it tightly.

"Matt. You're hurting my arm. Please let go," Alyssa pleaded. "I'm going to Charleston with you tomorrow morning. Let me just go to my meeting in peace."

Matt glared at her. "There's always somethin' more important than me, isn't there? You make me sick with your stupid wasted efforts. You know what you are? You're a do-better. Do you know what that is? That is someone who will never get anywhere in life. Haven't you lost enough time and money with those women? Let 'em help themselves. Stay home with me tonight. Help me."

She emotionally distanced herself from his selfish display of the moment, realizing that he simply didn't understand a huge part of who and what she was as a human being. There were aspects of their individual needs that were combatively opposed.

He intensified the squeeze of her arm and he even twisted it. She felt the burning sensation of her flesh being strangled and twisted, and the blood being unnaturally driven in the wrong directions on each side of his steel hand. Her bones underneath his intense pressure screamed in agony as if their snapping in half was imminent.

"Stop. You're hurting me."

He continued, ignoring her plea, "Why can't we ever just do somethin' together and be like we used to be? I want it crazy between us like it used to be."

He squeezed her arm even tighter and he backed her against the wall. "Don't go," he repeated.

She was suddenly transformed into that tragic and pure, frightened and vulnerable animal of nature that was cornered away from a secure place. She felt panic and fear, and her first natural reaction would have been an attempt to pull away and run through the front door as fast as she could. Instead, some instinctual drive to fight back overtook her, whether it was because she was in disbelief or that underneath it all she trusted him, she wasn't sure.

"You've been drinking. I can smell it reeking from your pores. You stink, Matthew. What are you doing to yourself?" Then again focusing on the agony of her violated flesh, she pleaded, "Please, you're hurting me. Let go of my arm."

"You're no wife to me. Do you even have a clue what

love is? I don't think so. You're a disgustin' and lost female who got all caught up in the glory of your title, doctor. They don't know your neglect, but I do. I'm your husband, not your thirty-minute office visit."

"Matthew, let go of my arm," she pleaded. "You're hurting me."

She cried, but he didn't let go. "Matt, please stop. You're drunk, and my arm really hurts." She was so caught up in that horrific moment of terror, that she shoved to the back of her mind the vision of her little girl, who was innocently sitting in the car, possibly hearing the violence inside the house.

Matt let go of her and he spun her around and away from him. "So what if I am? Do you care? Who cares about Matt Hunter? My kids haven't even called me for a month. You always have somewhere to go without me. So, I opened a couple of bottles of Antonio's weddin' present to us. If you had any romance left in you, you'd have a glass with me. Don't you remember the good times we had? What do I have to do to make you treat me fairly?"

As she inched toward the front door, she was filled with repugnance for what he had done. "You need help. You were spared your life and all you have to show for it is self-pity. You're alive and you're whole. Doesn't that mean anything to you? Do something. You didn't need to retire from life, you know. You can't depend on me for everything you need."

"How do you know what I need? You don't really even know me," he answered in a low voice as he gazed at the floor in surrender.

She retaliated, "I'm beginning to think you're right. Whatever you need, maybe you should look for it without me. Nothing I do is right in your mind."

He changed his demeanor to sweetness, and she watched him deviously twisting what had just happened into something trivial and misconstrued. He bracketed his cheeks with his hands, and opened his mouth in dismay. "Now look what we've done. This is silly."

Alyssa saw nothing silly in what he'd done. "Matt, don't ever grab me like that again. You don't have a right. You don't have a right to call me names and degrade me. I have to go."

She rubbed her reddened and swelling arm as she left the house. She hoped Lisa had missed it all as she was in the car waiting. Alyssa got in the car and drove away from the house.

Lisa's pleading eyes burned through her mother. "Mommy, what's wrong? Why were you guys yelling?"

Motherly instinct to protect her young drove dishonesty through her already broken spirit.

"Honey, I'm OK. Matt and Mommy are just having a misunderstanding tonight. Don't worry." Alyssa slipped her hand in Lisa's. "We'll always be OK. Matthew is the only daddy you've ever known. I know you love him very much."

Lisa returned her mother's hand squeeze. "Mommy, Jean-Marc is someone I love like a daddy, too. But I love you most of everyone."

She had not accepted that Matthew was her father, and she never called him Daddy.

Alyssa's cell phone rang. She answered it, "Hello, Matt."

He slurred, "Alyssa, come home. I've had enough. You

come home, now. Do you hear me? If you don't come home, I'll be gone when you get back. You can forget Charleston, too. I'll cancel our tickets. You don't deserve to go."

Alyssa knew Matt was bluffing. He might do a lot of crazy things, but he would never disappoint his mother. No matter what else could happen, he would be sure to pretend to her that everything was just perfect. He always made himself look good in front of his family, and he wasn't above lying in order to do just that. Alyssa began to question the theory that a great stable son makes a great stable husband.

"Matt, I can't talk to you right now. I'm taking Lisa to Mother's. I'll talk to you when I get home tonight." She clicked the cell cover closed.

Her arriving at the Harmony house as she had done for many months every other Thursday was a well-established routine. The night-blooming jasmine was radiant with a sensuous charisma that could only be captured by the summer's warm night air. Alyssa put herself together quickly as she entered the house. She felt lost in her position of coach and support person who was supposed to help women climb out of their pain. She needed to climb out of her own pain.

She had just endured an incredible experience that couldn't have been real. She needed to hide her emotions from the group. Her purpose was to help them. She would work out her own problems at home later. Besides, Matthew was different from the men discussed in these classes. He was a very complex person who had tremendous confusion because of bad luck with physical health. There was no way she would disclose her family problems to an environment that was reaching out to her for strength.

Alyssa needed someone to talk with and to confide in, but she was the professional. She couldn't be the one in need.

No matter what happened, she would be strong and figure out the way to handle Matthew's abuse on her own.

As she entered the front door, Denise greeted her. Alyssa made sure to appear cheerful and just fine.

Denise was a little blurry eyed, and announced that she was pregnant. That news guaranteed that Alyssa wouldn't reach out for help right then. How incredible to be in that phase of love. Denise was in full bloom with excitement. Her example of sweet and clean love was a healing influence on the ladies. Just because they had suffered abuse was not a statement about all love. She had a good husband who was a gentle man.

After the meeting, Alyssa left the Harmony House and drove along the ocean on the way home. She passed the beach where she and Matthew had spent part of their first date but felt nothing special about that spot. She didn't pay attention to the stars or the moon and there was no excitement in her heart. She hadn't called Matt and wasn't emotionally equipped to face her own marital despair that night. Lisa had wanted to have dinner at the Ocean Café and then spend the night with her grandmother since Alyssa and Matt were planning to leave for Charleston in the morning. Alyssa decided to stop by for a minute and join them for a quick salad if they were still there. She hurried into the restaurant and spotted her daughter reviewing the bill, obviously being taught how to figure it out by Jean-Marc, and Dionna was taking her last sip of decaf coffee.

"Hey, guys," Alyssa bubbled. "I just wanted to kiss you all good night before I go to Charleston. Matt is home resting before we leave in the morning."

Alyssa was becoming adept at hiding her problems from everyone.

"They wouldn't understand," she told herself.

Jean-Marc saw something in Alyssa's demeanor that bothered him. He scanned her totally within a second. "So, my little angel, what is wrong? Come outside with me for a few minutes."

Alyssa walked outside toward the ocean with Jean-Marc. "Matt is drinking again. I'm so afraid. He's just not right. I'm so scared for him. He needs to watch his health better or I'll lose him."

Jean-Marc answered her with a steady voice, "He needs to watch over you, or we'll all lose you. Be careful, Alyssa. You can't save him, he has to save himself. I worry about you a lot. He needs to go to AA or something."

That would never happen. "Matt would never let the world know he had a weakness like that. He won't even admit it to himself and he thinks everyone else is the problem. It would take more than a miracle to change things. I thought the heart attack would change things, and wake him up, but it didn't."

Jean-Marc reached for her hand and drew it to his lips, courting love with French finesse, then gently placing it once again at her side. "Alyssa, I love you. Do you know what love is? It is a form of caring about another person with no finite boundaries. It is like a sunrise that appears and then disappears for a while. But then it appears again in the form of a sunset. It's the beginning and the end of the day with everything in between. Even when the end of the Earth comes, my love for you will not end, it will only change form. You are my family. Remember when we were kids that summer in France?"

Alyssa stopped short in the sand. "Jean-Marc, you are

incredible."

"Alyssa, come to me anytime you're afraid. I am here for you. Don't be a fool for him. He could get crazy enough to hurt you or even kill you. You teach this stuff to other people, so why should I preach it to you? I am worried about you. Promise you won't stay near him if he starts to act violent."

"Of course I would leave at the first sign of danger. Jean-Marc, I would never put Lisa or myself in harm's way."

"Just go home to your house next door to me and yell out of your dining room glass. I will hear you," he laughed.

He always needed a joke to lighten up any serious moment. They walked inside and Alyssa kissed her little girl and her mother good night. She turned to Jean-Marc and hugged him tightly.

"Thank you," she whispered in his ear. "I'll see you in three days. Matt and I will call you in the morning," she said to Lisa.

She seemed reluctant to walk away, which Jean-Marc had not seen since they were teenagers one summer in France. They had promised that they would never love anyone else except each other. It was at the airport and Alyssa was thirteen. Jean-Marc was almost fifteen. She followed her parents to the plane and never stopped watching Jean-Marc until he was gone from view. Two years went by before they saw each other again. Their childhood romance had died. They became fast friends, almost family. They had never made reference to that summer again until tonight.

Jean-Marc sat back down at the table. "Dionna, is everything going OK with Alyssa and Matt? I worry about her."

Dionna gazed toward the exit. "I worry about her, too,

but they seem fine. Matt's been through so much since his heart attack. I think he needed to slow down, but he was too young to give up all that fame and fortune. I just think he's too young to retire. I know he has heart problems, but I think he'll get worse if he isn't constructive. He spends a lot of time doing nothing and I think it's driving him crazy. He needs to have an outlet to channel his creativity."

Jean-Marc took his girls home. Lisa wanted to sleep in her house next door in her old bedroom. Dionna agreed, and they did just that, together.

The next morning Jean-Marc came over and served breakfast for them in the glass dining room.

Lisa spoke up, "I miss it the way it used to be. I want us to be together again. I don't want Matthew to be my daddy. Uncle Marc, I just want you to be my daddy. Mommy is sad right now and I'm sad, too."

Lisa put her little hands over her face and cried like a baby. She was only seven years old. In a way, she was a baby.

Jean-Marc quickly grabbed her into his arms. "My little princess, I wish I could be your daddy, but I am not. I am your friend, I am your Uncle Marc, and that makes me kind of like your daddy. I love you."

"Uncle Marc," Lisa whimpered in his ear, "I love Matthew. I love Mommy. I love Grandmother. I love you, but I don't feel like I like anything right now."

She grasped him around the neck until she wilted, lying in his arms.

Jean-Marc took advantage of his rare opportunity to be with Lisa under such tender and heart-wrenching moments.

"Lisa, let's play hooky from school just this one time. I want to go to Sea World and touch the dolphins today. What do you say?"

"I guess that would be nice. Maybe we should ask Mommy and Matt, 'cause Matt doesn't ever want me to stay out of school."

Gently stroking her hair with his fingers, he answered, "No. We'll just go and not ask anyone. Mommy would say we could do it."

"OK, but right now I just want to hug you."

His thoughts were confused because he had become so involved with Alyssa, Lisa and Dionna. He wanted to return to France to be with his parents. He saw himself just getting older and awaiting crumbs from the leftovers of a family that should really be his and not Matthew's. He would never, ever do anything to make their life wrong. But he did cherish the friendship even without the sexual bonding and the babies he would like to create. He respected this little girl's mommy so much that he blocked his eyes from even scanning her figure or noticing her sexuality. He had never approved of, nor did he like Matthew. He tried to be fair with his criticism. He realized he was jealous. He fought his demons to overcome the sense of unfairness. His true love for Alyssa just wanted things to be right.

Jean-Marc cradled the little girl in his arms and smelled the sweet scent of shampoo in her hair as he held her, while his protective fatherly instinct roared within his chest. He felt unsettled as to the safety of this dear little girl and her mother.

Chapter Twenty-Two

$\mathcal{M}$att's family and Charleston, with bated breath, awaited the touchdown of Delta flight 4055 from Orlando.

"Honey," he kidded as they stepped off the plane, "Don't go buyin' everythin' you see. One house, that's all we need. I'm not workin' anymore."

Amy and Annie stood by the baggage claim, Annie swaying back and forth, anxiously awaiting the view of her aunt and uncle.

"Auntie Alyssa, Uncle Matt, I love you!" Spotting them as they turned the corner toward the baggage claim, she made a running beeline for them, arms stretched out like a quarterback's.

"I can't see Lisa," she pouted.

Alyssa reached for Annie's arms with one side of her body facing the other way, guarding her painful injury. "She couldn't come. She'll come next time because she loves you."

A big smile and a big hug were combined with a happy answer, "I love her, too."

Matt bear hugged Annie, "Hey. Where's my hug? Annie, how is Mommy?" He looked ahead at his sister coming toward him smiling, though much more reserved than her daughter.

"Mommy has a boyfriend."

Matt did a nervous double-take, "What?"

Amy laughed, and playfully grabbed the back of Annie's neck. "No, no. Mother's gardener came in the kitchen and sat with us for sweet tea this morning. No boyfriend, please. Last week I loved the mailman, and before that it was the bagboy at the supermarket."

"Uh-huh. Mama's got a boyfriend, Mama's got a boyfriend." Annie sang her tune with increasing volume until several people began staring.

"Annie, hush. Stop that right now. Mama does not have a boyfriend."

Matt slid his hand behind his sister's neck, and rubbed it. "Amy, let up a little. She doesn't mean any harm."

"She needs to learn some self control, and she needs to behave in public."

Amy's stern mannerism was unusual.

Alyssa nodded. "I agree with Amy. Besides, Amy, I like to see your spunk coming back."

Matt let go of Amy and reached for his niece. "Annie, gimme your hand. You and your Uncle Matt will sing together. Come on, Annie, sing with me. Mama's got a boyfriend, Mama's got a boyfriend." Annie, oblivious to all that was just said, joined her uncle skipping along and singing their new song all the way to the car.

Amy and Alyssa followed behind, smiling at the ridiculous music.

Then Amy sighed. "Annie got her period. It's really hard for me, because everything in her mind is about boyfriends. I've kept her away from school and other kids for so long now, I'm afraid to send her back. She really needs a normal social interaction, but I've broken that pattern for her since her father died. I'm afraid it's probably set her back. I've robbed her."

Alyssa couldn't imagine a sweeter or more supportive environment for Annie than the one Amy struggled so lovingly to provide. Craning her neck around to the front of Amy, she shook her head in disapproval. "You never robbed anyone in your life. Annie has it better than most children in this entire country. But you're right that socialization is important now that she's reached puberty. There's no reason in the world that she shouldn't feel all the natural feelings anyone else feels."

"I know that, I just worry about her because she's so innocent."

"Maybe I can help you pick out a good, safe school while we're here."

"Well. It's not like we have a Down Syndrome City in Charleston, but we have a few programs that might be OK. I work really hard with her at home, and I just want her to go to school part-time. I can't bear to be away from her for long. She's my rock."

When they were alone, Matt finally addressed the issue she suspected was first and foremost in his mind.

"You've been pamperin' that arm a lot. I want to see what hurts so much. You know I'd never intentionally hurt you." Alyssa allowed Matthew to reach down, moving her sleeve up her arm. She didn't resist his efforts, but she guarded him from touching her tender injury.

"I know that," she answered, "But sometimes you get so angry that you really frighten me. Matt, I spend a lot of time helping women so they'll stop getting hurt and I have an injury on my arm. You did this to me."

Looking down at her arm with disappointment, she carefully pulled up her sleeve, exposing an almost completely purple forearm.

"Alyssa, I love you. I worship you. Oh, no," he moaned as he gently lifted up her sleeve even higher, completely exposing her hideous injury.

His face tightened the way it had when they saw Amy's injuries that night on the hayride.

He slumped. "I feel so worthless. I have nothin' left to offer the world except fertilizer." He closed his eyes, and tears fell down his cheeks.

Alyssa felt his pain and died a little death with him. "Don't say such a terrible thing. Matt, I love you. We'll work it out. I know it was an accident. Please don't cry. Baby, I love you. I'm sorry."

"You're sorry? Look what I did to you. How am I supposed to live with myself? I don't believe in this stuff. My father did this to me and my sister and my mother all my growin'-up years. What? Am I cursed to be like him all over again? I'm goin' for a walk." He left the quarters, silently closing the screen door behind him.

"Matt, wait."

He didn't answer, but kept walking toward the water.

The great ace Alyssa held in her pocket was that she was a medical doctor. She knew psychiatry and psychotropic drugs, and with medications at her beck and call, there was hope. Matthew definitely would refuse psychiatric help, but maybe he would accept medical treatment because he saw with his own eyes how badly he had hurt her. Most women who had problems with men in pain didn't have the magic ingredients it took to help. Matthew had so much loss with his heart attack, and it was easy to understand why everyone around him needed to be a little flexible with regard to his behavior. She understood that, and she was committed to make life easier for him. Somehow, his illness made her love him more. Part of him was like a helpless child, and she wanted to mother that part in order to make it grow up and heal.

While Mother Hunter and Annie prepared a great barbeque and cooked fish in the fryer, Amy sauntered down to the bank and sat alone on the grass to watch the ripples on the water caused by the gentle breeze skating across its surface. Alyssa had seemed withdrawn earlier, and Amy hadn't been sure how to approach her.

Matt sprang up behind her. "Sis, can I join you?"

Turning around to welcome him, she invited him into the intense conversation she'd been holding in her mind. "When we were kids, I used to sit here and play a game counting the ripples in the water. Each ripple I counted was one less day I had live with his abuse. It was awful, you know that?"

"I know." He sat beside her and gazed across the water. "And I used to sit here dreamin' of goin' far away across that water and never comin' back. I just couldn't figure out how I would do it, 'cause I didn't want to leave you and Mama here alone with that monster."

He wrapped his arms around his legs and rested his chin on his knees. "Sometimes I think I'm like him. It's like, when he died, he jumped inside of me so his evil could continue. Amy, am I like him?"

She leaned into her brother, knocking him gently with her

side. "Not at all. You're such a wonderful man. Mother would never have had this home if you hadn't bought it. Nobody else can live like this and look at Fort Sumter while they swing on the porch. I've been staying in the slave quarters off and on since we got here. Annie loves being out there. It's hard to remember growing up in that building, because you did a great job changing everything and erasing the past from those walls."

Matt lay back on the grass. "Well, yeah. I had most of the walls knocked out, and added on the new bathroom and Jacuzzi." Turning his head, he faced the old weeping willow. "Boy, that tree got big. I'm surprised it lived with all those switches Mother broke off."

They burst out laughing thinking about their mother chasing them with a willow branch when they'd been bad.

Matt turned back around and faced her, the laugh lines fading from his face. "I just couldn't leave anythin' in that house like it was with all those memories. Amy, I know what Daddy did to you. I used to hear you cry in your bed at night after he hurt you. I hated him. I never told anyone, but before he died, he was sittin' on a chair outside. I came home from school, and he told me to get the soda pills. I thought he had indigestion or somethin'. I told him to get 'em himself. I walked past him feelin' hate, and I didn't help him. He was havin' a heart attack, not indigestion. Maybe I killed him. I've always felt responsible, but I never regretted it."

Amy reached down and plucked a piece of grass out of the ground. Matt sat back up and gazed forward. "History was forgiven in a small way, because we've all helped the dignity of the present heal the disgrace of the past."

With the grass blade hanging out the side of her mouth. Amy asked, "I bet you tell Alyssa all kinds of interesting stories about our childhood, don't you?"

Matt squinted at her. "When did you start readin' people's minds? I like it. Seriously, Amy. I only did for my family what you would have done if you could have done it. Come on, let's go back to the house."

"Yes. I need to check on Annie."

He helped her up and they could see their mother watching them from her rocking chair on the porch.

"Matt, it sure is nice out tonight."

"It sure is, Mother. Where's Alyssa and Annie? I'm gettin' hungry."

Just then, Alyssa appeared from around the building with Annie, who yelled to everyone, "Come, look at the flying fairies!" Her eternal innocence was a reminder to everyone of what they wished they could be.

The night was alive with fireflies lighting the garden.

Matt held Alyssa that night, gently protecting her bruised limb, kissing it with soft tender lips in order to cause her no discomfort. But she knew Matthew had problems beyond "I love you," and beyond "I'm sorry." He was unstable and uncontrollable. Maybe his seeing the bruises on her arm was the eye-opener for him, the catalyst that would force him to address his deeper problems and agree to get psychiatric help. She thought about his dangerous and uncalled-for anger and temper surges, and yet he was a man who understood love like nobody she had ever known.

"Matt, who ever taught you how to love a woman like that?" Alyssa whispered later as she wrapped her naked body around him and lay her head on his bare chest. This was what true bonding meant between two people.

Lying on his back, he tucked his arm behind her neck and lovingly ran his fingers through her sweat-moistened, hair. "Baby, I never knew what making love was until I met you." Matt breathed slowly, rhythmically, and fell asleep.

A good weekend ended, and as Alyssa hugged Amy good-bye, she remembered her intention when they first arrived.

"Amy, I feel terrible. We didn't do anything about Annie's school this weekend."

Amy linked her arm through her mother's. "Then come back next weekend, and we'll do it all then. Bring Lisa."

Annie mimicked her mother, "Bring Lisa."

Nobody had noticed Alyssa's huge bruise, as she'd carefully covered it up throughout the weekend. There would be a time to communicate further with Matt about his behavior. But they'd had such a great weekend, she wanted to take that energy home. Maybe something was really changing with him for the better. That unforgettable hunk she first met in her office had returned when they were in Charleston, and hopefully he would go home with her to Florida.

Matthew was renewed. He spent a couple of days relaxing in the home he had so meticulously built for Alyssa, and he called the cleaning crew for Dierdra II. His enthusiasm was at an all-time high, and he decided to surprise his wife and daughter with something different, something they had never done before, in a place where they had never been. He thumbed through a travel magazine he'd just received in the mail, and read an article, "Heaven in the Caymans." It looked enticing.

"That's it, maybe I'll surprise them with a trip to the

Grand Caymans for a couple of days next week."

Alyssa had just dropped Lisa off at the ballet studio, and she came home to talk to Matt in private about an idea she'd had. She was a little nervous; Matt had become so exclusive.

She spoke first, "Matt, I want to take Lisa out of school next week and go to Europe with Mother. Lisa's teachers said she can take a culture leave as long as she brings pictures and information home for the class about where she's been. Mother wants to visit the DeBussys, and I'd love to shop in Paris for a couple of days. Let's get away to Europe. We've never been to Europe together. Please, darling?"

Matt withdrew. "Next week? We don't need to go to France right now. I don't want to go. Besides, what if I have somethin' else planned?"

Alyssa said nothing. Her excitement deflated, she moved to the bathroom and turned on the bath, unzipped her dress, and let it fall to the floor.

Matthew followed her to the bedroom. "Turn off that bath for a minute," he demanded. "We need to talk. What's so important about France, anyway? Maybe what you really want is to go see your lousy French boyfriend, Jean-Marc."

Alyssa rolled her eyes and dipped her toes into the warm water. Matthew went to the tub and turned the water off in defiance. His face twisted in anger, and her heart raced.

He grabbed her and dragged her from the bathroom into their bedroom, where he backed her onto the bed. In a frenzy he pressed her down with his full weight and savaged her mouth with his. "Alyssa, do you have any idea of what total love is?" She strained against his arms, but he held her tightly. "You need to get a grip on the meanin' of marriage and bondin'. I'm your husband. I'm supposed to be the most important person in your life. You don't know anythin' about marriage and bondin'." He wrapped her hair around his fist, securing her head back on the pillow. "I've had better in the past."

The foul odor of whiskey flowed over her face. Alyssa gasped for air. "Matthew, you've been drinking again. Drinking isn't your reason for anger and abuse. Drinking is your excuse to be mean and not take the responsibility for it. Matthew, what is the matter?"

Matthew glared at her. "It's not about drinkin', Alyssa, it's about you. You just don't get it. You make me sick with your prissy little attitude."

He got up from the bed and left her crying on her pillow. "What is going on?" She wept. "I can't keep living on this roller coaster."

Matt slammed the door behind him. He walked to the water and gazed up to the stars. It was time he took Dierdra II out to the open seas and got away from this life, which was wrong for him. He walked up the gangplank, deciding to call his crew, but instead he flopped down on a couch.

Matthew passed out. He didn't leave the room for two days, and he didn't speak to Alyssa or anyone else.

He drank, though.

She knew that this time, like most of the other times, she had done nothing to provoke his exaggerated craziness. "I know he loves me, but I can't take it much longer. What's wrong with me? I'm abused and I can't let go. Why do I want him so much?" She thought of the Harmony House. "Oh, how could I ever face any of them again unless I do for myself exactly what I expect them to do for themselves."

Alyssa decided to board Dierdra II and talk to Matthew.

After all, he was ill and she wasn't. She could be big enough to be the one to go that extra mile and open communication. Maybe they should split up for a while. She could move back to her house while they sorted things out. Alyssa took a shower and washed her hair. She felt cleansed of pain as the water flowed over her face as if to wash dried tears from her cheeks. Determined to do the right thing for herself—and for Lisa—she dried off and slipped into a sundress.

The boat's master bedroom door was unlocked, and she found Matthew sitting alone in his hot tub. The curtains were drawn shut, and the stars were out in his fabricated night sky overhead. He was having a grand time, and didn't seem to be suffering at all. As she stood over the tub, he looked up.

"Hey, baby. Come in here with me," He spoke in that soft, low voice that was so sexy. "The water's great."

"Matthew, we need to talk."

"I agree with you. We need to talk. This whole thing is crazy. How can two people be so good together, yet they can't mix? Honey, do you want to split up for a while?"

Though she'd been about to suggest the same thing, his suggestion inexplicably hurt. "It might be a good idea. This isn't any fun."

He flexed his chest out of the water and commanded, "Get in here, and let's sort it out."

She slipped off her clothes and joined him. He rolled over onto her, raising the water over his back like a blanket, and she knew he was driven by passion. "I need you, baby."

Their mutual desire raged, and each one sought the other.

As they made love, Alyssa was torn between her natural desire to be with Matthew, the love of her life, and the professional reaction she would have if the relationship were one she learned of in the Harmony House. As he swallowed her with sensual pleasure, she found it difficult to assess her own motives.

Her first mistake was that she allowed him to woo her sexually when her purpose for even going to Dierdra II was to meet him on the grounds of separation. Why then did she shower before going to the dock, if she had no sexual intentions of her own? Neither one addressed the subject of wrongdoing that day. The worst tragedy was that Matthew obviously forgave himself totally. He didn't even mention his two-day disappearance. He must have felt entitled. "He really needs help," she told herself. Deep down, she knew her own behavior was becoming just a little pathologic.

She suddenly became nauseated and got out of the water, hurrying to the bathroom.

Matthew called after her. "Honey, are you OK? Did I hurt you? I would never be rough with you. Oh, baby. I love you."

Alyssa had been having light-headed moments for the last week. She had attributed it to nerves and stress. But maybe her troubled marriage wasn't all that was affecting her.

"Matt . . . I wonder if I could be pregnant. I'm late for my period and I feel so tired and lousy." she confessed.

Chapter Twenty-Three

*A*lyssa was pregnant. Her plans to separate from Matthew were dropped, and replaced during the next few months with serenity. Everyone paid extra tribute to Alyssa, thirty-five years old, pregnant, and borderline high risk because of her age. Amniocentesis and genetic testing indicated the baby would be normal and healthy, and a little girl was due in February. A nursery was created in one of the bedrooms near the couple in waiting, and a section of their own bedroom was dressed in a delicate pink-canopied crib. Lisa was ecstatic. Dionna spent her time buying gifts and knitting, even though they were in sunny, hot Florida. Matt and Alyssa walked on air and there was no sign of any past problems.

This was not a time for the Cayman Islands or French visits. This was a time for intimate family members at home. France was no longer an issue, and Matt felt neither threats nor jealousy. He had his three girls in his pocket. One was his wife, who obviously adored him; one was his little adopted girl; and the other was tucked away in a warm, healthy, and safe womb, awaiting the excitement of her first breath on Earth.

Matthew was probably the most excited of all. His expectations of the future were optimistic. This time he was getting it right. The heart attack thing was gone.

He often looked at his nude body in front of the mirror,

asking Alyssa with a grin, "Honey, y'all think I've become a lean, mean, sex machine?"

She always responded with something cute, like, "I'll lean, mean, sex machine you, if you don't behave."

Alyssa had taught Matt to eat right, and his blood pressure was in perfect control without medication. He was happy to have stopped working, and he was behaving very well. That tremendous stress had put him on the map, but it had also taken its toll. He would never really be the young invincible man he had been in the past. However, he finally had achieved the love of his life, and God — or fate — had even granted him another child. For the first time in his life he had time to watch football and do what he wanted to do with his days. He wanted to relax, and be a husband, and a father to his new baby and Lisa.

Lisa, who was almost eight, could hardly wait for her new baby sister to arrive. Alyssa and Matthew even put a little crib in her room with her favorite doll in it.

The summer months were quiet. With his approval, Dionna and Lisa went to France for two weeks. Alyssa and Matt flew to Charleston to see his family.

Surely, the Hunter clan had come to accept and even love Alyssa and Lisa. The new baby would bond the Hunters with them forever.

Matthew did some simple consulting work, but he avoided the stress of deadlines and megadeals, which he believed were the cause of his heart attack and most of his other problems with Alyssa. These were times of hope and new beginnings. He reflected on all that had happened, including his separation from Capezzio, who was so grateful for Matt's work on the project that he released the contract before

Matt crossed the actual finish line. Matt's relinquishing five hundred thousand dollars also helped to buy his pardon.

"Funny," Matt mused, "Now he thinks he owes me."

Lisa's eighth birthday was coming up, and Matt wanted to be in charge of the surprise party. He decided to do it all on Dierdra II.

"Honey," he reassured Alyssa, "I've got it handled. You rest and take care of our baby. I've already ordered the cake and ice cream, balloons, piñatas, and all kinds of stuff. We'll go about five miles out, and we'll have an ocean birthday bash. Hey. This'll be Lisa's last birthday as an only child, and I ordered eight hundred colorful helium balloons to release at the end of the party. How's that for a grand finale?"

"Now, that's a grand finale, and she won't ever forget it. I appreciate all you're doing, because these nausea and vomiting surges are so bad, and I couldn't do any of it right now. I think my pregnancy with Lisa was easier. Maybe it's my age."

Matthew gave her every bit of support and care she needed, even breakfast in bed, that is, when she could hold breakfast down. He quietly lay beside her, night after night, with his hand on her abdomen, touching it with his lips and talking to his unborn daughter, "How's Daddy's little angel in there, huh? You be a good little girl, and you'll come out real soon, OK? Night, night."

Then reaching for his wife, and cradling her head in his neck, he whispered, "Baby, I've never been happier in my life. You are my life, little one."

He was a perfect husband, a perfect father, and a perfectly sensitive human being who understood the needs of those around him, and he took pride in his ability to accommodate.

The birthday bash was going to be great. Matthew and Dionna had a ball together laughing in silliness while inviting all the children with their parents for a day of celebration at sea. Thirty-two children, with mostly their mothers, arrived in swimsuits with presents in their arms. The crew helped everyone load onto the ship and get settled before they lifted the anchor. Alyssa was able to trudge up the gangway with the help of Phenergan, an anti-nausea medicine he kept on board.

After the cake and ice cream were served, Matt sought out Alyssa sitting by the pool, dangling her swollen feet in the water.

"I'm gettin' really stressed, honey. The crew isn't controllin' the kids, and the parents are treatin' this like it's their personal vacation or somethin'. They forgot their own kids." He shook his head is dismay.

Alyssa grinned, "Well, it is a fun day. Isn't that what you planned?" It was clear she hadn't bothered to understand what he was going through.

"Yeah, but they're all slippin' and slidin' on the decks. I filled the pool for swimmin', not just splashin'. Everythin's a mess. Honey, I'm goin' crazy here. Maybe this was a bad idea. You got to help me here." His voice was getting louder.

"Shhh. Someone will hear you. Try not to get any more worked up, OK? Why don't you go inside for a while where you can be quiet and alone. Then maybe you'll feel better about everything. I'll try to help settle things down out here, OK?"

He entered the master bedroom and dropped onto the bed like a punished child.

"This was a bad, bad idea."

Alyssa went on deck to do her best, but it wasn't good enough.

Matt could still hear the loud squeals of the army outside, and he ended up in the living room pouring himself a glass of Capezzio's champagne and periodically checking out the window to see whether the children were being brought under control. Alyssa continued calming the waters outside, while Matt hid inside, drinking, during the last hour of the cruise. Dionna scurried around picking up what seemed like hundreds of towels missed by the crew, and nobody had any idea that stress was brewing behind the scenes.

Matt was melancholy after a couple of glasses of champagne. "I put a lot into this thing, and no Hunters were here to cheer me on. Annie would have made a big difference."

He moaned, "Why couldn't any Hunter have come to the party?" Then he reminded himself that Lisa was a Hunter, because he had adopted her, which meant he was the proud father of four and a half children. That felt a little better.

As if to confirm his commitment, Lisa opened the door to the living room and ran toward him.

"Daddy," she said so naturally, "I love you. Thank you for the best party ever." She leaned over and wrapped her little arms around his waist, squeezing tightly.

"Happy birthday, angel. In a minute we'll have another surprise."

"Oh, boy."

She jumped up and ran back out to the other children, and he wasn't sure if he should pinch himself or believe what just happened.

"She called me Daddy."

He connected with a couple of crewmembers on his walkie-talkie and ordered the balloons to be brought out for release. The children were seated on the deck around the pool, and Matthew came outside to watch the display. Suddenly, as if by magic, eight hundred colorful balls rose into the sky from nowhere. It was better than fireworks. A school of four dolphins appeared beside the yacht, the children squealed even louder, and Matt called to Alyssa.

"Honey, look. Four dolphins and four of us." He grinned at her and she blushed back.

He was getting drunk, and Alyssa was outside working the party, trying to stay away from vomiting over the side of the boat during the remainder of the four-hour voyage. They finally reached the dock, anchored, and everyone piled off to go home. Alyssa helped Matt into the house, and he sank into his leather chair near the window.

The phone rang, and Alyssa answered.

"When did you get in? You just missed Lisa's birthday party." Pausing, she glanced at Matt, then held the phone to her ear again. "Sure, I understand, but that's silly. Just a minute, he's right here." She handed the phone to Matt. "Jean-Marc's back in town. He waited for Lisa's party to end before seeing her, so he wouldn't disrupt the family day you planned."

Matt rolled his eyes, and snagged the phone from her hand, "Yes, Jean-Marc. What can I do for you?"

"Hello, Matt. I bought a puppy, and I would like to give it to Lisa for her birthday. May I?"

Matt felt sickened by this intrusive, disgusting excuse of a man. He wondered what was wrong that Jean-Marc didn't even have his own wife and daughter. "Sure, Jean-Marc. Give her anythin' you want. You know what? She called me Daddy today. You've always been jealous of Alyssa's and Lisa's love for me, and don't think I don't know about it. They're mine, and I'll never give them up, not to you or to anyone else. Givin' her the dog won't touch that." But Matt knew that Jean-Marc legitimately did have a piece of Lisa's heart, and he felt threatened.

Jean-Marc made a prissy noise. "It's obvious that you're drunk, Matthew. For the sake of Alyssa, Lisa, and your new baby, I hope some sense gets knocked into you. Stop drinking, or you will lose them all, not to me nor to anyone else. You will just lose them."

Alyssa missed the interaction between the two, as she had scurried back outside to bring in a few more items from the boat.

Matt put the phone down, staring into space. He had a gift, or maybe it was just luck, but his anger never played out in front of Lisa. She never witnessed her daddy's misbehavior, but she saw her mommy get sad sometimes, and she didn't understand why. Lisa was a very stable little girl, and Matthew wanted to keep her that way as much as everyone else around her did. The moment she called him Daddy, he knew he would protect her forever. She was his, and he was hers, and he would never let her suffer the same way his Dierdra had suffered from a broken family. His new baby girl would have the best, too. He decided it was time to call his lawyer and change his will.

Alyssa called Jean-Marc to tell him that she was too sick to go, but Dionna would take Lisa for a visit and to receive her new present. Alyssa would try to visit him in the morning.

"I love you, too," she answered and hung up.

After Lisa and Dionna left, Matt stirred from his torpor. "Just why are you talkin' to an outsider and tellin' him that you love him?"

"Jean-Marc is no stranger. He's been part of my family practically all my life. In fact, he probably knows more about my life than anyone else does, including you." She gulped hard, because she shouldn't have said that.

"It's not healthy for us for you to have him around. I don't like him stickin' his nose in our family business. I don't want him in my house anymore."

"Oh. Now it's your house, is it?" She wrapped her hands around her hips in defiance. "He has nothing to do with us. The last thing in the world he'd want to do is interfere with our life. He's like a brother to me and you know that. He and Lisa have a completely different relationship than you have with her. Please don't try to stop me from caring about other people. You can't isolate me from the rest of the world."

Matt's glare was, surely, his display of disgust. "I've never isolated you from anyone or anythin' that you haven't chosen to do yourself."

She watched him sway as he got up from the chair, and she followed him to the bedroom, where they met on mutual territory standing near their bed. She felt awful. "Matt, please let's not fight tonight. I feel so sick."

Matthew snorted. "I'm just sick of all your little extra security systems. Why can't it be enough that you have me?"

Alyssa felt his anger coming on, and she scrambled to allay his temper. "Matt, please don't do this tonight. We've had a lovely day."

"You think just because you're pregnant, that I have to

forget that your habits are wrong? You have no business talkin' to other men, do you hear?" Matt grabbed Alyssa's wrist and shoved her down. "You don't know anythin' about lovin' a man. I spent the last several days just takin' care of everythin'. This is no life for a man. I'm not happy, do you understand?"

Eyes glassy, he pinched her cheek and gave it a vicious twist.

Alyssa moved away. His callous disregard for her wellbeing made her cry. "That really hurt. I haven't done anything wrong for you to be so mean. You wanted Lisa to have that huge party. I never would have put that on you and I've been too sick with this pregnancy to offer much help. I can't handle the way you act anymore, and I warned you to never put your hands on me again. You have such a mean streak inside of you when you drink. I'm going to my house for a few days."

He lunged toward her, and she instinctively protected her arm. It hadn't been that long ago that her bruised and battered limb had healed.

Matt grabbed that same arm, squeezing it and forcefully twisting it, reviving her agonizing memory of his last tortuous abuse, only months ago.

She broke free and raced past him into the hallway.

Matthew yelled after her, mocking her, "Go ahead, you loser. You and your whole family are losers. I'm done with you. Run back to your little palace next to Mommy."

Alyssa grabbed her purse from the end table where it had been sitting, and hurried out the door.

She arrived in her driveway and felt safe. Then, trembling, she turned the key to that home which she had built for her little girl and herself. She smelled the warmth and felt the safety of her world before Matthew Hunter had turned it upside down.

She entered the foyer, gazed into the mirror, and saw the huge red, purpling bruise on her cheek. Her arm and her wrist were purple once again, too, and her pain was unbearable, a large part of that pain was due to the memory of the past. Now what would she do? She went to the refrigerator and made two ice packs, one for her face and one for her arm. She sat in a stupor for several hours, numb, unable to think or feel.

The baby moved for the first time. It was like butterfly wings brushing across her pelvis.

"How can something so miraculous and pure be growing from such confusion and pain?" She questioned the universe aloud in confusion. "Matthew, what's wrong with us? Where did we go wrong? This isn't us. You should be here to acknowledge the first movement of our angel."

The tears, one by one, fell onto her cheeks as she sat silently, with her hands over her pelvis. She was comforted in feeling movement, and she hoped the baby wasn't tuning in to the pain. Maybe the life within her was saying, "Mommy, I love you. Don't worry, it will all work out."

The front door opened, and Jean-Marc walked in through the doorway. "Hey, Alyssa, what are you doing here all alone?" He gasped at her ice packs. "What happened to you?"

She turned away, protecting her injuries. "It's nothing. I just got hurt. I'll be fine."

Then, knowing she couldn't fool him, she turned back around and began to cry. "What am I to do?"

Jean-Marc rushed to her and sat beside her. He gently placed his arm around her and moved her hand and the ice pack away from her purple, swollen cheek.

"Alyssa, what happened to you?" He laid light hands on either side of her face, as though cradling a most fragile treasure.

She fell onto him and wept. "It's Matthew. He twisted my cheek and hurt my arm because he was drunk, and because I told you that I loved you on the phone."

"Alyssa, you need to leave him. He's a sick person. He's not good for you or for Lisa. You are pregnant and you need a happy life right now. This is dangerous for you. My goodness, you are a doctor. You know you could lose the baby with violence and physical harm."

Alyssa squirmed out of his arms, allowing the tears to freely fall. "It's so easy for anyone to look at my situation and say I should leave him. I love the beautiful part of him that brings up the sun in the morning. I'm having his baby, Jean-Marc, but sometimes I wish I never even met him. Everything would have been so much easier."

"Alyssa, I've never said anything like this to you before. Do you ever wonder if you might have someday fallen in love with me had you not met him?" His voice cracked and his hands trembled. He squeezed them together trying to contain the shaking.

She grasped a throw pillow from the couch and hugged it tightly to her chest.

"I did think about that. Lisa and I would have been so much better off, and I've thought about that, too."

"Leave him, and let me take care of you. I'll do the right thing for you and I'll love both of your children with all of my heart. I'm not pushing romance, just live with me and let me keep you safe while you figure out what you're going to do. It's not good for the baby to live inside this stress, let alone the danger to both of you." She agonized in the quiet seconds that followed, realizing that he'd spoken but not really hearing a word he'd said.

She sank back into the couch, dazed by her sorrow, and sobs racked her body. "How can I wish I never met him when I feel this beautiful life moving within my body? The baby just moved for the first time today, as if to say, "Don't worry, Mommy. Everything will be OK. Daddy didn't mean it."

Alyssa paused, holding back tears. "This little baby girl is half of me and half of him." She lovingly caressed her abdomen with one hand. "He's not bad. He's just really messed up right now."

Jean-Marc's mouth dropped open. "It's not that he's bad? He can't help his behavior when it goes wacky? What do you call that? He makes you walk on eggshells because he could go off for any little reason, and you don't know what or when it will be. You will never change him. He doesn't really want to change, and he'll probably get worse. After he's maimed you or killed you, it will be too late for you and all of the rest of us who love you so deeply."

He cupped her shoulders with his hands. "How proud you were that day you read to me a poem you wrote for your ladies at the Harmony House. I think it was called, "Hey, Baby, I Love You." Alyssa, that's you in the poem. You wrote that poem for yourself and you didn't even know it when you wrote it."

She moaned. "That's not true. It's not true. He's not really bad. You don't know him. I think he's having a breakdown or something. Maybe after the heart attack he married me too soon. He quit working. I got pregnant. It's been a lot for him to handle."

"Oh, I didn't realize that when times are tough, men just start battering their wives, and it's OK. Sorry, Alyssa, how could I not understand such a fundamental and normal reaction to hard times? How stupid of me."

She held up her hand. "Don't, please."

"Why are you so desperate with excuses, fast excuses?" Jean-Marc gripped her hands. "I can't allow you to do this to yourself."

Just then Lisa came bouncing in with a little fluffy puppy in her arms. She spotted her mother, and came rushing toward her holding out her new Wheaten Terrier.

"Look, Mommy," Lisa giggled. "Jean-Marc gave me a puppy. Isn't he the most beautiful guy?"

As she drew nearer, her eyes widened in concern. "Mommy, what happened to your face?"

Jean-Marc spoke up fast. "Your mommy was getting something from the cabinet and she hit her cheek on the open cupboard door. We put ice on it and it will be fine."

Lisa responded, "Oh, Mommy, do you need my owie bear in the refrigerator?"

Alyssa turned the attention away from her face, "What an irresistible little guy." She reached for the cuddly pup. "What are you going to name him?"

"I'm going to find the best name in the world." Lisa grasped back her puppy and headed for the backyard.

She returned, puzzled. "Mommy, where's Daddy? I want to show him my puppy."

"Daddy's home."

"I want to go home and show him my puppy."

Alyssa and Jean-Marc shared a troubled glance.

That night Alyssa decided to stop participating in the support group at the Harmony house. She knew she was one of those ladies who should knock on that door and ask for help. She knew anyone hearing what Matthew had done would implore her to leave him. But she couldn't, not just yet. She still hoped his case was different. He wouldn't ever be a violent stalker. He wasn't homicidal. He just blew up and then he made mistakes. But how could she possibly stand in front of the ladies and convince them that her situation was different from theirs? Could she ever again, in good conscience, give them the very guidance that she herself couldn't follow? She made her choice to stop counseling rather than to be a hypocrite. She was battered and she was caught in the web of not walking away. It just wasn't time to say good-bye to Matthew forever. Surely, she, as a physician, could help him change. She returned her thoughts to the theories about abusers she'd considered what seemed like ages ago, when she was on the plane to visit Matthew at Napa. It couldn't be possible that such a wonderful man could have real live hidden demons inside of him. If he did have demons, then she would drive them out of him. But for now, it was better to stay away for a few days and allow him to cool down.

The baby moved inside of her again, and she mourned Matt's hand on her pelvis during this sacred moment. Exhausted, she prepared for bed, slid under the covers alone, and carefully avoided pressure on her new and sufferable facial injury. As she lay on her side, the combination of throbbing pain in her cheek and the gentle movement of new life within her womb almost blended together.

She reached over to the end table and turned the radio on low volume. A soft voice began to sing a song that Alyssa had always loved. It moved her to tears, once again, as many things did during these days. Taylor Dayne sang "I'll Always Love You."

"I'll always love him for the rest of my days," she whispered to herself."

Alyssa felt pain and pleasure, the yin and the yang of Matthew simultaneously, as her broken heart sank, as her eyes closed for sleep.

The battered woman syndrome was no different for her than it was for anyone else. Even with her education and basic emotional stability, she was sucked into that state of limbo that is mixed with denial, disbelief, fear, and a lot of love, with a little bit of hope for things to change.

After two days of total silence, Matthew suddenly showed up at Alyssa's house. "Alyssa, we need to talk." His shame denied eye contact with her.

"Yes we do," Alyssa responded with a low-key, sad voice. "I'm leaving you. I can't live on this roller coaster anymore. We rushed into this marriage without really knowing who we each were. I love that incredible representative of you, who I kissed on our wedding day. But he's gone. I'm pregnant and I need harmony to do the right thing for this little baby inside of me. You could end up killing the baby and me."

Matthew's shoulders dropped, he looked at the ground, and she saw his mouth quiver. She awaited tears, but instead he begged, "Honey, please. "Let's go to counselin'. I never believed in that stuff, but maybe it will get our heads straight so we can work things out. Alyssa, do you still love me? 'Cause if you do, then you sure don't try much to hold this relationship together. I'm the only one who tries all the time. You just don't put me first. I'm somewhere down the list after your mother, Lisa, your friends, and now the baby."

She looked up at him in shock. "How could you possibly think that? Matt, you see things from a really twisted place. There is no way to heal wounds that are just unfoundedly created. You accuse me of doing and feeling things that aren't true. You're so jealous and possessive that I'm strangled by your needs. I thought the violence was gone, but it's still there."

They stood in front of each other, holding eye contact in silence.

She wanted to lash out and say much more, but she knew that he would lose it if she did. He still hadn't faced the fact that he needed help.

But just staring into the blue of his eyes, seeing his face, and hearing his voice was all she needed to begin melting the tip of the iceberg again.

"The baby moved."

"And I wasn't with you to feel it the first time? It's all I've been waitin' for, honey."

"I can't believe you feel entitled to have been there after what you did to me." She said nothing more.

"OK," he answered, "If you want to do somethin' about our problems, you think about what I said, Alyssa. I love you and I love my daughters. Where's Lisa?"

He passed through the door, leaving his wife standing alone to close it behind her.

"Lisa, where are you?" Calling for her throughout the house, he glanced out the window toward the backyard, only to find her playing and running back and forth across the sand with her new puppy. He went outside and broke into a big smile.

"Daddy," she ran to his arms. "Look at my new puppy. His name is Teddy, because he looks like a teddy bear."

"Oh, baby, he's beautiful," he answered.

Matthew called the puppy to him and they ran together like a little boy playing with his dog. Teddy pulled on Matt's pant leg, and shook it furiously with his mouth. Lisa tried to pull Teddy's attention away from her father, but the puppy had just one intense mission. He wanted Matt's pant leg.

"Oh, Daddy, you're so funny."

The word Daddy came out of her mouth easily, as if she wanted to say it over and over again. He hoped it was so, because it had been so long since his other three children had called him that. He loved parenthood. It was a prestige symbol, not to mention the fulfillment of procreation and the mirror image thing. "It's really special when you love a woman so much that you would die for her, and she just happens to have an incredible little girl who loves you, too. When that child begins to call you Daddy, your world turns inside out. It's just as good as havin' your own blood. It's just different because you have to earn it," he told himself.

Alyssa watched through the window as they played. Lisa looked so happy. Alyssa wondered why dogs and children were so attracted to Matt Hunter. Dogs and children were so good at picking up good and bad energy. Especially dogs were supposed to have an extra sense to pick out danger. Obviously, Lisa and Teddy saw the same good qualities in him that she saw. But they, unlike her, never caught the brunt of his mean side. They saw the power he commanded over the domain of love. Her strength to separate was gone. Lisa's light heart had erased all of Alyssa's willpower. She wanted her marriage to turn around and be normal. Her heart was heavy with sadness.

That evening the Hunter family went home together. Matthew quickly glanced at Alyssa's injuries, and looked away from them, as if he knew what he'd done, but he never said a word. She knew he wanted them brushed into the past like all of his other mistakes, but she hoped he would do more than just believe he could move on from there and make things better without seeking the professional help he had promised to do. These were not just typical marital problems. These were problems seeded within domestic violence and the wrongful consequences of such behavior. She was back, once again, in the nest. But now there were criteria, established criteria that must be met in order to keep it together. She feared that Matthew, however, was comforted by the predictability of her loyalty, and maybe he would try to let the therapy slide.

Jean-Marc became an infrequent visitor to Menlo. He spent most of his time in Europe, working and playing the field with multitudes of French beauties by his side. He completely stopped talking with Alyssa, but making sure to keep close tabs on everyone, he directed his calls to Dionna's home. He never disclosed the extent of disgust he felt toward Matthew after their last conversation, and he worried that Alyssa had not seen the last of the Hunter wrath. Jean-Marc would be there to catch all of them if they fell, but in the meantime, he gave them space and hoped that his absence would help keep Matthew's mood stabilized. At least he would most likely not end up as one of Matthew's excuses for violence.

Lisa and Matthew grew closer together than ever within the short time that followed. Maybe for Matt it was a last stand, a way of holding Alyssa after such treachery. Maybe it was a conquest of something he had lost long ago with Dierdra. For Lisa, Matt was the welcomed father she hadn't known before he arrived. Maybe for her, it was combined with a competition with her new baby sister, who was only months away from possibly stealing first place in Matt's heart away from her. For whatever reason, Matt and Lisa had hit it off, appearing as two innocent people who happened to be quite alike in the good ways that bring two people together.

The second trimester of the pregnancy passed by in a flash. Alyssa was seven months pregnant and the nursery was coming together quite beautifully. The trio created a countdown calendar, and the routine morning ritual was to mark off one more day before the big event.

Lisa whined every time she crossed out another day with her gold crayon, "What's my baby sister's name?"

"Hey guys, remember the Matlyssa thing? Let's make it feminine again, and name her Marissa." Matt's idea was accepted as brilliant. With a high five in the air, Marissa it was.

Matt sat on the couch. "Come here, you guys, come sit beside me."

He waited until his audience took their seats.

"I never mentioned it on the plane that day, but there's an old slave story about a little girl named Marissa. I always loved that name. My mama used to tell me lots of old slave stories when I was a little boy."

Lisa perked up, "Daddy, tell us the story, please?"

"OK. Well, Marissa was a little slave child who suffered

the injustice of ignorant, white cruelty. On the plantation there was a little white girl with the same name. They became secret friends and bonded together as one when they pricked their fingers and pressed them together to mix their blood forever. In the story, the slave Marissa progressed to great freedom and success. She always felt that she was given a chance in the world because she was mixed with a little white blood from her friend. I always hated that part of the story. I hated that a slave had to feel that way. It wasn't fair. But I always loved the name, Marissa. It's really perfect for us, because it has all three of our names in it, and if we name her that, then all four of us are part of her name. It's really kind of cool."

Marissa Grace Hunter was born on February 11th. Matt and Lisa watched Marissa's first breath as she entered the world from her mother's womb. Matt cut the umbilical cord. The baby was placed on Alyssa's chest and then handed to him.

"Honey, look at our little angel," he whispered as tears filled his eyes. "We have everythin' that two people could ever want in this world. I love you so much. Thank you."

It was Lisa's turn to hold the new life. She pulled a chair up to her mother's bed and cradled her new baby sister in her arms.

"Mommy, she's so small. Look at her little fingers." She held out five little fingers with perfect little fingernails.

The Hunter home was an inviting environment. The harmony was almost corny. Dionna attended her daughter's every need for the first two weeks after the birth with great concern, because of Alyssa's last bout with postpartum depression. Even though some of her depression had been over Alex's death, the initial blues had begun almost immediately after Lisa's birth. Dionna understood very well what that was like, because she had suffered terrible depression after Alyssa was born.

Alyssa bounced back quickly this time. Matt had shown no signs of abnormal behavior for months. That feeling of a whole lot of love and a little bit of hope had faded and Alyssa let down her guard and allowed Matthew once again to enter the inside of her being. She wanted to forget everything that had ever gone wrong. Marissa Grace was living up to her name. The family was graced.

Though she experienced the greatest joy in her life with one little girl, she realized, that a mommy, a daddy and a child was a neat little package. A mommy, a daddy, and two children made a true family. A family was a little more cumbersome, but it was so much more rewarding. It was complete.

Chapter Twenty-Four

$\mathcal{M}$atthew was quieter than usual that morning as they lay side by side, and a fleeting moment of concern whispered in the back of Alyssa's mind. She brushed it away and nestled closer to her husband.

He moaned, "Alyssa, it's Saturday. Promise me you'll never leave me. I love you, honey." Turning toward her, and wrapping his arms around her so tightly that a crowbar couldn't have pulled him from her, he bared his soul. "You took a lost and broken man into your heart, and you breathed your precious life into him. That's why I'm here today. You must know that."

He pulled her on top of him and caressed her with all of his steel gentleness.

"Hold me, baby. Hold me back so tightly that you can't let go. Don't ever leave me, promise me, don't ever go."

"I promise," she breathed.

Alyssa and her sweetheart rhythmically made love, such perfect love that it would have inspired Beethoven to write one of his most romantic concertos. She loved her husband as much as she could, and she had done everything to forgive his evils of the past. Tasting him this morning was part of her sensuous dance performed for her lover. She had learned every trigger and every sensitive spot that he possessed, knowing him now in every way. Alyssa loved his heart, his mind, and his body, which stirred a passion that wasn't desperate, but rather a perfect drive to reach a sexual completeness that they had only ever obtained together. She remained on top of him, melted into his body, as he obediently massaged and kneaded her back until she dozed again, in peace. His total performance awaited her complete relaxation, and only then did he dare join her in sweet repose.

Matt was the first to stir. "It's Saturday," he whispered again.

Alyssa opened her eyes, and hearing his moan, she answered, "Honey, Saturday comes every week for us. What's wrong?"

Matt helped her roll off his body, and then turned sideways, facing her.

"Did I ever tell you how beautiful you are? Havin' an orgasm with you isn't about givin' me relief. It's about goin' straight to sex heaven. Do you know what I mean? I don't think I'd like havin' sex ever again, if it weren't with you."

"I know, me, too." She moved her hands up and down his body, gently feeling every contour, tickling him with her feather-light touch. "I love you, Matt Hunter."

Leaning back up, resting her elbow on the mattress, and facing him, she pressed the issue. "Honey, what does Saturday have to do with my never leaving you? Did something bad happen between us on a Saturday?"

Matt answered her with a sigh, "Like I said, baby. You took a broken man and you gave him new life. Without that, who knows what would have happened to me. You were the angel who saved me. That's why I love you so much."

Alyssa needed reassurance.

"I hope that's not the only reason you love me so much."

Matt leaned over and brushed her cheek with his lips, breathing out. "Silly. When I met you, I was kind of a broken man."

"Right. You were at the top of your game, and you knew it, and so did everyone else."

Matt shook his head. "You're wrong. I may have given everyone that impression, but I was hurtin' inside."

Alyssa grasped for something deeper in his praise of her, but he seemed unwilling to relinquish anything other than gratitude that she'd been his inspiration to try again, to get up and fight for better times. "You're even better and more handsome now than you were then. Every woman still wants you, but I have you, I'll never stop loving you, and I'll never let you go, never."

"Don't be silly. This conversation is absurd."

He reached over, grabbed her by the waist, and tickled her between the ribs until she could hardly bear another moment of uncontrollable laughter, reaching that intolerable point between pleasure and pain. "I'm all yours, 'cause now you're stuck with me."

She knew he wasn't better, nor was he more handsome than that Southern tycoon who pulled the little Romeo figurine out of a sack in her office a few years ago. His illnesses, both physical and mental, had taken their toll. It scared her as she looked into his face and saw a grayish cast in his deeply lined skin. He had lost some of his magic with her. So much had happened between them that she couldn't forget. She wanted all of the bad not to have been so, needing him to be the best love she ever had, and exerting every effort trying to make it true.

Her reassurance always helped his self-confidence, as he

seemed to reach inside of her, grasping a piece of the goodness in her soul, trying to make his own a better one. She wished she could lean on him for all those reasons a woman might lean on her partner, but she couldn't, not anymore.

Painfully, she knew all he ever wanted, just as she did, was to be loved totally by one special person for the rest of his life. When she met Matt, she saw him as a perfect man. Matt was supposed to be her dream come true, and in a way, he was, if the memory of his abuse would completely fade.

Usually Matt made Saturday a special day for the children. This day he'd planned nothing. He spoke little, and stared through the window at the water off and on all morning.

Dionna came to the house by Alyssa's request. "I wish I could take the children to Sea World, and spend the night in Orlando. It seems I never get enough time with them."

Alyssa winked at her mother as Matt smiled.

"Dionna, that's a great idea. I think my wife and I need a little long-overdue time alone together."

Dionna took the children, and Matt and Alyssa stayed home, walked on the beach, swam, and enjoyed the peace and quiet.

Matt's uneasiness and restlessness increased toward late afternoon.

"Honey," he called for Alyssa. "Let's have a drink. We don't drink much anymore. I'm gettin' antsy. I hate it without the kids here; I really miss them. Let's just open one of those bottles with the ribbons on them."

Alyssa had watched Matt drink lightly for almost three years without problems of anger or violence. Marissa was a two-and-a-half-year-old, and Lisa was almost eleven. It was hard to believe how quickly life was passing.

"OK," she answered. "Let's open a bottle of champagne."

She went to the bar and unlocked the cooler. Out came a bottle of Cristal. They poured two glasses, and then two more. Alyssa went into the kitchen to prepare broiled salmon, the bubbles tingling pleasantly in her head.

Matthew escaped to the cooler behind the bar. "Why that little devil."

The cooler had been locked to keep him from temptation, but Alyssa left the key in easy access, just to let him know she wasn't trying to rule him, but she was reminding him to try not to take that extra effort for a drink. He remembered that the key was in the martini glass to the right. He grasped the key and opened the latch with a click — making that extra effort for a drink. Like his old party-boy self, he popped open another bottle of champagne. He didn't really want salmon for dinner. He would rather have gone out to eat at a restaurant and danced in the moonlight, before returning to their home for some great sex in the Jacuzzi. Sex had always been first and foremost for him since he was a teenager, an instinct that was still very strong.

Alyssa worked hard to make the salmon just right. She marinated it in an herbal sauce, poured sautéed mushrooms over it, and broiled it slowly with a basil accent. When it was done, she served the fish over basmati rice with French-cut green beans, lined with tiny baby onions. She finished the presentation with a sprinkle of slivered almonds lightly dressing the fish. A tossed arugula salad on the side, with French bread, completed the meal.

Matt broke their silence as they sat together, eating and watching the sunset.

"Honey, this is delicious."

The phone rang, and he excused himself to answer it. "Hey, Amy. How are you?" He carried the phone outside. "Well, I'm sorry we couldn't be there. I'm happy for her, and I hope she has everythin' she ever wanted in life. Isn't that what it's all about? I mean, havin' the best in life?"

When he returned to the table, he was somber.

Alyssa took another small bite. "Is something wrong? How's Amy?"

Matt sipped his champagne.

"She's fine. She just wanted to say hello. She sent her love to you."

He didn't look at Alyssa, and there was a detectible irritability in his voice as he stood up from the table.

"Honey, leave the dishes for me to clear. You did the cookin', it's my turn."

Alyssa hadn't forgotten the cues of when to back away. Like riding a bike, she quickly remembered, and knew it was time. She quietly picked up her dish and took it to the kitchen.

Matthew left the table and turned on the TV, habitually clicking the channel changer to see what else was on. Though Alyssa wasn't in the room to get interested in a program and then sigh and make faces when he changed channels, he still found a measure of gratification in the action. He was restless, and he decided to make a real drink. He got up, still in possession of the liquor cabinet key, and poured himself a scotch. After a moment, he tipped the bottle again to make it a double.

He lifted his glass to the air and proposed a quiet toast,

"Here's to eternal love and happiness for everyone. May it begin today."

Nobody was there to share his toast. He wanted to be alone anyway, so it didn't matter.

Alyssa took a magazine from the kitchen nook and moved to the porch outside to read. She couldn't focus on the magazine, though. Matt's distant behavior troubled her.

He didn't join her, didn't go to the kitchen to wash dishes, but instead, he sat with one leg swung over the arm of the overstuffed chair, sipping from a tumbler of amber liquid.

It wasn't long before she reentered the house, intentionally avoiding confrontation.

Turning his head, he reached for her.

"Where you been? Come over here, please."

She neared him, focusing her eyes on his careless sprawl with his legs spread apart over the chair. Placing her magazine on the table, she stood in silence.

He looked back at her, winked, and slurred, "Baby, you are one fine woman, did you know that? I mean, I've had some fine women, but you got it all. I'm lucky I married you and nobody else. Let's have another honeymoon tonight."

"Matthew, you're smashed."

"I know, baby, but I'm OK. Come over here, and sit on Daddy's lap so I can feel you a little bit. Come and be my sexy girl."

Matthew was playful, and Alyssa sat on his lap. He slid his hand up and down her leg. "Oh, baby. Your legs are so smooth and your skin is so soft. I love you." He buried his face between her breasts, and then looked up at her with a wild glint in his eyes. "Let's go skinny dippin' in the pool."

They slid off their clothes and went outside. She giggled at the way he gazed at her beautiful, feminine silhouette partially hidden by the oncoming darkness. It was so obvious he wanted her.

They swam for an hour, floating on their backs, playing, relaxing under the stars, and then left the water to join together in the bedroom.

Matthew pulled her close to him. "Baby, let me bite an apple in the Garden of Eden."

But when they fell to the bed, he knew there was no such thing. His mind was all twisted from his past life and from the whiskey. He was too drunk to make sense of anything that had happened to him this day, and too drunk for the moment.

They slept peacefully, clinging together, until about three o'clock in the morning, when Alyssa stirred and reached for her husband. He wasn't there. She slid out of bed, still nude, and called his name as she went to the living room. He was sitting alone in a chair, with another drink in his hand. His eyes were glassy as he turned to her, glaring at her form, and she saw in his face the same saddened, gray look that worried her before. He looked old, tired, and miserable.

"Honey are you OK?"

Matthew attempted to stand, but his off-balance attempt failed. He slumped back into the chair.

"What are you doin' up? Go back to bed, baby. I'll be there in a minute."

Reluctantly, she returned to bed where she lay alone, hoping everything would remain quiet. Finally, she dozed off to sleep.

Suddenly, something shook her arm.

"Alyssa, wake up. I want to talk to you. Wake up."

She opened her eyes, and turned her head to face him. But before she could speak, he grabbed her lace nightgown and ripped it from her body.

Alyssa cowered at the anger on his face, and he sneered. "Don't you look at me that way."

He shoved her legs sideways, away from him with repulsion, and grabbed her by the shoulders. Pulling her torso toward him he lifted her up. Then he slammed her back against the headboard. Pain shrieked through her body. He snagged her by the ears, banging the back of her head on the hard hand-carved wood, over and over again.

Alyssa screamed, each cry punctuated by another blow, "Stop. Please. What are you doing? Matthew, please. Please stop hurting me, I'm begging you. Please don't kill me."

He pulled her back by her hair, and slapped her face. Her neck violently jerked in whiplash.

"Oh, please? Now make your poor little nose bleed." He continued slapping her furiously, and warm blood poured from her nostril. He spat in her hair and then on her face, still holding her immobile with steely power. She couldn't move. He reached down with demonic enjoyment crackling in his eyes, and kneaded her left breast in his clenched fist, giving it a vicious squeeze, sending stabbing pitchfork pain through her chest.

"Please stop," she screamed through the torture, writhing on the bed. "Please."

He continued spitting on her, and in between gobs of saliva, he mocked, "You love it, don't you? You force me to hurt you, because you love it, and you deserve it. Here, try this. Do you love this, too?"

He dug his fingernails into her thigh, scraping the skin off as his fingers raked a bloody trail down her leg. He shoved her back onto the bed, and then, focusing on her blood dripping onto the white sheet, he stopped.

Glassy eyed, he sat on her, holding her down with his unforgiving weight and his iron control, and staring at the flowing blood, as if he had snapped out of a nightmare.

Whether it was because he saw the blood on the sheets, the blood oozing from her nostril, the terror and agony in her eyes, or something else, he was done.

"Oh, my God," he moaned.

Her first instinct was to escape. She kicked him in the groin in order to disable him, but it only reawakened his rage. It did give her a few seconds to run to the bathroom, close the door, and lock it behind her.

She screamed through the door in terror, sobbing hysterically, "Matthew, what's wrong with you? Please go away, and don't hurt me anymore. I promise, I'll leave you alone. I won't ever bother you again, just don't kill me. Think of Lisa and Marissa, please."

He pounded on the door until it rattled and splintered in the frame. "You drive me crazy. You did this to yourself. You're the problem. You did this to me, and it's all your fault."

Lowering his volume, he continued his monologue, almost as if he were a brokenhearted soul who had surrendered. Every word was still audible through the door as he continued, now mumbling, "You've never been my wife, you're not my wife, and you never will be my wife. You're nothin' more than a bad replacement for the best I ever had. You're nothin' more than a fake replacement for true love."

Alyssa cried back, "What did I ever do to you? You and Carline broke up long before I ever even met you. If you still love her, I understand, but please, what did I do to deserve this?"

He said nothing more. Petrified, she listened to him stomping around the bedroom, breaking things. Suddenly, the loud sound of crashing glass stopped, and she heard the front door slam.

He was gone.

She sat on the bathroom floor, rolled into a ball, and sobbed for the next few hours. Sheer exhaustion overtook her. This was the nightmare that only other women experienced, like the women at the Harmony House.

What would she instruct another victim to do? Call the police. Survival was the first instinct she should follow. She had run to the bathroom, where now she was safe.

Speaking aloud, she agonized, "Not only does he need a restraining order, but at this point he needs jail."

The bathroom phone receiver easily lifted off of the wall, and her hand dropped it against her chest while she gathered her thoughts. The dial tone changed from a long, steady tone to broken fast busy signals. She slowly placed the receiver back on the wall without dialing 911.

Alyssa knew what she should have done, but calling the police would have been the ruination of Matthew's world. His name would have hit the papers, and the press worldwide, Capezzio might raise his head breathing his wrath, and her family could be in grave danger. His career ruination wasn't her goal. Sea Cliff Yachts would have become scandalous, and his financial empire would have crumbled. The children would have been cruelly humiliated and emotionally damaged at school, and she just couldn't do that to them. Instead, she would leave him.

It was eight o'clock before she found the physical strength to stand. She unlocked the bathroom door and hobbled to the bed. Her beautiful white lace nightgown was torn to shreds and half of it was bloody. Bloodstains were smeared on the sheets, and Matthew had thrown his clothes from the closet to the floor, in a hurry to grab a few things before leaving. A lead crystal lamp was broken into pieces, and their life-sized wedding oil painting had been ripped off the wall over their bed, sliced in half and thrown down for her to see. Its 24-karat gold leaf frame was smashed. The Tiffany chandelier had been hatefully transformed into tiny crystals strewn across the room and shattered into thousands of worthless sparkles.

Her throbbing ankle dragged behind her as she hobbled back to the bathroom. Gazing into the vanity mirror, she saw a horror of a person looking at her, a monster with a bloodstained face, a swollen bottom lip and nose, purple cheeks, and ratty hair. Her eyes followed the nightmare down her bloody, nude body to her battered left leg. The deep scratches followed the contour of her thigh, and had dripped streams of blood down her calf, pooling and drying on top of her foot. She turned on the shower and painfully stood in front of the warm water spray, which stung her open wounds like a thousand wasps as it cleansed her skin.

Her thoughts raced in a million directions. She spoke aloud, but under her breath, in fear of someone hearing her. "For sure he's crazy. He doesn't even know what he's doing. I can't help him anymore. He'll kill me before this is over."

She knew she had to leave Menlo. Where she would take the children to get away was still a question. It was too much to decide at the moment. She'd call Jean-Marc. He'd know what to do to make them safe.

After the shower she felt better. The dried blood had been washed off, her nose was red and swollen, and her face was black and blue.

She dressed her leg and wrapped her ankle. There was no way she, as a local physician, could call for help. This shame had to be kept quiet for the sake of everyone involved.

Alyssa picked up the telephone and called her mother.

"Hello, darling daughter, how are you?"

Leaning her face in her hands, Alyssa struggled to keep her voice calm. "I'm OK. How are my girls?"

"They're great. They loved Sea World, but touching the dolphins was their highlight. Now we're in the hotel room after our evening swim in the hotel pool. This is a wonderful place, and I took pictures of them all day long. We're having a ball. Do you guys want to say hi to them?"

Alyssa remained silent for a few seconds while she gathered her strength to confess.

"Mama, Matt left."

She could hardly get those words out before Dionna broke in.

"Alyssa, what happened? Are you all right?"

"Mother, he's really sick, and I'm leaving him. I'm fine, but he hit me again. Would you keep the girls with you for a few days? I'll order a police guard for your house, so if he comes he won't be able to take them. I need a couple of days at Susanna's to heal, while I make arrangements for us to leave Menlo. Don't worry, I'll stay safe. Call me later tonight, after they're in bed, OK?"

"Alyssa, I'm afraid. Honey, did you call the police this time?" Dionna's words trembled with the fear of a doting mother.

Alyssa lowered her voice. "No."

"Please, sweetheart, call the police. I'm so scared."

"Mama, make arrangements to take the children to France within the next couple of days, OK?"

"Of course I will, but is it that bad?"

Alyssa reluctantly answered, "Yes. It's over."

She knew that it really was over, and this time, she had to leave forever. She had plenty of time to figure out the past, and to plan for the long-term future. This wasn't the time for long-term decisions, only baby steps, as she used to instruct her ladies at the Harmony House.

It had been five lonely, painful days since Matt left. Alyssa remained in Susanna's supportive and protective home, was beginning to physically heal, and actually began to worry about him.

"Susanna, for all we know, he's lying in some hospital, or he might even have committed suicide somewhere. For sure, he's been drinking."

Susanna leaned over, while unwrapping her dear friend's leg wound for a dressing change.

"Looking at this makes me not care where he is, as long as he stays away from you and the girls. I almost hate him right now."

Alyssa flinched as Susanna removed the final gauze stuck to her leg.

"Don't say that, Sue."

"OK, I'll help you try to find him, only because I agree he

should know that you and the children are gone, and I mean gone for good."

Alyssa and Susanna tediously spent hours checking off names and places they had called in hopes of tracing his steps, to no avail. Racking her brain to remember any person or place they had left out during their fruitless search, Alyssa flashed on Napa Valley. Matt's rage in finding out that Peter hit Amy was ironic, especially if Matt had that same pattern of abuse in his own past.

"Susanna, I know I can't talk to Amy or Mrs. Hunter about this—they'd deny all of it and turn on me. But there is one person I might be able to talk to. Maybe Lena knows where he is."

Susanna put her pen down and stood up, stretching her arms.

"Maybe, but don't you think that's a little far-fetched?"

Alyssa cocked her head. "I don't know. Maybe not. I've never been able to get out of my head the way they acted together that morning on the terrace in Napa. I bet Lena knows plenty about Matt. Maybe he's been hiding something. Looking back, it seems strange that Lena's name never came up even once during our marriage. Besides, what do I have to lose by calling her?"

Susanna excused herself. "I need a rest. Want a soda?"

Alyssa shook her head, already in deep thought.

"Matt's precious black book. We'll get all kinds of clues from it. His mother even mentioned it to me when we first met. He always treasured it as a keepsake in memory of his historical conquests, and I believe it's tucked into bed in an old briefcase in back of his closet.

I'm going home to look for that book."

Even after being battered so severely, Alyssa decided returning to her and Matthew's home would put her in no danger. "Matthew isn't the type to plot out something ugly," she told herself. "He just has instant breaks, and plays them out until the energy has been released. He's not homicidal. He's a good man who has a short circuit that just keeps causing fuses to blow."

She entered the quiet and lonely house alone, and went directly to his closet, reached for the tattered briefcase, and carefully shuffled through the files. She came upon a black book, and sure enough, under Lena's name, there were multiple phone numbers scratched out and replaced with new ones. Alyssa scribbled down the most recent number, then tucked the black book back into the briefcase and moved away from it as if afraid someone might see her and fingerprint it.

Without looking at the destruction left behind in their beautiful bedroom from that terrible night, she turned away, left the room, and left the house. She drove her car to the beach and parked under the light of a lamppost. Rolling the window down for the cool, fresh air, she welcomed the sound of the waves rolling to shore, and they helped calm her pounding heart as she picked up her cell phone and dialed the number of Emelio de la Cruz in California.

A woman's voice answered the phone, "¿Bueno?"

Alyssa closed her eyes, groping. "Hello, is Lena there, please? This is Matthew's wife, Alyssa."

"Oh, no, senora, Marialena doesn't live here. She lives in La Jolla. Let me give you the number."

Alyssa's heartbeat quickened, as if tarot cards were being spread before her with bad news, as she wrote down the number.

Her shaky finger pressed the area code again, and the new number.

A friendly young voice answered the phone. "¿Bueno?"

Alyssa introduced herself and this time asked for Marialena.

Within seconds Lena answered the phone. "Is something wrong? Is Matt OK?"

Alyssa paused for a second to gather her senses. "I am so sorry to bother you, but I'm looking for him. I've called every single person, and every place I can think of, and he's nowhere to be found. I really need your help."

She counted on Lena's hearing the desperation in her voice.

"What's wrong?" Lena asked.

"Please tell me. Have you heard from him? Do you know where he is?"

"No. What's wrong?"

"I never forgot how he looked at you that morning we had breakfast in Napa. Since then, I was sure you knew something about him that nobody else knew."

Lena's tone was candid. "Did he ever tell you anything about me?"

"He never said much."

Lena answered softly, "I used to love him, too. It didn't work out, and we both went our separate ways."

"Oh." Alyssa knew her surprise was transparent, even through the phone. "I'm not calling you to pry. I guess I'm calling you because . . . I know you know him well." Alyssa began to cry.

Lena felt a faint alarm for Matthew's well-being, and she couldn't help feeling sorry for Alyssa. Still, she harbored resentment, because Matt had belonged, truly belonged, to someone else. Even though she knew back then he was wrong for her, now with the passage of time, things seemed different. Matt might have made it right, if he didn't have Alyssa to fall back on so easily.

Alyssa poured her heart out. "Matt has such treacherous mood swings, and violent behavior. I'm a doctor, and I know better, but I've been hopelessly weak for him."

Was Matt that good at his game that he blinded even the most educated and academically successful women? None of Alyssa's academics mattered. She was a woman who had fallen in love with Matthew Hunter, a male siren, a man no woman could resist once he had injected her with his passionate promises of ecstasy and eternal love. Another woman of the "battered woman syndrome"; a victim of domestic violence; Alyssa was his latest, most tortured soul.

Lena said nothing about the night in the vineyard, the miscarriage, the broken wedding promises, or their last encounter in Napa. Her privacy wasn't just for Matt, but for the sacred protection of her dead babies.

"Alyssa," Lena began. "Matthew is sick. He needs help. He's always been sick with temper. You're not the first woman he's hurt. I had to leave him for the same reason. You need to leave him, too. I know you love him, because everyone loves him. It doesn't matter. Leave him."

Alyssa ached with grief as she heard herself saying those same words over and over to other battered women at the shelter.

"Lena, I'm sorry if you've been hurt, too. I was a doctor who just went to work one day. An incredible man showed up, and I fell in love just like you, just like everybody else. I had no idea of his past, except for the few things he told me about Carline."

"Anything Matthew and I had ended almost nine years ago," Lena's soft, gentle voice continued, slightly tinged with a Latin flavor. "No woman who has ever fallen in love with Matthew James Hunter has stopped loving him, not ever. As life goes on pain fades, but if he has touched you, all it takes to break you down again is to hear one song that makes you remember. I still shut some music off when I hear it because it's too painful, and turning music off is hard for a Latin girl."

The next few seconds were painfully silent for both of them.

Switching the cell phone to the opposite ear, Alyssa looked up at the streetlamp, where hundreds of flying insects were mesmerized by the globe and its blinding-hot light. She saw Matthew as the light, and all of his fated loves were the pitiful bugs soaring toward their demise.

"I'm his wife, and the mother of his child. He's given me life, but at the same time he's killed me. This last time, he beat me up so badly that I should have called the police, but I was too weak to make that call, so I found every excuse in the world not to. I have Marissa, his little girl. He adopted my daughter who's ten now, and she sees him as her father."

"Alyssa," Lena asked, "Don't you believe anything you've taught to the ladies in your domestic violence counseling? You teach about red flags. Didn't you ever see any of your own?"

Alyssa whimpered again. "No."

Lena continued leading the conversation, "Matthew is a tragic and dangerous man. He will eventually hurt you, or kill you, if you don't get away. Maybe one of your children or both of them could be killed by his craziness. Is that what you're waiting for? Can you imagine how it would be for you if your two children died because Matt was violent to you? You have two beautiful little girls. Take them away, and save them from ever seeing suffering of that kind."

Pity colored Lena's voice, and Alyssa tried to draw strength from the fact that Lena had once been where she was now, yet had saved herself.

Alyssa cried, "He's changed me completely. I used to be strong and upright. Lena, I love him. He could have killed me a week ago, and I still love him."

"Alyssa, I'm so sorry for your suffering." She paused for several seconds. "It's easy to believe that his love is greater than his craziness, but it's not. All of us in the family think that Matt hired a hit man to kill Peter. We don't believe it was a jealous husband. We think his friend, Capezzio, orchestrated it for Matthew. Nobody will ever be able to prove anything. It's all hiding in Italy somewhere."

Alyssa sank into her seat, her reality spinning out of control. "He just uses his index finger to control the world around him." She'd known almost nothing of the man she'd loved for four and a half years.

Lena returned to the real subject at hand. "He's why women are born, but his sickness is his flaw, and it kills everything that is dear to him. He's a dangerous batterer. He is domestic violence. He doesn't want to be that, he just is."

Alyssa sat in dead silence, remembering, wanting to

forget.

"Alyssa, I got married one week ago. I sent an announcement to everyone including to you and Matthew. Amy was my maid of honor, and Annie was a flower girl. You didn't even send a card. Why?"

"You got married?" An ugly thought reared its head. "What day was your wedding?"

"Last Saturday."

Alyssa was stunned. "That was the day he went crazy drinking and almost killed me. He knew you were getting married that day, and it drove him crazy. That's exactly what happened. He started drinking again that day, because he was miserable over your wedding. Lena, that missing link in my marriage with him was you. He was still in love with you. He was upset all day because you were getting married. He never got over you." Gathering her senses, she fought the pain of the deadly knife that had just pierced her heart. "I never saw the announcement or the invitation. I had no idea. Congratulations, Lena. Be happy."

Marialena whispered in Spanish. "I feel terrible for you. I feel terrible for myself. I feel terrible for Matthew. Everyone is a loser in this. There is no happy ending for anyone here."

Somehow, they closed their cordial conversation with promises to keep each other informed of any news about Matthew.

Alyssa believed that Matt loved her. But now she realized he had other true loves, secret loyalties, and demons inside of him over which she had no control. The very bonding he demanded of her, he could never return. He had never stopped loving Lena, and she realized that the morning he left, he wasn't talking about Carline. He was comparing her with Lena. In Matt's mind, Lena was the wife for whom Alyssa was a fake replacement.

There in the car, at a beach just a few blocks from the restaurant where they'd had their first date, Alyssa ended the search for her missing husband. She believed Matthew would surface again at some point, but no matter what his alibis were, this time it couldn't matter. He had betrayed everything they had built, destroying the hopes and dreams of one more loving family, and he had added two more innocent children to his empty and abandoned fatherhood trail.

Their marriage couldn't now, or ever, hold on, even with life support. She was cutting the cord and pulling the plug.

She imagined her daughters and herself sitting on the dock, watching the dolphins gliding across the cove, breathing as they rose to the surface through the water's cool dimension, once again. She remembered the Hope For Harmony House, and she realized she hadn't failed those precious ladies at all. Now she, as one of them, could do more for their safety and dignity than ever before, because now she did understand, as she hadn't back then. She would take her family to France and write about what she had learned, hopefully reaching thousands of battered human beings, rather than just dozens, as she had before.

She started the engine and touched the accelerator with her foot. The glassy sheen the lamplight cast across the hood of her car reminded her of that Christmas morning when Lisa found it in her driveway. On her way to Susanna's house, she drove past the Bistro and glanced back at the beach on the other side of the street. Her chest throbbed with loneliness to experience those glorious moments of perfect new love again. Maybe it wasn't Matthew, the man, she missed, but rather the dream of completing the perfect mating dance; escaping her battered dreams broke her heart, yet gave her strength that night.

Chapter Twenty-Five

*I*t had been a year since Alyssa, her children, and Dionna relocated in Nice, France, to live within the protective arms of Jean-Marc.

She remained haunted by Matthew's memory, her emotions flipping back and forth from longing for his love to nightmarish terror of his sadistic and horrific cruelty. She would never forget that incredible first date with him dining at the Bistro, with Dierdra II in the background, followed by the spontaneous late-night swim in the ocean, and their first kiss as they lay in the sand on the shore. She still hadn't let go of that first night they made love in his starlit Jacuzzi on his yacht, or his boyish proposal of marriage to her and Lisa in Central Park. The romantic hot air balloon ride in Napa and his surprise visit to Acapulco were now all part of a fairy tale. How could she forget the fear of loss, sitting up all night lovingly holding his hand, after his heart attack? The wedding, Charleston, building their new home together, and most important, their love culminating in the birth of Marissa, their daughter, his image, whom she held in her arms every day.

Marissa called him Daddy the last time she saw him, as she and her sister bounced out of the door to Sea World. Her beautiful big blue eyes looked into his beautiful big blue eyes, and Alyssa remembered how grateful to God she was, that this child, and her father, were able to share that moment together. Marissa was everything good about Matt, though she had a huge temper, sloughed off by everyone around her as part of the terrible twos. Alyssa sometimes worried that it was inherited.

During that past year, like clockwork, on the first day of every month, Alyssa received a letter from Matthew. She remained steadfast, never opening even one of them, for fear of weakening and responding to him. For the children, and mostly because she couldn't totally let go, she tucked them inside a small suitcase in back of her closet, reminiscent of Matthew's little black book. Not reading them was a reminder, like the locked liquor cabinet had been for Matthew. The dangerous side, the side that could have killed her that last night she saw him, was only an action away, and her choice not to read those letters was her key to safety. The temptation gnawed at her.

Leaving reality behind, and entering the realm of her own imagination, she helped herself heal by writing a steamy novel of domestic violence and love gone wrong. Now she had lived through horrifying abuse from a man who was driven by two separate forces, those of sick and treacherous behavior, and those of healthy, tender love. Her hero in the book resembled Matthew, which vicariously allowed her to hold him again, and relive the love and passion that drove them to each other, and bound them together for those few short years.

Her own true story would never be told. His family, especially his mother, would never have accepted the truth. Alyssa believed he had twisted the facts to them, that it was she whose behavior forced him leave rather than the other way around. She wanted to hold sacred the public name of her children's father, and so she protected his memory.

Lisa, twelve years old, excelled in a private French dance school, and she was stable and popular, not to ignore that she was beautiful. The boys were already going nuts over the American beauty Lisa Kippler-Hunter. She appeared to thrive within the security and attention of her loving grandmother and Jean-Marc. Still, on her nightstand was a framed photo of Matt, Teddy, and her together, running on the beach in Menlo.

It was five o'clock on a Friday evening, and Alyssa was preparing Jean-Marc's favorite French dish. The aroma of buttery sautéed onions filled the kitchen as she mixed in minced parsley and garlic into the smooth cream sauce. The last and most important touch was adding the extravagant black truffles. Cooking for Jean-Marc brought her pleasure. He was a gourmet and patiently taught her the secrets of fine cuisine. She caught a noodle on a spoon to test its readiness, knowing he would soon come through the door and compliment her efforts.

"My dear, how you do perform miracles to create banquets for a king."

She was beginning to move on, though she hadn't filed for divorce. Part of her still loved Matthew in spite of all she knew and in spite of all that he had done.

The television was on in the living room, and the French News Network was broadcasting. Alyssa's French was still not fluent, but she caught the gist of what she heard. Marissa was in front of it, oblivious to it, playing with her Barbies as she waited for Jean-Marc to bring Lisa home from her dance class.

The broadcaster's voice pierced through the walls. "Matthew James Hunter, the internationally known nautical designer, and founder of Sea Cliff Yachts, is missing at sea.

His ship capsized in the Caribbean off the coast of Grand Cayman yesterday. An all-effort search-and-rescue mission has been in force during the last six hours, though so far, there has been no rescue, nor sign of recovery. Again, Matthew James Hunter missing at sea at the age of forty-eight."

A sharp dagger drove through Alyssa's pounding heart, and she cried out.

"Oh, no. Oh, dear God, no," she moaned. "It's a mistake." She stood over the stove, paralyzed for several seconds, holding the saucepan top in the air over the pot.

She rushed from the kitchen to the living room, where Matt's face flashed across the TV screen. The love of her life was very alive in that picture she recognized from his mother's nightstand—handsome, and smiling, and he was looking straight at her through the screen. She reached down in front of her and lifted up her little four-year-old daughter.

Marissa's huge blue eyes caught her mother's agony. "Mummy, what is wrong?"

Alyssa closed her eyes and held her little girl tightly, recapturing some of his essence. The tears she had been holding back for months flooded her cheeks.

"Oh, my dear God, tell me what have we all done wrong," she mourned.

Just then Jean-Marc and Lisa came through the door. Alyssa looked up and couldn't speak. Lisa ran into her room and slammed the door behind her. Jean-Marc grasped Marissa from Alyssa's arms and gently placed her down. As he wrapped himself around her shocked and stiffened body, she collapsed in his arms.

He lifted her, carrying her to the couch, where he laid

her down, positioning her awkward limbs. Gently placing a throw pillow under her head, he whispered, "I am so, so sorry."

Within seconds, Alyssa raised her head. "Where's Lisa?"

Pushing herself up from the couch, she reached for Jean-Marc's strength to stand.

Lisa had locked her bedroom door.

"Let me in, baby," Alyssa pleaded.

The lock clicked, and the knob turned. A delicate and broken little person appeared in the doorway.

"Mommy, I want Daddy," she sobbed. The two of them clung together, tragic victims. "I want him to turn me upside-down. I want to smell his parfum and feel him kiss my neck and tell me I'm his princess. Mommy, every night I beg God to bring him home to us. I miss him so much."

Alyssa had no answer for her daughter. She struggled to put coherent order to her thoughts.

"Why didn't I call him or respond to even one of his letters? He wrote so many letters and I never even opened one of them. Oh, dear God, his letters. Maybe he was trying to tell me something about his health, or something that I could have done to save him."

Shaking, she walked Lisa back into her room, guiding her to sit on the bed.

"We don't know for sure what's happened. We need to pray for him right now, and maybe they'll still find him."

Lisa fell back on her bed, burying her face in a pillow.

"Please, dear God, save my dad. Save my dad. Don't let him die."

Alyssa called for Jean-Marc, who was out on the terrace

with Marissa, trying to help her little young mind withstand the trauma in the house.

"Jean-Marc. The letters, I need to read them."

He had tried to encourage Alyssa to read them all along, but she wouldn't. Right now, she had no fear of Matt, but only desperation to be close to him in any way that she could.

Jean-Marc entered Lisa's room, Marissa cradled in his arms. "Alyssa, if you want, I will take the girls for a little while."

Alyssa nodded her thanks, and then rushed to her room. She reached for the small suitcase in the closet and pulled it out, only to sit on the floor with her arms wrapped around it, caressing it, and rocking it as if it were an infant in distress.

While Jean-Marc took the girls for a walk in the park across the street, Alyssa sat on the terrace alone, the precious envelopes clasped to her breast. She watched the three of them disappear through the trees, and then began reading the letters one by one.

Letter 1

My Dearest Three Little Women,

I love you all more every day that I have lost you. My days are empty because you are not here with me. I don't deserve you because I'm not worthy of angels.

Alyssa, how can I fix what I've destroyed?

Lisa, my little darling I want to watch TV with you, and do your homework with you, because you're too sleepy to finish it alone. I love you. Daddy misses you so much, you can't imagine.

Marissa, how's Daddy's baby girl? I love you. You are too small to ever know how happy I am that Daddy and Mommy made you from our love for each other.

Alyssa, I'm not asking you to forget the evil things I have done to you, you shouldn't. No matter what I have said or done to you, you are the greatest love of my life. In losing you, I have lost myself. I have done and said unforgivable things, and I lost my soul. I am fighting every minute to earn it back. I'd give anything in the universe to be feeling some part of you right now, to be inside of your warm walls, holding me tightly within.

Matthew, a would-be Romeo

Letter 2

Alyssa,

I am lying in our bed tonight. I can feel your mouth on me and I want to cry. I love you. I was so stupid. I realize I have an alcohol problem. I need to stop drinking for myself first, if I can ever be worthy of you and the girls again.

I'll never forget that first night on the beach. I didn't feel drunk, not on alcohol. I was drunk on falling in love with the most beautiful woman on Earth. What can I do to fix what I destroyed? I replaced everything I smashed in our room that night. I even had the oil painting of us duplicated and placed back up over the bed. Maybe we should just sell this house, and get a brand-new one.

Baby, help me change. I'll do anything to save us. I need you. I swear on my own life that I will never hurt you again. Please, please, please let me come back.

Every night I fall to sleep imagining the four of us together. I love Lisa as if she were my own blood. I want to see her laughing with Teddy, and I want to help her grow into the beautiful woman she already is as a little girl. I want to be the last one to flip her upside-down and kiss her little neck. I guess she's getting a little big for that. How is her dancing going? Just to hear her giggle would make my day. You can't imagine the pain I feel because of my mistakes.

Little Marissa, I love her, and I want to hold her, and close my eyes while I breathe the smell of her hair. I remember most nights when I slept with you, I put my face near you, just to smell your beautiful, clean hair. It helped me fall asleep.

Alyssa, you're a doctor. Help me. I am reaching out to you, please. I've wronged you so. Help me help myself. I've always been wrong with something or someone in my life. I can't stand it anymore. The only right thing I ever had was you.

Matt

Letter 3

Alyssa,

It's been three months. I'm dying, because I killed us. I love you. I worship you. Be weak. Take me back. I'll do anything to be in your world again. I am a lonely man with nothing to live for unless I'm with you.

I have decided to sell my favorite toy, Dierdra II. She's no fun anymore without you and the children. I'm getting help. I'm seeing a psychiatrist. I want to change I guess my daddy taught me to hurt people. Do you know he never told me even one time that he loved me? I remember he used to tell me that Amy was the best, and I didn't deserve anything. Maybe that's why being rich meant so much to me.

My father tried to reduce me by convincing me I never would be a success. I never learned anything about being a good person, just a rich one. I need to be a better man for our children. I need to earn you back. I'm trying so hard to change. I miss you. Can't we just try to talk a little?

Baby, write to me, please. Better yet, call me with the time of your flight home, please.

Remember my secret number (011-773-709-0000)? I'm waiting for you.

Matt

Letter 4

I'm in the hospital right now, but I'm going to be released today. I had some chest pain the other day, but the cardiologist said it wasn't my heart. I had a stress test this morning, he said I passed it, but he changed my blood pressure medicine. I felt lonely because I couldn't ask you if it was a good thing to do.

I don't know what to do. I would get on a plane and come to you, but that wouldn't be right. I've always just taken anything I wanted, but this time I'm trying to give you the space to make up your mind without my force. I hope you will get to a place where you are willing to try one more time. I'm begging you with these letters. Please don't keep me away from the girls forever. That would mean I lost five out of five children.

I want to call you, but I can't. Nobody here will give me your number. I could still get it within minutes if I tried. I don't know who they think they're kidding. But I don't want your number if it means I need to pull strings to get it. I'm so ashamed of all the strings I've pulled in the past, and all the terrible things I've done to other people.

Right now, I just have to get help with my nerves. I've been put on a medication to slow down those ugly mood swings I get. I think it's helping but probably stopping drinking has helped me the most. Alcohol has become like a poison for my brain.

Please answer me.

Matt

Letter 5

Honey,

I sold Dierdra II today. It was like she and I were both crying when she moved away from the dock. We had been great friends for a long time, and I loved her. She's on her way to Italy right now, belonging to Antonio Capezzio. I thought if I let her go to him, at least I could borrow her once in a while, and she wouldn't totally be lost from me. I've lost so much that all I have left are Mama, Amy, and Annie. I thank God for them.

I'm so depressed. I don't even know if this new medicine is helping me. I still have temper surges for no reason, but at least they're better than they used to be. My psychiatrist is going to strengthen my pills a little in two weeks, if this dose doesn't kick in. It makes me feel tired, but he says it's because I don't have all that extra manic energy, so I just think I'm tired, when I'm really feeling the way normal people feel. All I can say is that all you normal folks must be exhausted all the time. How do you get anything done? Ha!

How's Teddy? How's Mittens? Tell our girls that Daddy loves them and hopes to see them real soon, if Mommy will stop shutting me out.

Matt

Letter 6

Happy Halloween.

I'm in Charleston with Mother. She had a heart attack last week. She just got home from the hospital, and she's not doing so well. I came up to be with Amy and help out.

I wish you were here to give us your medical guidance. It always seems that if you're the doctor, things go better. You're such a great doctor.

Mother and Amy asked me to give you their love the next time I talked with you. I guess they wonder why we don't live together anymore. I just tell them that I visit you a lot, but you're working out some personal stuff. I can't make myself admit to them that most of our problems were my fault.

I'm still getting those chest pains. They're going to do a cardiac catheterization again. I didn't want to do it right now because of Mother's health. I'm not sure it's my heart, anyway. I'm getting a lot of indigestion. Anyway, it's scary with Mother's heart being bad, and then I have chest pains, too.

That medicine for my mood swings still makes me tired. For the first time in my life though, I'm starting to see things differently. I want to be a responsible man. I want to be a good man.

Maybe you and I could start out as friends and grow together until we could fall in love in a new way. I could prove to you that I'm changing. I'll never hurt you again, I swear it. You're the last person in the world that I would ever hurt. I love you.

Matt

Letter 7

Happy Thanksgiving!

I'm thinking of going to Grand Cayman for a couple of weeks. I have some money there that I need to transfer. Robert said he'd go with me. He's going to be out of school in December, and we're taking off together. I can't wait to see him.

We'll be back for the Christmas holiday. Carline does some traditional thing with all the kids, so I guess I'll just go to Charleston.

Alyssa, it's been seven months since I heard from you. I heard your mother was visiting the states, and I called her yesterday in Menlo. She said she doesn't want us back together, because she's afraid I'll hurt you. I tried to convince her that I got help, and I'm not that same crazy guy I was. I could tell that she still cares for me, and she did finally admit that she believes you still love me. You'll never know what that has done for the last twenty-four hours of my life. I can't continue this forever. I need you. Give the children a big kiss for me.

Say hello to Jean-Marc. Close your eyes and feel the good part of me, please.

Matt

Letter 8

Merry Christmas!

I hope this letter finds you all having a good time. I hope Santa Claus has been good to you. I hoped he would put something under my tree from you, but he didn't.

Mother isn't doing so well right now. I think she's depressed. They did an echocardiogram and her heart isn't very strong, something like congestive heart failure? I'm worried about her. She'd like to see you and the children.

I hope you all got the presents I sent to you for Christmas from Grand Cayman.

I wish I could be with you this year.

Matt

Letter 9

January 1

Happy New Year!

Alyssa, Happy Anniversary.

I can't believe we took our wedding vows five years ago. I miss you so much. I'm beginning to think that I've really lost you all. I actually picked up the phone to order a plane ticket to France today. I didn't do it. Under the circumstances, that could have been a disaster. Maybe you've even met someone else. Or maybe you're with Jean-Marc now. I don't blame you if you are. He is a really good guy, that's why I was always so jealous of him. For myself, I don't want to ever meet anyone else again. You brought the curtains down for me, baby. Maybe I should say I almost brought the curtains down for you. Thank God I didn't do that.

I still love you with everything I've got.

Matt

Letter 10

February 7

Dear Marissa,

Happy birthday, little one. You are four years old now. What a big girl. I hope you got the money Daddy sent you, so you can buy anything you want for your special day. I miss you, and I love you very much. Give Lisa and Mommy a great big kiss for me.

Daddy

Letter 11

My dearest Alyssa,

My mother died last week. Life in Charleston is depressing. She didn't suffer at the end. Her heart just gave out. We were all there, even Lena and her new adopted baby girl were there. You were the only important person who was missing.

Lena sent you her best. I admitted to her that my craziness drove you away, and I told her how sorry I was, and how much I love you more than I ever loved anyone in my life, and how much I miss you. I told her that it was all my fault, and you were the purest soul I ever knew.

I've bought a little Hatteras and I'm taking her to sea for a while. I need to get away. Matthew Jr. might go with me to sail around the Caribbean.

I can't stop thinking of Mama for even one minute. Without you, she was all I really had.

I miss you so much,

Matt

Letter 12

Alyssa, My Darling Wife,

This is my last letter to you. I'm giving you a divorce. I've had papers drawn up and they're waiting for your signature. However, I want visitation rights with my children, and I must have that.

You are all handsomely taken care of in my will. I know you never have looked for anything, nor have you ever needed anything. Maybe that was my problem. You were never a "thing" person. Things and sex were all I ever understood about giving love. Somehow you knew that, but you were the one who pushed me to the edge while you stretched my awareness to include a little spiritual understanding. I will never be able to repay you for that.

Anyway, none of my five children will ever have to worry about things in their life. They will share more money than they can ever spend. I am coming to France soon to see the children and you. I am bringing the papers with me for you to sign. It's been a year now, and I have had no word from you. I don't blame you, but I really have changed for the better.

I haven't had a drink for a year and I don't want one. I'm not all charged up inside anymore. I'm starting to feel good about me for the first time in a long time, maybe for the first time ever. I actually went to a cathedral in Charleston the other day, and felt some kind of spiritual power that I've never felt before. It was really a good thing for me. I'm going to go to church again sometime.

I don't know what it will be, but I feel a great change coming. It's almost as if I can feel the breeze blowing against my face, as you would describe it, "kissing my cheek."

Oh, I want you so bad. Will it ever be different for me, I hope so, and I'll just have to believe that it will all turn out the way it's supposed to be.

This will be my last letter to you. I said that already, didn't I? I've always been a little too obsessive about things I want. Some things we just can't have. It took me forty-eight years to catch on. You know that old saying about accepting the things you can't change, and changing the things you can, and having the wisdom to know the difference? I think I can do it for the first time in my life. I'm trying, that's all. Hey baby, just remember that I love you. I'll always love you.

Forever,

Matthew

Afterword

National Domestic Violence Hotline:

1-800-799-SAFE (7233) or TTY 1-800-787-3224

Intimately Betrayed is much more than a page-turning love story. It is also intended as a tool to help others see and recognize the dangers of violent and abusive relationships. If you doubt the seriousness of this issue, consider the information below.

First Annual Allstate Foundation National Poll on Domestic Violence Executive Summary

The following are survey questions and responses that provide an understanding of attitudes and perceptions of domestic violence in the United States:

Question:

In your own words, how would you define domestic violence?

Respondents' definitions of domestic violence tended to fall into three categories: abuse among family members, abuse in general and abuse/violence between two people (not necessarily family).

The following are a selection of verbatim responses from respondents:

- "I guess it's when spouses disagree and hit each other."

- "It's the use of physical or emotional abuse within somebody in your household".

- "Violence at home against any family member. It is one of the worst things that have happened to women and men in America and we don't realize how far it reaches."

- "What is domestic violence? I've lived it."

- "Uncontrolled anger."

- "Any act of aggression used against someone else that resides in the same household."

- "It's a power grab by one over the other. They use pain and strength over a weaker person to make themselves fell stronger or better than them."

- "Violence in the household."

- "I've been through it, I've seen it and it's horrible."

- "Just somebody hitting on somebody."

- "Loss of self control and acts of ill will toward people who live within the same dwelling."

- "I'm a victim of domestic violence and it's the worst thing. You never know what will happen and when you ask for help it's treated like nothing. Sometimes the people don't believe you and that's why a lot of women are scared to go to the police. You go back and continue to be a victim because it's better than trying to get people to help you and believe you. Even the police don't believe you. If you call you have to be black and blue. They don't do anything."

Question:

In your opinion, which of the following statistics do you feel most accurately describes the number of adult women living in the United States who will experience domestic violence at least once in her lifetime?

25% of the survey respondents accurately estimated the incidence of domestic violence in the United States. According to the Centers for Disease Control, one out of four women will experience domestic violence in her lifetime.

Signs of Domestic Violence

$\mathcal{I}$n 1996, Vice President Joe Biden (then Senator), authored the landmark Violence Against Women Act, the strongest legislation to date criminalizing domestic violators and holding batterers responsible and accountable for their actions.

Multiple foundations and Councils world-wide have been established to assist victims against domestic violence, yet on many levels of domestic and criminal justice, this remains a subject of disbelief and neglect.

The following warning signs are keys in recognizing potential dangers in relationships with other people:

1. **QUICK INVOLVEMENT** – The abusive personality often gets serious very quickly and presses for extreme closeness and commitment very early in the relationship.

2. **JEALOUSY** – Signs of severe jealousy and relationship insecurity blown out of proportion, most often involving the opposite sex, but often accusing family members or friends of interfering with the relationship.

3. **CONTROLLING BEHAVIOR** – The abuser prefers to make the major relationship decisions, and may work to separate you from anyone who could take away that control. You may need to check-in frequently throughout the day, he may show up at your work or time your activity away from him.

4. **ISOLATION** – One by one your friends seem to disappear, and socialization slows down. Family or friendship support systems may begin to decrease as he finds fault with other people close to you. Men are the usual primary targets, especially fathers, brothers, or uncles. He may even make plans to move far away from your outside support systems.

5. **HYPERSENSITIVITY** - Sensitivity to any type of criticism, even constructive suggestions, flying off the handle over little things, and blaming you.

6. **THE JEKYLL AND HYDE PERSONALITY** – Normal behavior one minute, then suddenly without apparent reason or warning, irritation, furious or violent outbursts ensue. Punching walls, breaking objects, especially little things that you hold sentimental, or just storming away, even driving away or disappearing for a while are common traits.

7. **MINIMIZING BAD BEHAVIOR OR ABUSE** – Rudeness, cruelty or hurtful exchanges are common, then dropped, or later described as nothing, making fun of your reaction to the misbehavior. New body bruises may be sloughed off as easy-bruising.

8. **DENIAL OF RESPONSIBILITY** – Never admitting fault, being sure that the blame for quarrels, problems, or outbursts are because you did something to provoke

the behavior. If physical injury takes place, you may be told that you deserved it, you wanted it, or you needed it.

9. **SEXUAL ABUSE** - Some abusers find it very important to abuse sexually. They may make fun of your style, or try to force you to play games in bed that you find offensive. They may show signs of sadism or enjoy spanking you. Forcing sexual exchange or denying it as punishment for something you did wrong is not uncommon. Making fun of your appearance, your weight, your hair, your clothes are all part of gender put-downs to gain power. Hurting your feelings or demeaning your sexuality may decrease your self-worth and unconsciously increase dependence on the abuser's power.

These are nine of the most common personality traits of potential domestic violators. Most abusers don't display all of these traits, yet often before the violence, they display at least three or four of these elements.

The subject of human and animal behavior is fascinating, though cruel and brutal when it involves harming another. Nobody has the right to violate the dignity, pride or physical space of another. Most authorities on the subject of Domestic violence will agree that it is a learned and developed behavior. Violent behavior is like a raging forest fire. The strike of a match makes a spark which ends up destroying everything in its path. If it's not stopped, it will grow and grow and destroy. Very rarely does a batterer simply change because he's sorry. Domestic violators behave in cycles. After they strike, they're remorseful, and go through a period of loving, gentle and kind behavior. Then the crescendo begins until there is a new outburst. The cycle plays over and over, until there is frequently a tragic ending, often the death of a female or a child.

Very rarely does domestic violence just disappear. If it does go away, the violator must begin to take responsibility for his behavior. Professional help, serious intervention, and years of therapy are required to change this insidious behavior, and only a small percentage of batterers ever actually change.

It is not right to live in a violent relationship. There are no excuses for anyone to abuse another, neither emotionally nor physically.

The **first step** in changing violence in the home is to **STOP ALLOWING IT TO HAPPEN** by getting away from it and seeking safety. It is not right to live in a violent relationship. **There are no excuses for anyone to abuse another, neither emotionally nor physically.**

If domestic violence touches your life or is a threat, I recommend *When Violence Begins At Home (A Comprehensive Guide to Understanding and Ending Domestic Violence)* by K.J. Wilson, Ed.D., Hunter House Publishers, 1997. This book is an excellent resource and I recommend you purchase it or borrow it through your local library.

About The Author

*R*oxanna P. Platt, MD, is a masterful new author, publishing her first dramatic romance, Intimately Betrayed. A Korean Conflict war orphan, and one of three siblings, Dr. Platt was raised by her loving widowed mother, who provided a childhood studded with multilingual training, and world travel. It was during her travels that she first became interested in the diverse cultural differences and attitudes surrounding the female gender.

Dr. Platt has been an advocate against domestic violence, helping her own patients with issues related to the "battered woman's syndrome." Having grown up within an almost fairy-tale childhood, she wasn't prepared for her own personal encounter with domestic violence, which tragically, virtually brought part of her adult life to a paralyzed standstill. Intimately Betrayed was originally penned as an outcry for help, instead, becoming her beacon, spearheading her intense involvement in the subject of domestic violence.

A victim of the very cause for which she fights now, Dr. Platt married a man whom she believed was a loving and good man, only to discover he harbored a very dark side, a secret he hid from the outside world. After multiple episodes behind closed doors of his shocking mental and physical abuse, she separated from him with intensions of divorce, while shielding her young pre-teen daughter from further exposure to violence and possible physical harm.

One evening, she received a phone call from him promising her that he would seek both psychological and medical help if she would meet him to discuss salvaging their shattered relationship. Still very much in love with his good side, she agreed. Dr. Platt chose to drive, only to be violated by her husband's quick temper, as he violently reached across the van, turning the wheel into an oncoming semi-tractor trailer. He was killed, and she was trauma hawked on life support to continue her fight for survival, this time, as the victim of a brutal automobile accident. Much of her left torso was crushed and fractured with severe internal bleeding. Within the next two years, Dr. Platt developed a malignant sarcoma in her traumatized breast, beginning another fight for her life. The tragedy didn't stop with his death and her difficult physical recovery from the accident, as she was charged with causing the accident. Her recovery during the next several years was threaded with poignant and painful repercussions from living with domestic abuse, near death, and legal entanglement. This experience has directed her to continue writing and working diligently against all human abuse, most recently focusing her attention on the abused elderly.

As a practicing Family Practice physician, with extensive training and experience in women's issues, she also serves on The Council Against Domestic Violence. The council uses her home for unpublicized events, preparing abused women, many with children, to re-enter society after recovering in battered women's shelters. Dr. Platt is presently developing programs to educate and protect violated and battered women and children, as she continues her campaign to help raise money for their cause.

If you or someone you know is caught in a domestic violence situation, get help. The National Domestic Violence Hotline is available to help callers 24 hours a day and 365 days a year. Hotline advocates are available, for victims and anyone calling on their behalf to provide crisis intervention, safety planning, information and referrals to agencies in all 50 states, Puerto Rico and the Virgin Islands. Assistance is available in English and Spanish with access to more than 170 languages through interpreter services. If you or someone you know is frightened about something in your relationship, then please call the National Domestic Violence Hotline at 1-800-799-SAFE (7233) or TTY 1-800-787-3224, or online get help and information at: www.ndvh.org.